$ 16.50

Urbanization and
the Developing Countries

edited by
Raanan Weitz

Published in cooperation with the
Continuation Committee of the
Rehovot Conference

The Praeger Special Studies program—utilizing the most modern and efficient book production techniques and a selective worldwide distribution network—makes available to the academic, government, and business communities significant, timely research in U.S. and international economic, social, and political development.

Urbanization and the Developing Countries

Report on the Sixth Rehovot Conference

Praeger Publishers New York Washington London

PRAEGER SPECIAL STUDIES IN INTERNATIONAL ECONOMICS AND DEVELOPMENT

Library of Congress Cataloging in Publication Data

Rehovot Conference on Urbanization and Develop-
    ment in Developing Countries, Jerusalem and
    Rehovot, Israel, 1971.
    Urbanization and the developing countries.

    (Praeger special studies in international
economics and development)
    "Published in cooperation with the Continuation
Committee of the Rehovot Conference."
    Bibliography: p.
    1. Underdeveloped areas—Urbanization—
Congresses. I. Weitz, Raanan, 1913-   ed.
II. International Conference on Science in the
Advancement of New States. Continuation Com-
mittee. III. Title.
HT169.5.R43   1971a   309.2'62'09124   77-186202

PRAEGER PUBLISHERS
111 Fourth Avenue, New York, N.Y. 10003, U.S.A.
5, Cromwell Place, London S.W.7, England

Published in the United States of America in 1973
by Praeger Publishers, Inc.

Printed in the United States of America

CONTENTS

PART I. REALITY

Chapter

LIST OF TABLES

The process of urbanization—like its product, the city—is a tumultuous phenomenon, mostly disorganized but also uniquely fascinating. So was the Sixth Rehovot Conference, which was devoted to it.

The topics that were discussed and analyzed during that Conference were myriad. Everything having the remotest connection with the subject was dragged in or brought up: people and population, cities and villages, economic organization, man and his family, size of cities and metropolitan clusters, policies, strategies, and methods, urban and regional approaches, governments, policies and policymakers, scholars and planners—in sum, every aspect of humanity in our time.

Formally, the Conference was organized around plenary sessions and three study groups: One had to deal with "The Role of Urbanization"; the second, with "Size of Cities"; and the third had to discuss "Regional Development and Urbanization." In reality, however, all the groups dealt with all the topics.

Out of the proceedings of the Conference and the papers submitted to it, I undertook to mold a report that would reflect the Conference faithfully. After several months of struggle, I came out with an entirely different creation.

The book presented here is neither a report nor proceedings of the Conference but represents the subject matter presented in the form of papers or discussions as seen through the eyes of the editor. Obviously this form of editing cannot be entirely objective, as it reflects the opinion of the editor and his collaborators in the selection and writing up of the material. This might be considered a shortcoming, but, on the other hand, it avoids duplication and presents the subject matter in an orderly and logical sequence, thus allowing each chapter to be dedicated to a definite subject. The reader can, therefore, follow the opinions of the participants in a concise and easily accessible manner. For better or worse, this is it.

The Sixth Rehovot Conference was convened by Abba Eban, Foreign Minister of Israel and Chairman of the Continuation Committee of the International Conference on Science in the Advancement of New States. It was held in order to enable the professionals and policy-makers of the developing countries to exchange views and establish meaningful communication on the over-all topic of "Urbanization and Development in the Developing Countries." The Conference included 166 representatives from 62 countries, among them 40 from

Africa, 38 from Asia and the Mediterranean, 33 from Central and South America, and 13 from North America. A number of major international organizations, such as the World Bank, the International Labour Office (ILO), the Organization of American States (OAS), the Organization for Economic Cooperation and Development (OECD), and the United Nations Development Program (UNDP), were represented.

The opening ceremony was addressed by Mrs. Golda Meir, Prime Minister of Israel; Mr. Abba Eban; H. E. Sheriff M. Dibba, Vice-President and Minister of Finance of The Gambia; H. E. Eugene Lechat, Vice-President of the Malagasy Republic; and H. E. Gonzalo Facio Segreda, Foreign Minister of Costa Rica. The professional keynote addresses were delivered by Professor Lloyd Rodwin, Head of the Department of Urban Studies and Planning, MIT, and Mr. David Morse, Senior Consultant, United Nations Development Program. Throughout three days of plenary sessions, general problems were discussed on the basis of the working papers submitted. The final days of the Conference were devoted to three study groups, each allocated one subject to discuss in detail, despite the fact that it soon became apparent that the topics were closely interwoven.

The work of the Plenary Sessions and Committees was ably summarized by the rapporteurs: Professor Y. Elon, Department of Architecture, Haifa Technion; Professor C. Rapkin, School of Architecture, Urban Planning Division, Columbia University, New York; Dr. A. Solow, Project Director, Municipal Administration and Development, UNDP, Venezuela; Professor A. Shachar, Department of Geography, Hebrew University of Jerusalem; and Dr. Erick Cohen, of the Department of Sociology, Hebrew University of Jerusalem.

The editor wishes to thank his collaborators who undertook the initial selection of editing the material: Mr. Michael Hopp, who edited Chapters 1 to 5, Mr. Avshalom Rokach, who edited Chapters 6, 7, and 9, Mr. Joseph Slyper, who edited Chapters 11 and 12, and Dr. David Pines, who wrote Chapter 12; and to thank Dr. Amos Manor for his sound and practical advice, Mrs. Lily Beyrakc-Cohen for her laudable effort in the language editing of the final manuscript, and Esther Hammerman for the strenuous work of putting the manuscript into printed form.

In the final session, the delegates unanimously passed a proposal that there should be follow-up regional conferences in Africa, Asia, and Latin America, correlated with the plans of other bodies and organizations, to be more practical in outlook, dealing with specific problems and not academic models. The need to distinguish between the problems of the various continents as well as those within the continents themselves, should be emphasized.

In the final analysis, the editor takes full responsibility for the somewhat unorthodox way of treating scientific material, taking the position that readers will find it useful and interesting.

Raanan Weitz

1

PEOPLE
AND
CITIES

The vast, often incredible rate of world population increase and the even faster growth of towns, cities, and urban agglomerations all over the world are phenomena that have taken place only fairly recently. ROBERT C. WEAVER has noted that

Slightly less than a century ago no nation could have been described as predominantly urbanized. It was not until the twentieth century that one nation, Great Britain, was in that category. By the mid-1960s all industrial nations were highly urbanized, and the process was growing increasingly in developing areas.

The statistics of world demography are staggering when expressed in numbers: From an estimated 900 million in 1800 the world population had climbed to 1 billion in 1900 and to 3.3 billion in 1960, and a world population of 6.3 billion at the close of the century is projected.

Urban population has grown at an even more startling rate. The estimated 1.7 percent of world population living in cities of more than 100,000 residents in 1800 had grown to 5.5 percent at the beginning of this century and to 22 percent by the beginning of the 1970s. When expressed in numbers this is even more impressive: From 15 million "urban" residents in 1800, the figure has jumped to almost 800 million today.

The last hundred years have brought about so immense and unique a revision in the affairs of man that it threatens the world with total change before the century is over. Patterns of life that have taken centuries to shape are being shattered in one decade. Traditional societies are being phased out in country after country. A new culture, the urban society, is on the rise, aided by modern technology and mass communication, and it is surprisingly uniform.

Scientists, philosophers, politicians, and technicians alike are trying to come to grips with this new entity. New disciplines are emerging to deal with it—urban studies, urban sociology, urban planning.

The effects of high-density human concentrations are being studied and evaluated, and attempts are being made to isolate and identify their economic, social, and physical potentialities and handicaps.

It has now become clear that, if the constant growth of population and mushrooming of cities are left unchecked, the situation is liable to get out of hand. Congestion, pollution, slums, environmental decay, and social atrophy loom large on the horizon and threaten to overshadow the benefits of modern life. Countries in which technology and enlightenment have reached heights unprecedented in human annals are threatened by social disintegration and technological strangulation. Other less developed countries will face explosive economic disasters if the enormous pressures of urban concentrations are not alleviated. Dr. WEAVER continued:

The rapid growth in the size of cities and the number of city-dwellers began with the industrialization of Western Europe. The transfer of workers from agriculture to industry and services was accompanied by a movement of population from the villages to the towns. Occupational mobility, which was the outcome of more efficient methods of production in all three economic sectors, was directly linked to geographical mobility.

The connection between economic development and the growth of cities in the Western world was not accidental. The survival of an urban population is primarily dependent on a regular supply of food. As long as agriculture was based on subsistence farming there were limits to the possibility of any growth in the urban population. Moreover, transport facilities were such that towns could rely only on their immediate surroundings as a source of agricultural produce. It was only when scientific and technological progress led to improvements in agricultural efficiency, the development of a supporting structure, and the extension of commerce and industry that the way was cleared for the growth of urban centers. The acceleration of this process during the last three decades led to the formation of giant cities stretching over increasingly large areas and encroaching on rural districts. Such giant cities rely on the largest hinterland possible—in fact, it may be said that the whole world is their hinterland.

Weaver pondered on a further aspect:

. . . Early in the industrialization process mortality rates were higher and birth rates lower in the cities than elsewhere in the involved nation. The consequence was that rural-urban migration was the basic source of city population growth. At the time, industrializing cities were unable even to maintain, much less augment, population by reproduction. Thus their growth usually occasioned an absolute and relative decline in rural population.

The cities in undeveloped areas are now growing at a rate greater than that which characterized the industrializing areas in the nineteenth century. Today there is a different type of urbanization. It is attributable more to rapid rise in total population than to economic development. And the current worldwide rapid growth of cities is due mainly to events in the developing countries, since the rate of urbanization is slackening in the industrialized nations.

Taking up these processes KINGSLEY DAVIS attempted an analysis of past and current forces of urbanization in developed and developing countries alike.

. . . The wide gulf separating the industrialized countries is clearly revealed in our data. Only about one-fourth of the people in underdeveloped countries live in urban places, whereas nearly seven-tenths of those in industrial countries do so. The proportion in cities is only one-third as great in the underdeveloped as in the developed countries.

Given this sharp difference in the level of urbanization already reached, one would expect the urban fraction to be increasing more rapidly in the underdeveloped countries. After all, many of the advanced nations are near the end of the transition; they have few agriculturists left to migrate to cities. The rate of change in the urban proportion of the underdeveloped countries is almost double that of the developed countries. However, since the base from which they start is much lower, the situation is reversed in terms of percentage points: The gain in the underdeveloped countries is only slightly over half that of the advanced countries. I think there is a damper on the shift in the urban fraction in underdeveloped countries, but, before explaining why, let me compare the growth in the absolute population.

If the recent mushrooming of town and city populations has been impressive in the world as a whole, it has been startling in the underdeveloped regions. The urban population in the 171 underdeveloped countries more than doubled between 1950 and 1970, and the city population increased more than one and three-quarters times. The rate of increase was twice that in the developed countries.

5

It is commonly assumed that the rapid growth of towns and cities in the underdeveloped countries is due exclusively to rural-urban migration. When thinking of sprawling and spreading districts of squatters in cities throughout the underdeveloped world, one automatically attributes the ballooning of these cities to a mass influx of people from the countryside. Actually, for the underdeveloped countries as a whole we do not know the relative contribution of migration to city growth, because for many cities vital statistics are lacking. However, by assuming that the rural areas have a natural increase 20 percent higher than the urban areas (a maximum assumption, as we shall see later), we derive an estimate that during 1950-60 rural-urban migration contributed slightly more than half of the urban population growth. According to our estimates, reclassification (that is, the transformation of rural villages into urban places from sheer population growth) contributed about 10.7 percent to urban population increase, and the rest, 36.4 percent, was contributed by the urban population's own excess of births over deaths. The actual direct contribution of migration may well be less than 52.9 percent, but the indirect contribution (from births to migrants after they get to the city) may make it more. In any case, it is clear that close to half the growth in the urban population of the underdeveloped countries is due to over-all population growth, not to migration.

Curiously, using the same assumption regarding superior natural increase in the rural sector, we find that 49 percent of the urban growth in the developed countries is directly attributable to rural-urban migration, with 41.7 percent contributed by the urban population's own natural increase and 9.3 percent contributed by reclassification. At first glance it seems incredible that rural-urban migration is playing almost as great a role in urban growth in highly developed nations as it is in poorly developed ones, because the agricultural source of migrants is drying up. In 1950 the industrialized societies as a whole were only 47 percent rural, whereas the non-industrial societies were 83 percent rural. In the latter countries a small rate of out-migration calculated against the population in the countryside would automatically yield a big rate calculated against the population already in the cities. Thus, in terms of their potentialities, the underdeveloped countries seem to be getting less rural-urban migration than might be expected and the industrial countries more.

In the eighteenth and much of the nineteenth centuries, cities were deadly places because, with people crowding together, infectious diseases could spread rapidly at a time when medical control was not possible. At the same time the cities had fewer children per woman than the countryside, both because of the high opportunity costs of children in the competitive urban milieu and because of infecundity and widowhood as a result of ill health and high mortality. As a consequence, although the cities had more births than deaths in normal years, the occasional occurrence of epidemics or other calamities left them with no long-run gain. If they had had to depend on their own natural increase most of them would not have increased in population. The fact that they did grow—and during the Industrial Revolution they grew rapidly—demonstrates the power they had to attract rural migrants. The migrants were endless in number because they came from a huge population reservoir that dwarfed the city population. Although the rate of natural increase of this rural reservoir was not great, even a modest growth was enough to distress the rural economy and furnish a flood of migrants to the cities.

Although economic development and public sanitation doubtless had some effect in bringing down city death rates, improvement was extremely slow, even long after the urban transition had been under way. As late as 1872 the expectation of life in Glasgow was 36 years, the same as in London in 1841. The slowness derived from the fact that the technology of both medicine and science was only gradually invented and applied.

In 1850, when London already had 2.3 million inhabitants, the city was "honeycombed with cesspools, some of them like lakes." After 1848 owners could be compelled to connect house drainage to sewers, but the sewers themselves were defective and their contents were discharged into the Thames or its tributaries or into ditches. There was no system of refuse collection or disposal. The dead were buried in overcrowded grounds surrounded by houses. London was being regularly ravaged by cholera, which killed more than 14,000 in 1849 and nearly 10,000 in 1854. Thousands of homes depended on public pumps or on wells (aptly called "slaughter wells") that drained cesspools, graveyards, and tidal areas of the river. This was at a time when Great Britain was already over 40 percent urban, a level far above the average of 26 percent found in underdeveloped countries today. As late as 1871-75, when Britain was as highly urbanized as many countries are today, the infant mortality in Manchester was 198 per 1,000 live births; in 1901 it was still 176 in Birmingham.

The age structure of the early cities, bulging with young adults who had migrated in, should have given them a high crude birth rate, a low crude death rate, and hence a high rate of natural increase, but for the most part countervailing conditions were too powerful. Mortality seems not to have declined substantially in the cities until the latter half of the nineteenth century, and by then fertility was beginning to follow suit. In 1861, Liverpool, a city of half a million, had a birth rate of 34.2 per 1,000 inhabitants. This sounds high; but the death rate was 29.0 per 1,000, leaving a natural increase of only 0.5 percent per year. At first city death rates generally declined faster than birth rates, but near the end of the nineteenth century the reverse was true. By the 1920s and 1930s most large cities in the industrialized countries had negative rates of natural increase, especially when correction is made for their age structures.

After the Great Depression the recovery of the birth rate in urban-industrial countries was greater in the urban than in the rural population, while mortality, already at a low ebb, kept on declining (the decline has shown signs of slackening only in the last few years). As a consequence the cities of the industrialized world have generally had an extended postwar era of high natural increase—probably the highest natural increase many of them have ever had in their entire history.

The urban birth rate rose because, among other reasons, modern cities, despite their great size, have been made more amenable to rearing children. Above all, the deconcentration of cities—that is, a faster increase in their population, a process that has been going on for many decades but that gained momentum after 1920—has facilitated parenthood. Also, there has been a general tendency in industrialized countries to shift the economic burdens of parents onto others, notably taxpayers; and a number of factors in modern urban society have conspired to lower the age of marriage for women and to increase the proportion who marry.

Whatever its causes, the rise in the capacity of cities in advanced countries to generate their own population growth has come just when the agricultural population was diminishing to numerical insignificance and could no longer furnish mass migration. As a consequence, perhaps for the first time in the history of advanced nations, city growth is primarily due to city population. I have given you my estimate that recently migration has directly supplied 49 percent of urban growth in developed countries. This estimate is more than confirmed by United States data. Between 1950 and 1960, 11 of our largest metropolitan areas gained 8.2 million inhabitants. Of these, 5.5 million, or 67 percent, came from the excess of births over deaths within the areas themselves, and 33 percent came from migration. If births to migrants during the decade are allocated to migration, the contribution of migration rises to about 40 percent of the decade increase.

In advanced nations during the first half of the urban transition the agricultural population could furnish migrants to the cities and still expand itself. Agricultural density did not increase, because the cultivated area generally expanded faster than the agricultural population; but the cities, not able to fill their ranks from their own births, offered opportunities sufficiently attractive to lure many rustics to their streets. As city population eventually became sizable in relation to rural, and as rural fertility itself began to fall, the countryside could no longer fill the urban void and maintain its own growth. Consequently, in country after country the agricultural population began to decline in absolute numbers, usually when the country was 50 to 55 percent urban. In England the decline started around 1870, when 26 percent of the population was in cities of 100,000 or more; in the United States it started around 1917, when 25 percent were in cities of 100,000 or more and 50 percent were urban. Throughout the history of this change the size of the urban or city population was the determining factor: It was like a magnet, pulling in migrants according to its size, regardless of the size of the rural population. As the urban population became massive in relation to the rural, it maintained its growth, and maintains it now, by robbing the countryside of more than its natural increase. Agricultural density continued to fall, now from the loss of farmers rather than from the expansion of the cultivated area, as agricultural production could more easily be modernized.

DEMOGRAPHIC ASPECTS OF THE RECENT PATTERN

When we turn to contemporary underdeveloped countries, we find a fundamental difference in the demographic situation. First, the cities of these countries are not death-traps; on the contrary, they are usually more healthful than their rural hinterlands and are almost as healthful as cities in the most advanced countries. They have participated disproportionately in the miraculous fall in mortality that has occurred generally in nonindustrial countries since 1940— a fall that has enabled them to make gains in 20 years that industrial countries starting at a similar level required 70 to 80 years to achieve. The cities have been the main recipient of this new death control because they are the places to which medical and scientific techniques, expert personnel, and funds from the advanced nations are first imported and where the largest number of people are reached at the smallest cost.

Nor do conditions in cities of nonindustrial countries seem as hostile to reproduction as those of the nineteenth and early twentieth centuries were. In general, urban fertility is lower than rural fertility, but not much lower; and both are higher than they ever were in most of the industrial countries. Among Moslem couples interviewed in 1957 in Lebanon, those who were living in a city both before and after marriage had a fertility that would yield 6.6 children for each wife if she lived through the reproductive period. In Accra, the capital of Ghana, the figure was 6 children in 1960. In Bangalore City in 1950 the average woman aged 45 or over had borne 5.3 children. Surveys in 1960 in five cities in five Latin American countries found the average number of children born to women aged 40-44 to be 5.1.

To some extent this city fertility is a function of good health and low mortality, but it is also a function of some of the very changes that make better health possible. Economic improvement, public welfare, international aid, subsidized housing, and free education make the penalties for having children less than they once were. Giving priority in housing to larger families, maintaining maternal and child-health clinics, and discouraging labor-force participation by married women are additional props to urban reproduction. More important are old institutional structures with built-in incentives for prolific breeding—structures that persist in the cities because the paternalism of the times treats them as sacred.

Although existing levels of fertility will probably fall in these cities, they have a long way to go before they yield a low rate of increase. Also there is no indication that they will go that far within the foreseeable future. In the Latin American city surveys just cited, the number of children considered ideal by young women aged 20-24 was close to the average number that women aged 35-39 had actually borne. The ideal was only 8 percent lower than the actual. The inhabitants of cities in nonindustrial areas can hardly be expected to reduce their fertility below that of cities in industrial countries. American cities of 100,000 and over had a natural increase of 13.1 per 1,000 in 1960—enough by itself to double their population every 54 years.

The cities of the underdeveloped world are caught in a trap. Currently, with a combination of preindustrial fertility and post-industrial mortality, they have the greatest natural increase ever found in big cities. Around 1960 in Chile the natural increase in cities of 100,000 or more was 26.1, in Mexico, 30.3, and in Venezuela, 32.8. The excess of city births is so great that few opportunities are left for rural migrants. If the people already in the cities reduce their fertility substantially in the next three decades, as they probably will, the effect will be in part nullified by further improvements in mortality as a result of medical gains and an age structure that remains extremely young by virtue of past high fertility. The effect will be further nullified by the fact that, as the city people reduce their rate of reproduction, migrants from the swollen rural reservoir will flood into urban areas. This influx will keep the cities growing at the maximum pace that economic development will allow. As the migrants come in, they will not exhibit the reproductive restraint of the people already accustomed to the city but will start at a higher point, thus breaking the over-all decline of the city birth rate in proportion to their numbers. There thus seems no chance that the cities will reduce their rate of growth except by economic stagnation.

Yet, even so, they will not be able to grow fast enough to siphon off the rural excess of births over deaths, much less begin to reduce the rural population in absolute terms. The cities are already growing at close to the maximum rate that seems tolerable; for them to reduce the agricultural population as the cities of the past did they would have to grow at an intolerable pace.

Approximately 200 years have elapsed since Britain first started the urban-industrial transition in the late eighteenth century. During that time some forty-odd other countries have made the transition to a high urban fraction, but today these embrace less than one-third of the world's people. The other two-thirds are in various phases of the early stages; on an average they are at the point where Britain was in 1825 and the United States in 1870. They thus have a long way to go. In the meantime the character of human demography has undergone revolutionary changes that make completion of the transition much more difficult for these countries. Indeed, completion along evolutionary paths similar to those in the past may be impossible.

Most of the participants, however, concerned themselves directly with the problems of urbanization in developing countries, expressing grave concern at the current situation. ROBERT SADOVE, in the introduction to his paper, expressed an opinion shared by many at the Conference.

. . . Almost every major city in the world has slums, unemployment, housing shortages, inadequate transport systems, and congestion of people and traffic. And every major metropolitan area is increasing in size. These are the liabilities of urban living everywhere. Consequently one might ask why this paper focuses on urbanization in the developing, rather than the developed, part of the world. The reason lies in relative magnitudes. Greater population increases, lower per capita income, fewer capital resources, greater unemployment, and less developed urban infrastructure characterize the cities of the developing world.

The magnitude of these problems´compared with the paucity of available resources to deal with them demonstrates that the developing urban world faces a situation radically different from that of cities in developed countries.

Urban population growth is the principal source of the problems, particularly as the result of rural-urban migration. There has been an alarming rate of rural-urban migration, in major part caused by technological advances in agriculture. The various "green revolutions" have permitted increased food production with a reduced farm labor force. Surplus agricultural laborers crowd into the cities, which offer better employment opportunities. Although urban amenities may be lacking, those that are available appear highly attractive to the migrants when compared with living conditions prevalent in rural areas.

The rapid influx of immigration has perpetuated urban poverty, unemployment, and grossly inadequate housing. It has also created an urgent need to create additional urban infrastructure.

This needed infrastructure is costly and competes for priority with government efforts to allocate scarce resources into directly productive investments. Moreover, capital formation for any purpose is especially difficult. The low level of per capita income does not allow the developing countries, particularly the poorest, to accumulate sufficient savings either for productive enterprises or for urban infrastructure.

The unsolved problem of masses of people living in deprived conditions threatens political stability, a sine qua non of socioeconomic development.

Sadove saw the crux of the problem in the extremely rapid growth of cities in developing countries: the growth rate of the larger towns. An average of 4.5 percent rate of growth is shown over the last decade for towns that had 100,000 or more population in 1960, or 4.9 percent excluding India. An even faster rate is estimated for most towns in developing countries of over half a million inhabitants, the number of which grew from 56 to 106 during the decade. For many of these towns the average rate of growth was as high as 6 percent per annum, or a doubling every 12 years. Still more alarming growth rates are estimated for some cities that have been investigated.

Sadove was sustained in this view by JORGE E. HARDOY of Argentina, who put much of the blame on the demographic structure of developing countries.

Distribution of Population. Two major demographic differences between developed and developing countries are the much lower rate of population growth and the higher percentages of urban population in relation to total population that developed countries have. Developing countries present a much higher rate of urbanization than developed countries. According to the United Nations 85.7 percent of the world's population growth between 1970 and 2000 will be absorbed by the four less developed major areas: Latin America, Africa, and East and South Asia. The percentage of the population of the four more developed major areas—Europe, North America, the Soviet Union, and Oceania—which in 1970 represented 26.4 percent of the world's total population, will decrease to 20.7 percent by the year 2000.

The annual rate of increase of the world's population in 1970 was 2.0 percent. But, while Latin America grew at the rate of 2.9 percent per year, Africa at 2.6 percent, and East and South Asia combined at 2.3 percent per year, Europe grew at 0.8 percent per year, North America at 1.1 percent, Oceania at 2 percent, and the Soviet Union at 1 percent per year. We have to acknowledge these realities and recognize that developing countries cannot depend on emigration to other countries to solve their population pressures.

In 1968 the world had 153 metropolitan areas with 1 million inhabitants or more; sixty-six, or 43.7 percent, were located in developing countries: eighteen in China alone, twenty-seven in other Asian countries, sixteen in Latin America, and five in Africa. Of these 153 metropolitan areas eighteen had 5 million inhabitants or more; eight, or 44.4 percent, were located in developing countries: one in China, two in Asia (both in India), one in Africa, and four in Latin America.

In 1960 the four more developed major areas had 51 percent of the world's urban population while the four less developed major areas had 49 percent. However, regional differences in rates of population growth are changing so rapidly that by the year 2000 the four less developed major areas will have 67 percent of the world's urban population. A recent United Nations report estimates the growth of the world's urban population between 1970 and 2000 at 1,977 million, or an average of 65.9 million per year; 1,520 million, or 76.88 percent of the total expected urban growth, will be concentrated in the four less developed regions. This means that the cities and towns of the developing countries will have to absorb an average of 50.6 million people every year during the next 30 years.

In 1970 the annual rate of increase of the urban population of Colombia, Ecuador, Honduras, the Dominican Republic, Algeria, Morocco, Cameroon, Angola, the Democratic Republic of Congo, Zambia, Southern Rhodesia, Uganda, Kenya, Tanzania, the Ivory Coast, Ghana, Albania, Turkey, Saudi Arabia, Lebanon, Syria, Iraq, West Malaysia, Thailand, Nepal, Pakistan, North Korea, the Republic of Korea, and Mongolia was 5 percent or more. Such rapid urbanization poses heavy burdens on those countries. However, some countries are troubled by a rapid rate of urbanization and by a large national population. For example, China will have to absorb an average of 6.8 million urban dwellers per year during the next 15 years; India, 6.3 million; Brazil, 3.2 million; Mexico, 1.8 million; Pakistan, 1.4 million; and Indonesia, 1.3 million per year.

TOWN AND COUNTRY: AN IMBALANCE

Many speakers attached great importance to an understanding of the sources of rural-urban migration. As Professor FINKEL put it,

. . . Urbanization is a result of either a push or a pull. The trend of urban migration is a universal phenomenon in all countries, but for different reasons.

In some countries it is for positive reasons, in some for negative reasons. We must make this distinction from the very beginning, or else anything else that follows may, in some cases, be irrelevant.

The positive reasons are (1) the attraction of the town, and (2) the increased efficiency of the farm, so that a certain number of the population is redundant and therefore free to go to the city.

These are both positive reasons, one based on the development of industry, commerce, and services in the town, the other on improved agricultural techniques.

There is another group of reasons, which I would call negative—not the attraction of the town but the repulsion of the rural scene. There are people in many countries who leave the rural scene for the towns knowing that there is nothing awaiting them in town.

Yet they do not leave because they have become unnecessary. They leave because the farm standard of living is intolerable in every sense of the word. They work from dawn to dusk, with most of the profit going to the trader, the middleman. They see well-produced crops rotting because the marketing system is inadequate. They see the other ills of underdeveloped farming, of which we are constantly aware.

They go to the city for negative reasons. When you have a situation of this kind there is no symbiosis between urbanization and agricultural development. The people living close to starvation levels in the city do not increase the market demand for farm products. By concentrating in the cities they may be organized into political parties and very often drawn into left-wing parties, thus becoming more important politically but not for rural causes. The slum-dwellers in the cities in South America are not going to use their new-found political power to improve rural conditions, because they have crossed the line and will fight for a minimum wage level and for all sorts of benefits.

So you have a loss on the one hand: These individuals have more political power but it is no longer rural power, which means a loss of political power on the rural scene. The best talents among the young people, those who show initiative, who can break away from tradition, escape from this intolerable situation and go to the city facing uncertainty. These are people who under other conditions might have made very good farmers, willing to face the uncertainty of trying a new kind of tree or new agricultural techniques, which requires courage when farming is based on tradition. The rural scene is then depleted. You have a decline in the generation of the farm population in every sense of the word.

This continued mass immigration to the towns was regarded by most participants as the first and foremost problem of urbanization in developing countries. With an over-all annual urban growth of up to 6 percent and growth of individual cities in excess of 10 percent per year, such countries face insurmountable problems aggravated in large measure by the fact that many of the immigrants do not better their lot at all and become social and economic burdens. This provoked RANAAN WEITZ to comment that

. . . The various forms of malaise that have come to the fore in rich countries have an even deeper impact on traditional societies. Many assumptions that were regarded as gospel only a decade ago prove to be quite different in reality. Thus, rapid concentrated urbanization neither reduced the gap between town and country nor brought more and more people within the sphere of influence of the town. The rate of population growth in most developing countries is so high that, in spite of increased migration to the towns, the rural population is still growing, while a considerable percentage of the migrants who reach the towns do not improve their standards of living and merely exchange rural poverty for urban subsistence living.

WALTER SEDWITZ carried the point further, maintaining that

. . . Attempts to deal with the multifaceted development problem have led to chronic inflation and overvalued exchange rates. This situation, together with controls over the prices of "essential products," has helped to displace large numbers of agricultural workers who have migrated to the cities in search of a better life. Since industry cannot absorb them, partly at least because it is capital-intensive in type, the migrants have typically found employment in sectors where productivity and wages are low, have been forced into cheap and rudimentary shelter, and have contributed to the over-burdening of urban facilities. Advances in public health have simultaneously produced sharp declines in death rates, which, in the face of relatively constant birth rates, have led to rapid urban and rural population growth. One result of these trends has been the creation of only a very few major urban centers. During the early 1960s 14 out of 19 Latin American countries belonging to the OAS had 10 percent or more of their populations in the principal nucleus or metropolitan area, and in 5 of these the largest city accounts for at least 20 percent of the total population. Although urban birth rates are both lower than rural and declining, the expansion of the cities will not thereby be arrested, because it is based on migration from areas where the natural population growth is still high.

Examining these problems, JORGE HARDOY arrived at quite a startling observation.

. . . The problem of most of the world is the underdeveloped city—but what is an underdeveloped city? Just a week or two ago I read in an Argentine newspaper that, though the second largest city of Argentina is Rosario with 900,000 inhabitants, the second largest city of Argentina is, in fact, the population that lives in the shanty-towns of Buenos Aires. These people form the second largest city of a relatively well-developed country. The same is true of the second largest city in Mexico—it is not Guadalajara, it is the population living in the shantytown of Mexico City. The same is true of Lima and of most of our underdeveloped countries. Both developed and developing countries complain that their cities are underdeveloped. This is a dual situation: My colleagues in the United States talk about underdevelopment, but our type of underdevelopment is entirely different—it is not the type of underdevelopment of New York, San Francisco, or Los Angeles.
What then is an underdeveloped city? It is largely a self-built city with a high rate of unemployment and underemployment; with insufficient resources, services, community equipment; with absolutely no control over its pattern of physical expansion.

CONCLUSIONS

HARDOY, in continuation of the preceding notes, made an observation characteristic of the mood in the Conference.

. . . The most oft-repeated word in recent literature dealing with problems of urbanization published in developed countries is "crisis." What do we mean by a "crisis?" Implicit in the word is the existence of a disease, but who is affected by the disease, the cities or the urban and social systems that leave their impact on them? Which is the crucial decision, to produce a different city or to change society?

The world demographic explosion and growth of cities are a reality. They are easy to analyze historically and to find excuses for, but they offer no easy solutions to voluminous and pressing problems. Never, in fact, has the present looked so hopeful and so foreboding at the very same time; and never were so many people engaged in looking for solutions for a better future for all mankind.

2

URBANIZATION
AND ECONOMIC
GROWTH

Urban growth and economic growth have for a long time been referred to as synonymous. Much theoretical discussion has been devoted to the question of which preceded which, but it was fundamentally accepted in classical theory that the two are closely connected. This stems from the fact that the classical theories were formulated almost exclusively on the basis of statistical data and historical evidence accumulated in the developed countries of Europe and America, where the theory often holds true.

In recent years, however, the notion that economic and urban growth go hand in hand has come increasingly under fire. The growing concern with underdeveloped and developing countries has produced new evidence that often refutes accepted formulas. New processes of urbanization have come to light in which economic development plays little or no part and in which particular urban relations hinder economic progress. It is also now understood that the accelerated economies of fast-growing cities do not necessarily always imply corresponding development of the whole country.

Furthermore, effects of environmental and social decay in many developed countries have brought the long-accepted theories into considerable disfavor in well-advanced economies as well. It appears that the concepts of economic growth are not as straightforward as they may seem, and that progress in one field may well be offset in another.

THEORIES OF URBAN AND ECONOMIC GROWTH

The complexity of economic and urban relationships was one of the issues to which participants at the Rehovot Conference

17

devoted much time and thought. It was generally agreed that the interrelation of the two is far more complex than was hitherto believed and that the current theories are quite inadequate, especially in developing countries.

BRIAN BERRY, writing about urban hierarchies, outlined the historical background of the economic development of cities in the developed countries according to their spatial organization.

Common Growth Characteristics of Developed Countries. The developed countries have experienced high rates of increase in per capita product and substantial rates of population growth. Much of the economic growth has been sustained as a result of improved production techniques—largely improvements in the quality of inputs and greater efficiency traceable to increases in useful knowledge and improved institutional arrangements. All sectors of their economies have participated in the increase of efficiency, manufacturing in particular, while at the same time sustained growth has involved changes in the relative importance of the sectors. A declining share of total product is attributable to agriculture, rising shares to manufacturing and public utilities, and rapidly increasing shares to personal, professional, and governmental services. Significant changes have occurred in the structure of final demand. These changes have been both the effect and the cause of changes in the productive process, and have included important shifts in the regional allocation of resources and increasing size of production units as both product and labor have shifted from smaller to larger firms and organizations. These, of course, have led to increased concentration of people in cities. Shifts in capital allocation, in product, and in labor have in turn depended on rapid institutional adjustments and mobility in factor inputs, and it is here that urbanization has played a critical role in facilitating shifts in population and the labor force, both among and within regions and by type.

Regional Implications of the Growth Process. Rapid increases in total product have also implied greater pressure on natural resources, while increasing scale and concentration imply wide differentials in types and rates of growth among different social and economic groups in different regions, the interregional mobility of labor and capital, and the emergence of a geographic pattern of core (or heartland) and periphery (or hinterlands).

Large-scale industry has tended to concentrate in a limited number of cities in a limited region that serves as the polity's industrial heartland and, because of the large numbers of industrial workers employed, the center of national demand. Such a concentration develops a self-generating momentum as complementary services

18

and activities are established, each helping the other to pyramid the productive process; increasing numbers of workers further concentrate the scale of the local market and pull even more strongly activities seeking optimal national market access.

This cumulative causation extends outward to the hinterlands, for once the core-periphery pattern is set the core region becomes the lever for development of peripheral regions, reaching out to them for their resources as its input requirements increase, stimulating their growth differentially in accordance with its resource demands and the resource endowment of the regions. The result of this core-centered pattern of growth and expansion is regional differentiation— the specialization of regional roles in the national economy.

Cities are the instruments whereby specialized subregions are articulated in a national space-economy. They are the centers of activity and innovation, focal points of the transport network, locations of superior accessibility at which firms can most easily reap scale economies and at which industrial complexes can obtain the economies of localization and urbanization. Agricultural enterprise is more efficient in the vicinity of cities. The more prosperous commercialized agricultures encircle the major cities, whereas the inaccessible peripheries of the great urban regions are characterized by backward, subsistence economic systems.

Two major elements characterize this spatial organization of the developed countries: (1) a system of cities arranged in a hierarchy according to the functions performed by each; and (2) corresponding areas of urban influence, or urban fields, surrounding each of the cities in the system.

Generally, the size and functions of a city and the extent of its urban field are proportional. Each region within the national economy focuses on a center of metropolitan rank, and it is the network of intermetropolitan connections that articulates the whole. The spatial incidence of economic growth is a function of distance from the metropolis. Troughs of economic backwardness lie in the most inaccessible areas along the intermetropolitan peripheries. Further subregional articulation is provided by successively smaller centers at progressively lower levels of the hierarchy—smaller cities, towns, villages, etc.

Economic change is patterned by the urban hierarchy. Impulses of economic change are transmitted in such a system simultaneously along three planes: (1) outward from heartland metropolises to those of the regional hinterlands; (2) from centers of higher to centers of lower level in the hierarchy, in a pattern of "hierarchical diffusion"; and (3) outward from urban centers into their surrounding urban fields.

Part of the diffusion mechanism is to be found in the operation of urban labor markets. When growth is sustained over long periods, regional income inequality, for example, should be reduced because the higher the capital/labor ratio in a region, the higher the employment level of the unskilled at any wage rate and at any given social minimum and, therefore, the smaller the number of involuntarily unemployed. With a general expansion in a high income area, some industries will be priced out of the high-income labor market, and there will be a shift of that industry to low-income regions, i.e., to smaller urban or more peripheral areas. The significance of this "filtering" or "trickle-down" process lies not only in its direct but also in its indirect effects. If the boom originated in the high-income region, as is highly likely, the multiplier effects will be larger in the initiating region, although the relative rise in income may be greater in the underdeveloped region. But the induced effects on real income and employment may be considerably greater in the low-income region if prices there are likely to rise less and/or if the increase in output per worker would be greater. Both are likely, because of decreasing cost due to external economies stemming from urbanization of the labor force. If the boom can be maintained, industries of higher labor productivity will shift units into lower-income areas and the low-wage industries will be forced to move into even smaller towns and more isolated areas.

The significance of these diffusion mechanisms is that if economic growth is sustained over long periods it results in progressive integration of the space-economy. Regional differences in levels of welfare are progressively eliminated, since demands for and supplies of labor are adjusted by outward flows of growth impulses through the urban hierarchy and the inward migration of labor to central cities. Troughs of economic backwardness are reduced in intensity, and each area finds itself within the fields of influence of a variety of urban centers of a variety of sizes. Sufficient growth impulses will move through the system so that each region and each city can expect to grow at about the same rate as the nation, although local factors may cause seemingly random variations above and below this national expectation when viewed from the national perspective.

THE CITY AS AN INSTRUMENT OF ECONOMIC
GROWTH AND OVERGROWTH

Referring to the process in developed countries, EDMUNDO FLORES said,

. . . Until approximately 30 years ago the relationship between economic growth and urbanization could be stated in firm, clear terms.

20

As Schumpeter put it, "Modern economic processes are to a great extent contingent upon agglomerations of population in cities and upon the facilities put at the disposal of the business community by public action."

Or, as Kingsley Davis wrote, "Urban growth is an excellent indicator to measure the economic and social development of a region. . . . The city reflects the changes that take place in each sphere of social life. . . . Its growth is nurtured by all the factors that turn agricultural illiteracy into industrial literacy. . . ."

In the classical argument, urban growth produced substantial external economies and externalities, and the fast spread of cities, in turn, triggered far-reaching changes in the subsistence pattern of land utilization.

The preindustrial subsistence pattern was subject to simultaneous and disparate pressures exerted by the new and varied use of possibilities inherent in modern technology. Concepts such as "optimum location" or "fertility" became increasingly elusive, since the new margins of substitution and the possibilities of duplication invalidated notions built on supposedly static attributes.

The usefulness of space, in the classical argument, became associated with new functions, which, far from depending on Marshall's "free gifts of nature," were linked to man-made circumstances, to individual wants, and to social objectives. Technology made possible the swift removal of many previous resistances to land use. Sanitation and pest and disease control rendered usable land that before was void. Irrigation and efficient transportation and communication facilities converted frontiers and remote hinterlands into integrated market areas. The cumulative discovery of more uses for old and new materials shifted the optimum site of previously established industries and plants. The land utilization pattern assumed a new dimension as vertical deployment was added to horizontal spread. Principal land uses achieved unprecedented degrees of intensity in the ever expanding metropolis, while at the same time they became exposed to rapid obsolescence.

Virtually in every case the economies of agglomeration exceeded its diseconomies, and therefore urbanization on an ever growing scale was generally hailed as a beneficial symptom and one to be proud of. For instance, when the 1970 census revealed that the population of the metropolitan area of Mexico City had reached 8.5 million, the newspapers wrote excited stories about this pretended landmark in the country's development.

Flores then introduced his first doubts about the validity of this theory.

. . . Then this rosy, optimistic picture began to deteriorate
alarmingly, particularly in the developing world. The joint and
cumulative effects of the population explosion; Duesenberry's demonstration effect; the new, devastating progress in communications,
which I call the "McLuhan effect"; the emergence of automation; the
appearance of ubiquitous environmental disruptions, e.g., smog, water
and sea pollution; and, finally, the emergence of large-scale, massive
rural and urban unemployment—all these powerfully disrupting forces
converged in the expanding cities of the developing nations and turned
accelerated urbanization into one of the most baffling and acute
problems of our times.

Jay Forrester's warning concerning the flaws of contemporary
urban development policies seems an apt starting point for outlining
national policies with positive repercussions in the cities: ". . . efforts
to improve the condition of our cities will result primarily in increasing the population of the cities and causing the population of the country
to concentrate in the cities. The over-all condition of urban life for
any particular economic class or population, cannot be appreciably
better or worse than that of the remainder of the country to and from
which people may come. Programs aimed at improving the city can
succeed only if they result in eventually raising the average quality
of life for the country as a whole."

Various Speakers at the Conference explained the shortcomings of the accepted theories of interrelated urban and economic
growth in the underdeveloped countries. The external manifestations of what had become known as "overurbanization," such as
unemployment, slums, squalor, diminishing standards of living,
and environmental decay, are mainly dealt with in other chapters
of this book. Flores' discussion of unemployment, however,
put the subject into perspective.

. . . Unemployment is a modern malady born with the Industrial
Revolution. In feudal times it did not exist. There were, to be sure,
idleness, hunger, and famine, but not unemployment. However, as
soon as a traditional society begins to industrialize and to urbanize,
unemployment rears its ugly head. The new productive techniques
and communications, and the temptations created by the enormous
variety of trinkets, novelties, and services produced by industry and
towns, make many people, especially women, feel unemployed. At the
same time the towns and factories begin to attract an ever growing
flow of peasants and their families. Thus accelerated industrialization increases the number of the unemployed at higher rates than
those of population growth.

URBANIZATION WITHOUT ECONOMIC GROWTH

One of the reasons for this seeming paradox may lie in the "unnatural" growth of cities in developing countries—unnatural insofar as many of these cities did not arise as a result of integral internal needs but in order to fulfill secondary external functions. The point was well illustrated by speakers from Africa, South America, and Asia.

AKIN MABOGUNJE spoke on the rise of cities in Africa.

Urbanization in Africa: A Consumer Innovation. It is the main thesis of this paper that the primary reason why urbanization represents such a disturbing factor in many African countries today is that it is essentially a consumer innovation, a new form of social organization that encourages an attitude of mind negative to or at least inconsistent with real economic development. Although urban development has had a long history in Africa, notably in northern and western Africa and along the East African coast, its modern manifestation can be said to be essentially due to active European penetration of the continent in the last decades of the nineteenth century. Fresh from the trans-forming experience of the growing Industrial Revolution of the eighteenth and nineteenth centuries, the various European powers scrambled among themselves to carve out in Africa complementary trading areas for collecting greatly needed industrial raw material. The African's role in this intercontinental economic relationship was that of the blind seller, doggedly producing goods about whose utility or monetary value he had hardly any idea. However, when he received the scanty amount paid in exchange for these goods, he could feel the pleasure of self-aggrandizement in spending the money on a wide variety of unusual but cheap, mass-produced articles from distant European factories. These articles were to be bought in the new growing urban centers where the European merchants concentrated. Hence from the very beginning, modern European-induced cities in Africa were seen as places where people spent their hard-earned income or showed off their capacity to consume.

A striking contrast thus distinguishes the role of the city in Europe and in Africa. For Europe, cities were, in the words of Haig, optimum points for production and consumption, especially when considered from the point of view of transfer efficiency. With respect to their role as production centers, Mantoux noted that "the factory system brought about the rise of those mighty centers of population whose monstrous growth is still going on under our own eyes." Lampard further observed that "the most significant feature of the early urban-industrialization in England, the Netherlands, and northern France, was that it permitted experiments in the organization and promotion of business several decades before any widespread application of the power-technology." In other words, the rise and growth of the modern industrial city in Europe was the occasion of significant transformation in the technology of production and transportation and in the organization of business and other enterprises.

In Africa no such fundamental transformation was consequent on the growth of the modern city. Although the collection, bulking, and exporting of industrial raw material required a high degree of organization and business skills, the logic of a colonial relationship was such that the opportunities for doing this were jealously guarded and restricted to citizens of the metropolitan country. In short, urbanization during the colonial period denied the African not only the opportunity of acquiring modern productive skills for processing the produce of his farms, forests, and mines but also the chance of learning organizational skills needed for ensuring the smooth flow and delivery of this produce to foreign markets.

For most urban Africans in the colonial period, therefore, the city was simply the place where they did a set of not very meaningful jobs for which they were paid wages and salaries to spend on goods and services whose production they knew little about. This relation of the African to the city was further underlined by the type of education he came to be given. This was an education that taught him to read and write in a foreign language and to acquire literary and numerical skills that freed him from the guiding constraints of his own culture or at the least had little relevance to it. It is true that this education was in the best tradition of Western European civilization, whose essence, according to Evans, was "to reject all that tends to hold the human spirit in bondage." Yet this rejection in the African context meant an escape not only from the onerous life of the farmer but from virtually any hard work. And for this relatively slothful life in the cities the African was paid handsomely, certainly at a relatively much higher level than his compeers in the rural areas. It is thus no wonder that the image of Western education that was conjured up in the minds of most Africans was as a means of escape from strenuous manual work to a life of relative luxury. And the city was the place where this easily acquired wealth was spent to best advantage. Virtually every African farmer, every African parent, prayed that his son might be educated so that he could turn away from farming and go to the city to enjoy "the good life."

The point, then, is that, while European-type education and European-induced urbanization taught the African how to enjoy "the good life," they equipped him only minimally with the skills to create the wealth needed for this enjoyment on the basis of self-sustained growth. However, for as long as the colonial regime lasted, the rush to the cities was kept under moderate control by the simple expedient of restricting the opportunities available for education and creating conditions that discouraged massive migration from rural to urban areas. Such restraints by their very nature are inconsistent with democracy and self-rule. Hence with the independence of most African countries the floodgates of migration from rural to urban areas seem to have been thrown wide open. In order to appreciate the nature of the urbanization problems in Africa today it is therefore necessary to examine some of the socioeconomic changes that followed hard on the heels of political self-government in most of these countries.

Commenting on Mabogunje's ideas, RAM MALHOTRA outlined the processes taking place in Asia.

. . . I think that what Mr. Mabogunje conveyed was that there is a gulf between city life and rural life in the developing countries. After having listened to him I think that we have had a meeting of minds here, and that he spoke not only for Africa but also for Asia — as a matter of fact, he has spoken for all the developing countries. Definitely, then, the consumption-oriented cities present a contrast. We speak of the rich countries getting richer and of the growing gulf between the richer and the poorer countries of the world. When the cities of the developing countries become the centers of consumption, they are really becoming parasites, and this creates a struggle; it is a kind of unrest, a kind of explosion of rising expectations on the part of the rural people, but at the same time a feeling of frustration. I have had several people from the rural areas come and ask, "Why do you have every facility in the capital city, and why are the rural areas so backward?"

When I reflect that our capital city is so backward compared with any city in an advanced country, I can understand this. As far as the rural people are concerned, for them the gap is very big and has to be bridged. I wholeheartedly support the views expressed by Mr. Waterston regarding rural development, as I, too, think that the urbanization problem has to be regarded in the totality of the problem of economic development.

URBANIZATION AND THE STRUCTURE OF
ECONOMIC SECTORS

WALTER SEDWITZ then examined the rise of cities in South America from a similar angle.

. . . It is well known that cities in Latin America were originally located for trade, communications, or military purposes. During a subsequent inward-looking stage, industries seeking markets settled in or near these ready-made urban areas, further contributing to their growth. The concentration of leading sectors and wealth in the cities meant that they progressed in step with the country and that their housing and urban infrastructure could therefore generally be of good quality. The initial outward-looking growth, together with the cost of overcoming adverse geography (mountains, jungles, or distances), produced urbanization oriented toward the coastal periphery, with a few exceptions, and a loosely related though accelerating non-urban population. Cities therefore were intended to facilitate the exploitation of a few natural resources for which there was some demand on the world market or else for the assembly of consumer goods. They were structured to serve these activities and those of government. By the time major efforts were made to guide and accelerate social and economic development, the principal urban centers were firmly established on the basis of those earlier objectives and were already of such a size that they absorbed vast quantities of capital that would otherwise have been available for the development of food supplies, domestically required raw materials and minerals, power and water supplies, and other purposes.

The rise of cities in developing countries has often created a spatial organization that is neither functional nor optimal. BRIAN BERRY examined this in his paper and explained the phenomenon of primacy.

. . . In every country urban centers are organized functionally into a hierarchy; the hierarchy is the instrument whereby society, polity, and economy are integrated over space. In traditional societies hierarchical organization was based as much on purposive sacerdotal, juridical, military, or administrative principles as on economic grounds, however. But, whatever the principles, status of towns within the hierarchy determines their sphere of influence and depends upon the power residing in their level of the hierarchy. Status and sphere, in turn, vary from level to level depending upon the organizing principle. City size remains the simplest and best index to this power. Differences in the numbers of cities in different population-size classes should therefore reveal differences in the nature of hierarchical organization, and these in turn should relate to developmental differences and variations in the degree of urbanization and the proportion of population concentrated in the largest cities.

In the developed nations the distribution of cities by size follows the rank-size distribution, i.e., the distribution is approximately log-normal. The rank-size pattern has thus been interpreted as the "functional" outcome of economic growth, with the result that deviations from the rank-size distribution have excited the greatest interest in the developing nations. The argument is that a rank-size distribution should be characteristic of any well-defined system of cities in which growth has, as a minimum, obeyed the law of proportionate effect for some period of time.

One particular deviation has been of overwhelming concern. Where the actual population of the largest city exceeds that expected on the basis of the rank-size rule, a condition of "primacy" is said to exist. Such deviation is thought by many to be dysfunctional. Colin Clark uses the additional term "oligarchy" to describe situations such as prevail in Japan, India, Australia, or Brazil, where the towns of over 100,000 population have a bigger share of the total urban population than would be expected from the straight-line relationship, but where at the same time the primacy of the leading city is kept in check. Clark also defines as "counterprimacy" either declining primacy of the largest city through time or increasing negative deviation of the population of the largest city from predictions based on the rank-size rule under conditions of national planning directed at achieving such outcomes as goals.

The idea of primacy as initially formulated by Mark Jefferson was very simple. He argued that everywhere "nationalism crystallizes in primate cities . . . supereminent . . . not merely in size, but in national influence." He assessed the degree of eminence of cities within countries by computing the ratios of size of the second- and third-ranking cities to that of the largest place. But immediately after Jefferson's papers had appeared Zipf directed attention to the entire system of cities, focusing in particular on the case of the rank-size rule. Such, he argued, was the situation to be expected in any "homogeneous socioeconomic system" that had reached a harmonious equilibrium state.

It remained for discussants at a series of postwar UNESCO conferences on urbanization in Asia, in the Far East, and in Latin America to put the two together. Cases deviating from the rule were said to arise from "overurbanization" of the economies of lesser developed countries because of "excessive" in-migration and super-imposition of limited economic development of a colonial type, creating "dual economies" characterized by "primate cities" that tend to have "paralytic" effects on the development of smaller urban places and to be "parasitic" in relation to the remainder of the national economy.

Obviously, each of the words in quotation marks involves a value judgment; but nonetheless the idea of the primate city from this point on was firmly established as a malignant deviation from expectations about hierarchical organization derived from the rank-size rule, with strong pejorative connotations. The value-laden attitude is illustrated in the following quotation from Lampard's work:

"Its growth and maintenance have been somewhat parasitical in the sense that profits of trade, capital accumulated in agriculture and other primary pursuits, have been dissipated in grandiose urban construction, servicing, and consumption. . . . The labor and enterprise which might otherwise have been invested in some form of light manufacturing or material processing . . . are drawn off to the great city by the attractive dazzle of a million lights."

Measurement of primacy has subsequently become a textbook exercise in urban studies (see for example the volume by Jack P. Gibbs). To planners such as John Friedmann and T. Lackington primacy cannot be separated from the idea of "hyperurbanization": ". . . a society exhibiting a high measure of disequilibrium between its levels of urbanization and per capita income is likely to experience serious internal tensions. . . . [This] hyperurbanization . . . takes the form of increasing concentration of urban activities. This may be established in several ways. . . . the degree of urban primacy [may be measured] according to . . . the relation of the largest to the second urban complex. . . . Another possible measure of primacy is in relation to the rank-size rule which describes a standardized distribution of a country's population among its cities."

To many planners and policy-makers in the developing countries "gigantism" of the largest cities is a characteristic to be feared, even when the principal city is small relative to cities in other areas.

The reason for primacy is to be found in the filtering mechanism that produces hierarchical diffusion. This mechanism works poorly, if at all, in many parts of the world. Instead of development "trickling down" the urban size-ratchet and spreading its effects outward within urban fields, growth is concentrated in a few metropolitan centers and a wide gulf between metropolis and smaller city is apparent. Rather than articulation there is polarization. Why?

There are two classes of reasons, one institutional, the other functional. Under colonial rule most empires were controlled by holding key cities and strategic points: "head links" that connected the colonial net. For colonial powers to extend and consolidate their authority in alien social and geographical territories, cities were the necessary base of action. British rule in India, for example, centered on capital and provincial cities both for maintaining an integrated and authoritarian administrative structure and for securing the economic base of its power—the collection of taxes and control over the export of raw materials and the import of British manufactured goods. Elsewhere in Southeast Asia, McGee writes, the structure of the colonial economy did not permit the cities to be generative of economic growth. The colonial cities were subordinate to the metropolis and world trade, acting as foci for the alien middleman and effectively inhibiting economic growth.

However, the colonial cities did help create modern indigenous elites. They gave birth to nationalist movements, and they restructured traditional economic patterns to focus on the cities, initiating massive inward flows of rural migrants. The resulting high rate of population growth outstripped rates of economic growth in the cities after independence and confounded the trickle-down process. The result was to worsen the way of life outside the metropolis and simultaneously increase the urban labor supply, at all levels but particularly among the unskilled, at a pace that has never permitted economic expansion to come up against (ever rising) metropolitan wage-rate floors; thus growth cannot decentralize naturally. This systematic confounding of trickle-down mechanisms is particularly acute where, either because of the very small size of a political unit or because of a critical dependency of the polity upon external trade relationships, there is a single national focus and sizable alternative growth centers are absent.

THE COMPLEXITY OF ECONOMIC AND URBAN GROWTH

The evidence and data that have been accumulating in developing countries have given rise to much doubt as to what the actual relations between economic growth and urbanization are. LOWDON WINGO expressed uncertainty in his paper on national development objectives.

. . . We have come to accept as fact the proposition that in the process of economic development a fairly strong relationship exists among levels of development, measures of social welfare, and degree of urbanization. It is no mystery that among nations such variables as the proportion of male labor force gainfully employed in non-agricultural pursuits, the percentage of the total population living in urban settlements (however defined), and per capita incomes exhibit very strong intercorrelation; indeed, such variables are frequently used interchangeably to describe differential levels of economic development.
Nevertheless, the precise relationship among these phenomena is sufficiently obscure as to leave unresolved at least two key questions: (1) how are rates of change of these variables related, and (2) how are characteristics of these variables related? Uncertainty about the answers to these questions has given rise to a great deal of controversy about the consequences of government programs and policies tending to influence the way in which urbanization takes place. Some argue that the rate of change of urbanization variables

can be retarded without either affecting the rate of growth of welfare measures like Gross Domestic Product (GDP) or impairing the rate of the agricultural-industrial transformation that lies at the heart of our conventional view of economic development. Others argue that a given national urban population can be distributed in different ways among cities of various sizes without any loss in welfare or in the rate of economic development. Both these questions are brought to the fore in the current controversies taking place in a number of developing countries, centering on the relative scale and rate of growth of their principal metropolitan regions.

The same doubts were voiced by Dr. DELGATE.

. . . My contribution to this discussion is mainly based on my West African experience. The question I would like to raise is fundamental to the whole approach of linking urban structure with economic development in a dynamic sense, and I consider it a great improvement that we are talking about the processes involved, identifying what really happens in the course of time and not, as used to be done in textbooks 5 or 10 years ago, without knowing exactly what the controlling mechanisms are.

An attempt is being made to pinpoint these controlling mechanisms and to suggest a way of rational interference with the processes in order to achieve a certain policy objective. Since we are talking about mechanisms, my first question is whether it would be right openly to admit that there is not one single mechanism that relates economic development to urban structure but at least two mechanisms: one that functioned a hundred years ago and ended in the early part of this century, and another that is operating at present, particularly in underdeveloped countries. Are these two extensions of each other or are we talking about a different world? For dimensional history, once it is introduced, carries irreversibility with it.

EDWIN MILLS, on the other hand, wrote a compelling thesis disavowing any connection at all between urbanization and economic growth.

. . . Almost as pervasive as urbanization is the belief of public officials and, to a lesser extent, of urban specialists in universities that migration from rural to urban areas, and especially to the large cities, is excessive and that public policies should attempt to retard the growth of at least the largest urban areas. This paper, and the empirical research on the subject of overurbanization surveyed in the next section, are concerned with the less developed countries (LDC's). But it is worth noting here that similar concern is frequently voiced in many developed countries. Many Western European nations have tried in various ways to inhibit the growth of their largest metropolitan area. For example, in England it has been government policy to discourage growth in the London area for most of the period since World War II. In the United States it is now almost official policy of the national administration that the largest metropolitan areas, especially on the eastern seaboard, are too big and that their growth should be discouraged. As a final example, the strength of the forces producing urbanization is suggested by the fact that public officials worry about overurbanization even in countries where, unlike the United States, governments appear to have almost complete control over the growth of urban areas.

It is important at the outset to distinguish two strands of concern with overurbanization in LDC's. One group of people believes that an excessively large fraction of the population in many LDC's lives in urban areas. A second group believes that there is an excessive concentration of the urban population in the largest urban area. The first concern is with the extent of urbanization and the second is with the size distribution of urban areas. Neither phenomenon implies the other. Although the main focus of this paper is on the second concern, I shall start with brief comments on the first issue.

1. Those who believe that many LDC's are overurbanized base their contention on the alleged relationship between urbanization and industrialization. Several writers have correlated the percentage of the labor force employed in industry. Sample data are values of the two variables from a variety of developed and less developed countries during the 1950s and 1960s. It has been found that many LDC's lie above the average relationship, or regression line, between the two variables. Many people have concluded that such countries are more urbanized than is justified by their levels of industrialization and that overurbanization produces parasitic urban areas that become pockets of misery.

The first criticism of such studies is somewhat technical. The correlation methods employed measure the straight-line relationship between the variables. But, even if one believed that urbanization and industrialization should be closely related, the relationship should not be expected to be a straight line. A more plausible form for the relationship would be a logistic, or S-shaped, curve. Countries with little industrial employment should be expected to have some urban areas, because urban areas perform functions other than providing places for industrial activity. Until industrial employment reaches a substantial level it would probably have relatively little effect on the extent of urbanization. Likewise, countries with very large industrial sectors should be expected to have some rural population, because agriculture and other activities take place in rural areas.

31

When industrial employment reaches a high level it will probably
have relatively little further effect on urbanization. But in the middle
range of levels of industrial employment it may have substantial
effect on urbanization. The situation is as shown in the figure below.

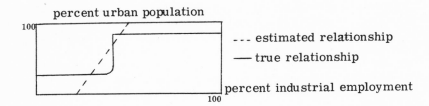

The estimated straight-line relationship will have a slope
similar to that over the middle range of true curved relationship,
because that is where most of the sample observations lie. It is then
inevitable that most countries with little industrial employment will
be more urbanized than is indicated by the straight line. But the conclusion that little-industrialized countries are therefore overurbanized
reflects the mistaken assumption that the true relationship is a
straight line. Such studies provide no evidence of overurbanization.

It cannot be doubted that urbanization is related to industrialization in the broadest sense. Rapid urbanization in Europe and North
America during the nineteenth century was undoubtedly spurred by
the rapid industrialization of the times. But the relationship has
never been very close. In the United States, whose data I know best,
urbanization was substantial before the period of rapid industrialization that began about 1840. More important, urbanization has proceeded
rapidly since 1920, although the percentage of the labor force that
is in manufacturing is almost the same now as it was in 1920. Likewise, urbanization and industrialization are not highly correlated in
Europe. Sovani has shown that the correlation between urbanization
and industrialization is only about 0.40 in Western Europe and North
America, whereas it is about 0.85 in the LDC's.

In fact, there is no strong reason to expect urbanization and
industrialization to be closely related, and I am at a loss to know why
so much attention has been paid to the issue. Urban areas have many
functions, of which industrial production is only one, although it is
an important one.

2. The second strand of concern with overurbanization has to
do with primacy, or the allegedly excessive concentration of urban
population in the country's largest urban areas.

There is a voluminous literature on the size distribution of urban areas, which cannot be reviewed here. It is well established that the size distribution of urban areas is highly skewed in all countries and at all times for which data are available. The skew is to the right, indicating that there are a few very large urban areas and a much larger group of small urban areas. Some writers used to believe that the size distribution of urban areas obeyed the "rank-size rule," which says that the second largest urban area is half the size of the largest, the third is one-third as large as the largest, and so on. But it is now recognized that a variety of skewed distributions, including the Pareto and the log-normal, fit most data about equally well.

Whatever the exact distribution, it is widely believed that the largest urban area is considerably larger relative to other urban areas in LDC's than elsewhere. The fact is often attributed to colonialism or other political factors, and the primate city is believed to be parasitic and generally harmful to the development of the country.

Earlier studies of alleged excessive primacy in LDC's were based on fragmentary data. During the 1960s much better data on worldwide urbanization became available, and recent studies have shown that primacy is not related to economic development in a simple fashion.

Kingsley Davis has recently published a valuable monograph of world urbanization data. The monograph shows 1950, 1960, and projected 1970 data for total population, urban population, and population density for all countries for which data are available. It also contains a primacy index for every country that had at least four urban areas with populations of 100,000 or more. In 1960 there were 46 such countries. Davis's primacy index is the population of the largest urban area divided by the sum of populations of the next three largest urban areas.

THE NEED FOR NEW AND COMPREHENSIVE
THEORIES

NATHANIEL LICHFIELD's analysis of economic growth and urbanization best expresses the current preoccupation with the problem under discussion. Pondering the question of whether developing countries should follow in the steps of developed countries, Lichfield wrote:

. . . As literature shows, there are compelling reasons for thinking that the correlation between economic growth and urbanization for developing countries in the future will not necessarily be the same as for developed countries in the past. For one thing, the

33

indicators mentioned show that, while there are clearly common
underlying tendencies, the urbanization of developing countries is
proceeding more rapidly than it did in developed countries in the
past (national population growth is faster and also the rate of rural
migration from the land) compared with improvements in the socioeconomic indicators. This divergence might have all kinds of explanations, including the possibility that many developing countries are
overurbanizing for their stage of economic development.

Another reason is the differing political climates of developed
and developing countries during their developing stage. While in
Europe economic change was the catalyst for political change, in
developing countries since World War II it is political developments,
in particular the independence from colonial rule, that are themselves
forcing social and economic changes.

Other not unrelated reasons are the greater political maturity
of the developing countries and the fact that economic growth in the
contemporary world is not regarded as narrowly as economic growth
in the last century. There is greater consciousness today of the aims
of more equal distribution of wealth as well as of economic efficiency,
and also of the indirect costs of economic growth that are not shown
in national income accounts, to overcome which a slowing in the rate
of economic growth is desirable. Finally, there is the influence of
planning in contemporary developing countries at the three levels
that are of significance here (national, regional, and local), which
was absent in the corresponding stages of growth in the developed
countries.

Perhaps it is this last reason for the divergence between the
history of the developed countries and the future of the developing
countries that is the most important. It is now possible for countries
to attempt to shape their future in the social, economic, physical, and
locational spheres. While experiments in this direction since World
War II have shown the difficulties as much as the solutions, they
nonetheless demonstrate sufficient achievement to give some confidence that in the not too distant future comprehensive planning of
the kind indicated will become a reality. The signs are hopeful; let
an economic rather than an urban planner testify in relation to towns:
"Urbanization is not the result of cosmic forces or organic growth
following immutable laws of nature which can be observed but not
influenced by human behavior. Within limits, man can control his
environment . . . a need for problem-solving where urbanization
occurs has produced increasingly successful efforts towards social
control through planning."

For the reasons just indicated it is not thought profitable to
trace from historical analysis the contribution that urbanization has
made to past economic development and simply to apply the results
to the future of developing countries.

As has been pointed out, "the search for a positive urbanization policy needs more detached analyses of the dynamic relationship between urbanization and industrial development, analyses which go beyond statistical correlations." Since these do not exist, it is only possible to speak in general terms. The same point could be put another way. Common observation of the urbanization patterns and problems of the developed countries spells caution in following historical paths, a caution that is reinforced by the fact that the very aims of contemporary urban and regional planning in developed countries are to remedy the consequences of past economic development and industrialization. Indeed, so serious are the problems in developed countries that the content of urban and regional planning itself is being extended to cover the social crises in the cities and also the threat of pollution in the urban and rural environment.

If the experience and practice in economic growth and urbanization of the developed countries are not to be taken as the guide for the developing countries, however, then perhaps economic theory can help.

Lichfield then went on to examine the gaps in economic theory relating to economic growth and urbanization and voiced the urgent need for better and more applicable theories.

. . . As might be expected, many different branches of economic theory have a bearing on the relation between economic growth and urbanization. Examples are those relating to the growth of economic activity itself; to the location of the firm; to the spatial distribution of economic activity, relating to both services and production; to growth poles and areas; to growth poles in the regional context. A perusal of this literature leads to the following points of relevance to the theme of this paper.

Economic growth theory has changed emphasis from the classical location theories to recognition of "growth poles" and "growth centers" as tools of research into the dynamics of economic growth in a spatial context. But the concepts have so far been only loosely defined and are not yet clear. A fairly common theme is that of linkage effects, the interconnection between firms and industries and the economics of agglomeration in nonspatial terms. The shortcomings of the discussion in nonspatial terms were recognized by distinguishing between economic space (in which poles were defined) and geographical space (in which poles were located). Boudeville showed the existence of a growth "pole" as abstract space and a "center" as the condition for its appearance and location in a geographic sense. Isard and Schooler demonstrated a link between a pole and its location by developing an interactivity input-output matrix for the elements in an industrial complex, in which they dealt with the choice of investment with regard to consideration of optimum size, of scale and transport costs. But, in contrast, Hirschmann has suggested that the notion of "pole" has a limited theoretical value in a locational context and as an inducement to economic growth.

Alongside uncertainty in theory, there has been only limited empirical research on growth centers in practice. However, this has not daunted those concerned in regional economic development and the regional allocation of investments in time and space. This has mainly been discussed in France, where national and regional planning calls for definition of regions and spatial as well as sectoral distribution of resources. In this connection Boudeville's concepts of three types of region (homogenous, polarized, and planning/programing regions) were incorporated into French planning. He developed a model that makes possible the definition of boundaries of regions polarized around major cities by the application of an information-flow gravity model with the inputs of population and distance only.

However, despite this bold excursion from theory into the applied field, a comprehensive theory still has to be developed on the relationship between economic growth and urbanization. It would seem that some important gaps in the theory occur in such fields as the following, all of which are highly relevant to the evolution of a more satisfactory theory of economic growth and urbanization that could be applicable in developing countries:

(1) relations between agglomeration and external economics, particularly when not only the direct costs and benefits to the firm are concerned but also the indirect costs and benefits to others, the externalities;

(2) location of optimal growth centers, having regard not only to past performance but also to potential and to empirical irregularities within the countries;

(3) optimal rate of growth centers, having regard to insufficiency of export-based industry within a country to sustain growth, or need for rural sectors to retain labor in a region;

(4) determination of take-off point in particular localities and whether theory in urban growth corresponds to economic growth in this respect;

(5) optimal size for a city or industrial complex to provide an "adequate" range of external economies to firms; and

(6) nature of costs incurred by preventing expansion in particular growth areas to the benefit of expansion in others.

Thus considerable steps are needed for the formulation of adequate theory. Indeed, at this stage of knowledge it would be a useful exercise simply to set out what a theory of spatial incidence of development would have to attempt to explain. In this regard, in the view of one review author, the theory should be sufficiently developed to "identify and quantify the specific areas in which the present structure of economic space falls short of that structure needed to implement the goals of the society under consideration and lead to the formulation of policies which will help the society to achieve optimum distribution of population, industry, investments, and urban equipment consistent with the achievement of its goals."

CONCLUSIONS

The rise of the cities and the economic development that have taken place during the last century in the Western world have for a long time been regarded as two sides of the same coin.

This has often led to the largely erroneous and unfortunate conclusion that building large cities will in itself guarantee economic progress. The developing countries in particular are suffering from the serious implications of these misconceptions, which often result from the best intentions or are inherited from past colonial history.

It has been realized now that, though they are closely related, it is wrong to confuse urban and economic growth. Unchecked urban growth may cause economic stagnation or even economic collapse. Economic misplanning on the other hand may well cause overurbanization.

Instead of the old ones, new theories are therefore required that will apply to the developing countries, as well as new techniques to interrelate economic growth with urbanization in a meaningful and effective manner.

3

**CITY
AND
SOCIETY**

The vast changes in human habitation that are taking place in virtually all countries at an ever increasing pace are not only revising the physical and occupational environments of man but shaking the very pillars of his society. Traditional social structures formed in the rural village and the small town, and molded on tribal and family ties, are being shattered in the large city while other social entities, hitherto often undefined, are formed instead. Much of the misery of modern life in developed and developing countries alike can be traced directly to its social origins, and many of the evils of the past are being replaced in the huge city by new and no less awesome burdens.

The fine arts and philosophy have traditionally been the realms for the study of man in his society. The scientific study of societies and social structures is a relatively recent but constantly developing innovation. The adaptation of these new disciplines to urban studies and urban regional planning is an even more recent practice in which there is still much uncharted terrain.

SOCIAL ASPECTS OF URBANIZATION

Speakers at the Rehovot Conference concentrated on those characteristics most typical of the developing world when tackling the questions of urbanization and its impact on society. A number of speakers made an attempt to put the process of urbanization into historical and perceptual perspective from the social point of view.

ROBERT WEAVER dealt with this subject in his paper.

. . . The inevitable short-run economic and social costs of rapid and large-scale urban migration have frequently been documented.

They are expressed in high rates of unemployment and underemployment, inadequate volume and low quality of housing and supportive
facilities, high mortality and morbidity rates, broken families, juvenile
delinquency, and associated ills. Why, then, do people flock to the
cities? The answer, obviously, is that cities hold out attractions. An
urban environment seems to be the setting to raise living and work
standards and provide educational and cultural facilities and programs
that can elevate man from the dull drudgery and meagerness of peasant
life. It is this promise of economic and social mobility and opportunity
for greater realization of one's potential that primarily motivates the
movement from the countryside to the city. The push of the drabness
and economic, political, cultural, and social poverty of rural environments accelerates the process. But more important is the potential
of urbanization. Urban growth is both a basic condition and an inherent
consequence of social and economic development. More, the success
of population control and rural modernization is largely dependent on
urbanization and the dissemination of urban attitudes. Sober reflection
forces one to recognize that migration to cities will not only continue
but also grow in force.

Social Aspects of Urbanization in the Western World. Man has a tendency to identify the problems of his generation as unique—a tendency
that is greatly accentuated by the disdain for history so often expressed
by some of today's youth. Yet history is instructive, providing many
insights into contemporary behavior.

The cities of industrializing England were centers of crime,
pestilence, filth, and human suffering. William Blake wrote of them
in these words:

> I wander thro' each charter'd street,
> Near where the charter'd Thames does flow,
> And mark in every face I meet
> Marks of weakness, marks of woe.

Hogarth and Dickens painted pictures of urban misery and poverty, of social disorganization and disease, that were frightening. In
the United States European immigrants were crowded into the cities
with the familiar toll of disruption of families, illegitimacy, desertion
by husbands, disease, alcoholism, and madness.

Subsequently Negroes began to move out of the social backlash
of southern agriculture into the northern cities in large numbers.
They faced the same problems plus additional ones of past deprivation
of unique intensity and continuing racial discrimination. Recently they
have felt the adverse consequences of the cessation of a strong demand
for unskilled factory labor as well as a much more complicated urban
environment. Why did they continue to come?

Movement to the city afforded many their first opportunity for industrial employment, and some of them became a functioning part of organized labor. While the rate of unemployment among nonwhites still remains twice as high as for whites—and the differential is much greater among youth—the vast majority of the black migrants are working and earning wages much higher than they could in the rural South. Currently, for example, the economic benefits of urban migration are both more immediate and greater for blacks than for whites. The city, too, provides excitement and, for some, a greater sense of personal worth.

The transfer of disadvantaged blacks in the United States to areas of the country where people have more advantages represents a long-term gain. It brings the problems they face to light, forcing the attention of society to the contrast between their and most others' status, thereby causing acute discomfort in a society that likes to believe it affords equal opportunity. In rural America, as in all rural societies, poverty can be hidden. When the poor move to the city they cannot and will not be hidden. An attempt can be made to sweep them into slums, but they will and do ultimately emerge, because in the city men are interdependent and interact sooner or later. In a word, the urbanization of the rural southern blacks has created a situation that has more potential for improvement than their continued isolation from the mainstream of society.

For all the economic and social problems measured by statistical averages and, more important, those that cannot be quantified, it is in the urban environment that hundreds of thousands of Negroes have achieved upward educational, social, and economic mobility. It is primarily in the cities, too, that blacks have won political influence in the nation. Urbanization has occasioned many problems of adjustment and generated serious and baffling economic difficulties—not the least of which is dope addiction. Yet it is also the sine qua non of Negroes' participation in the mainstream of national life. If the color line is eradicated, that, like most progress in race relations, will occur in urban areas. The revolt of the Negro against second-class status is practically exclusively an urban phenomenon, as is the black militant movement.

Urbanization everywhere creates expectations and raises levels of aspiration. It often occasions a new social structure by facilitating greater economic and social mobility. It is either a consequence of industrialization or, at the least, a force to encourage industrialization. It provides better services to those involved. It often enables neglected people to become more effective in influencing government, thereby upgrading their status and helping to create a more effective national effort to deal with economic and social problems.

Significantly, in Latin America, according to Professor Francine F. Rabinovitz of the University of California in Los Angeles, "even the twentieth-century peasant movements were organized by urban-based political groups or parties which sent revolutionaries out to the countryside. The big city is thus a command post for the nation, as well as a container for specifically urban activities."

Ernest Weissmann, formerly with the United Nations, has expressed the situation well in a world setting:

"Urbanization is indeed the principal means by which the benefits of development reach increasingly larger sections of a country's population. . . . Yesterday's ignorant peasants are learning quickly how to manage their community democratically with their own and their families' shelter and livelihood as incentive.

"Wherever the marginal migrant settles, whether as transient or as permanent settler, he has undergone a radical change. Modern science and technology applied in health, agriculture and industry have profoundly altered conditions in country and town and the 'push' away from a declining rural life combines with the 'pull' of the city to change his outlook and aspirations. As 'urban man' he has moved from the traditional landlord/peasant relationship to a new, as yet unchartered social environment of the squatter town (more often than not via the city slum). He now joins with others to promote his and his family's interest collectively."

Urbanization and Traditional Social Structure in Developing Countries. Literature and conventional wisdom are replete with the list of social disintegrations incident to urbanization. All of you who are a part of the process in developing countries know the items well. Those who, like myself, have been involved with them in industrial nations cannot but recognize the serious impact they have, particularly for the young and the old.

The social consequences of rapid urbanization result from being uprooted from the closed static pattern of the rural agricultural community or small town; being thrust into the uncertain turbulence of the city, where every man is a stranger and yet all are dependent on each other; a culture, thousands of years in the making, disintegrating in a generation under the impact of new ideas, new concepts, and new values; learning to survive in an environment created by men yet beyond the ability of men to understand and control; losing the sense of community, of identification, of continuity; trying to find creative satisfaction in a life that often is the constant repetition of a specialized function the significance of which can rarely be understood or explained.

Rather than repeat the inimical social consequences of urbanization, I propose to discuss the question of whether or not we can, in the foreseeable future, do away with the grossest of these ills. Two elements are crucial: the resources available and the impact of population growth. Availability of resources determines the level of employment through its impact on investment and industrialization. It also sets a ceiling on expenditures for housing, infrastructure, health, food, education, and associated social needs. The size and rate of growth of the population determine the magnitude of these needs.

In this context it becomes apparent that the potential of the West differs from that in most developing countries. By way of illustration, consider the United States. Its resources are sufficient to finance full employment and, with rearrangement of priorities, provide sufficient housing and health and social services to upgrade materially the status of newcomers to the cities. Although there has been consistent prediction of a population explosion that would double the population in 40 years, the demographers were again in error.

Preliminary census data suggest that by the year 2000 the population will be closer to 260 million than the 300 million figure previously prophesied some three years ago. And, contrary to many forecasts, the birth rate has declined from about 3.35 children for each family of child-bearing age in the early 1960s to about 2.7. However, because of the postwar baby boom we shall be faced with a large increase in family formation in the next decade.

Regardless of the exact figures involved, the population of the United States will increase appreciably, placing pressure on the supply of resources—water, air, open spaces, transportation, and the like. We will require a large increase in electric power and will probably continue rapidly to expand the number of automobiles and other motor vehicles, augmenting the pollution potential. All this emphasizes the problems of controlling the environment, but it does not spell a lack of resource capabilities to meet the social problems that plague our cities.

There is a tendency in the United States to assume that, because greater expenditures are required to solve the social problems of our cities, enlarged expenditures alone will suffice. But current experience does not support this position. As mentioned above, we can afford to do the job, but, if it is to be accomplished, we shall have to augment appreciably our understanding of these problems and probe deeply into methods for attacking them efficiently. (Indeed, some who recognize this and many who are disillusioned by our program difficulties of the past have consciously or unconsciously shifted from emphasis on social issues to concentration on environmental matters.) Urban problems are so complex and interrelated that a series of intrinsically sound but uncoordinated actions will not suffice, and changing situations call for changing institutions.

European industrial nations are experiencing a migration somewhat similar to that in the United States in the pre-World War I era. It is a movement of people from country to country. In the current situation, the receiving countries—including Great Britain, France, Germany, and Switzerland—are highly industrialized and economically expanding. As always, those migrating have experienced both advantages and grievous social problems. Steadier and higher-paying jobs, although often hard and unpleasant, represent economic improvement, but separation from families, isolation from the larger population, frequent concentration in virtual ghettos, and substandard housing create social costs that were seldom anticipated. The very affluence that attracted these newcomers to European centers of industrial expansion suggests that the receiving areas have the resources, if they so direct them, to modify substantially the impact of displacement and neglect.

The developing nations have both inadequate resources to provide needed economic opportunity and social services for existing urban populations and higher rates of urbanization than Western nations. In some of the developing nations living conditions in town and country are rapidly declining under the impact of the population growth and migration. There are many nations where gross national product increases less rapidly than the rate of population growth and urbanization. These countries will need outside financial and technical assistance. These nations will have to develop urban strategies for national and international development. Few, I am advised, have national policies for housing and urban development or effective machinery, including financial institutions, for dealing with such problems. This suggests that the international community needs not only to envision financial assistance, often in the form of seed capital and other resources, but also to concern itself with helping the undeveloped nations devise and administer appropriate programs to deal with rapid urbanization.

The rapid growth of population is an ever pressing situation, serving to dilute progress. It is this latter variable that the developing nations can affect internally, and what they do in this regard will influence greatly the extent to which the expectations of those who migrate to the cities will be realized either by the present adults or by their children.

Given the resources and their productive utilization, effective population control, institutional changes, and a great deal more understanding and knowledge, the potential of urbanization could be realized. Where the rate of urbanization is rapid, progress will be slower because the intensity of the problem is greater. But the very places where this occurs are societies in which standards of progress are less exacting than in areas with greater resources and the consequent capacity to effect rapid change.

This, however, provides only limited solace in today's dynamic society. According to a recent study, the labor force is expected to grow by 1 percent per year over the next decade in the industrial countries; the annual rate in the developing nations is projected to 2.3 percent. For the latter countries it is expected that the urban labor force will grow 4.6 percent annually. How long a growing mass of unemployed, ill-housed, and generally disadvantaged population, in close proximity to each other, will accept the resulting social situation is uncertain. But one can agree with the study of the Organization for Economic Cooperation and Development when it affirms that this restless, alienated force represents a basic threat to political and social stability.

Reference was made above to the paucity of resources to provide jobs, housing, and services in many developing countries. Yet, as one views some of the nations involved, it becomes clear that outside assistance, while usually an indispensable ingredient, is not sufficient alone: Institutional changes—both economic and political—are called for if there is to be a more equitable distribution of wealth and if expansion in output is to be to the benefit of the masses and increase employment opportunities. Frequently, over the short run, greater social benefits will flow from immediate development of industries requiring many workers rather than rapid industrialization that occasions manpower displacement. Maximization of production can, under certain conditions, accentuate social disorganization and social ills.

It must be recognized that industrialization today occurs in a much more technically advanced setting than formerly. Early industrialization was still largely labor-intensive. Industry needed hands, supplemented by crude forms of energy and machinery. By the time technology became capital-intensive, population growth had stabilized, educational standards were rising, and the first full infrastructure of an industrial economy had been laid. Today, technology is highly capital-intensive, and to utilize it fully in developing countries calls for more capital than is available, while utilizing far less manpower than is available. What many developing nations need is an approach that will do the reverse—occasion less capital and utilize more manpower.

The gravity of the social implications of migration is awesome. Its manifestations in an industrialized nation such as the United States flow from the existence of pockets of poverty in a society that is generally affluent. Largely because of America's industrial progress, its people—including the poor and the disadvantaged—are conversant with its economic achievements and potential. This makes poverty even more intolerable to those exposed to it.

In the less developed countries people are being crowded together in cities without an industrial base to provide employment. In situations where a fourth or fifth of adult males are unemployed, where a third or more of the people are without water service, where as many as four out of five families live in a single room, it is inevitable that social tension and serious political unrest occur. As to the degree of tolerance of these deprivations, one can only observe that it varies from place to place. One can speculate, however, with a degree of certainty that it gets less and less each year and that each explosion in one locality shortens the fuse elsewhere.

Undeveloped nations are no longer isolated. Just as the disadvantaged in industrialized nations contrast their relative poverty with the general affluence that surrounds them, so the undeveloped nations contrast their poverty with the plenty in other parts of the world. The greatest ferment is, and will be, in the cities and among the urban poor.

Social problems associated with urbanization are of three types:

(1) those that arise from a transfer, through migration, of rural problems—poverty, illiteracy, unemployment—to urban areas, where they become more conspicuous;

(2) those that result from the process of rapid change inherent in rapid urbanization created by sheer increase in physical numbers, more congested living, more complex social institutions, and by the difficulties of transition from the rural to the urban way of life; and

(3) those that flow from the inherent nature of the urban environment and way of life.

Discussions of rapid urbanization emphasize the first two groups of problems. But, of course, the last cannot be ignored, for it undergirds the others and will persist as long as man lives in cities. Even if and when the migrant is sophisticated in the ways of the urban setting and overcomes joblessness, illiteracy, malnutrition, and poverty, he will still be subjected to the strains and stresses of city life. He, like others around him, will react to the impersonality of social relations caused by the transience of contact that urbanization implies.

The city not only raises the migrant's hopes and expectations but, sooner or later, greatly increases his and other poor residents' impatience. It also provides them with a setting in which they learn to act collectively. Modern technology, too, with radio and television, is closing the communication gap, which has further increased the impatience of the urban poor in all parts of the world.

Urbanization, by occasioning and exposing social problems, becomes both an instrument for galvanizing discontent into community pressure and a setting in which the concentration of resources and knowledge can accelerate action to effect change. The challenge of urbanization everywhere is to act intelligently and promptly to effect sufficient change so that hope will outweigh despair and those now disadvantaged will have a sense of their not-too-distant realization of a truly better life.

URBANIZATION AND SOCIAL CHANGE IN THE
DEVELOPING COUNTRIES

Historical processes of social change were also approached, from a slightly different angle, by <u>JORGE HARDOY</u>.

. . . Between the sixteenth and nineteenth centuries, five European powers moved to control by conquest what are now the developing continents, their trade, and the exploitation of their natural resources. They founded thousands of new cities and towns or redefined the functions of existing ones. When they established contacts with a world that had cities as large as those of Europe at that time, they modified the settlement pattern to serve their objectives better. When they moved to open territories sometimes occupied by primitive cultures, they established a completely new settlement pattern to serve their own purposes.

Most settlement patterns in the developing nations of Asia and Latin America and in some countries of Africa are centuries old, as are most of their largest cities. Some existed prior to the arrival of the Europeans; others were founded by them as trading posts or administrative centers. The settlement patterns favored by the colonialist powers, as well as the key centers in those regional urban systems of cities and towns, were built with the main objective of serving the metropolis first and the interests of the people in the territories afterwards.

Political participation was discouraged or repressed. Much of the best agricultural land was kept in the hands of foreign interests or in the hands of their local allies; banks, insurance companies, and national services were mostly in foreign hands.

Political independence with economic dependency is not enough to change such a situation. The struggle for independence and self-respect is now followed by the struggle for survival and development.

Many authors have emphasized their hope that urbanization will bring modernization to developing countries. Vague as those concepts are, honest as their appreciation may be, I wonder how effective urbanization is, as it is now taking place in developing countries, for the development of underdeveloped economies.

In each country the process of urbanization is basically taking place on two scales: a macrospatial scale, formed by the regional urban systems in each nation, which are interrelated with other regional systems within the country and with those of other countries; and a microspatial scale, which is limited to very small geographical areas and is formed by the elements of the larger systems—in other words, by towns, cities, metropolitan areas, and conurbations and their hinterlands.

Different political and socioeconomic models have different approaches toward the development of natural resources and industrialization, of power and transportation, of the use of technology and human resources. Those are the main factors of urbanization, and the location and growth of human agglomerations depend on their rational use.

AKIN MABOGUNJE in his speech, excerpted in Chapter 2, stressed the importance of historical perspective in assessing the disturbing impact of urbanization in many African countries. Progressing from these observations, he outlined some of the present evils of life in the city as reflected in social conditions.

. . . Social welfare problems are given short shrift under such management conditions as have been [earlier] described. There is hardly any arrangement for the reception of new migrants to the city, who have to deal with their adjustment problems as best they can. Even for veteran residents only very limited social amenities are available. There are hardly any municipal playgrounds for children and few organizations or recreational places for teen-agers outside the school or church where these exist. For the adults there may be the football fields and the cinema, the public bars and the dance halls, but, again, hardly any facilities outside of the church or workplace for real cultural activities and social contacts. Nor are there open spaces or parks for solitude and self-communion or for a brisk, pleasant walk.

In a context in which most of the traditional social supports (the extended family, kinsmen, age-group organizations of the migrants' rural background) are no longer relevant or operative, the weakness of urban centers in providing substitutes creates problems of mental stress, personal disorientation, and social disorganization for many people. This has come to be regarded as partly responsible for the heightened incidence of crime, delinquency, and other psychopathological phenomena in urban areas of Africa. Concern with these problems is only gradually receiving attention, although some of the initial studies emphasize caution in ascribing these manifestations to the urban environment per se rather than seeing them as reactions to the stress conditions involved in any process of socioeconomic transformation.

These varied problems are especially compounded in the primate cities of most African countries. Today these rapidly expanding metropolitan areas are some of the most stress-inducing places to live in the world. The rapid rate at which most of these places have grown, their "explosion" beyond their legal administrative boundaries, the pressure being exerted on infrastructural facilities by the increasing number of industries, all these and many other problems identify these

cities as areas of maximum frustration in many African countries.
Yet, because these places also have a disproportionate share of all the
talents and expertise in the country, it is hoped that, if they successfully resolve these urban problems, the experience so gained may serve
for dealing with the other pressing problems of the nation as a whole.

SOCIAL ADAPTATION AND SOCIAL DEVIATION

DENNIS JOHN DWYER seconded these remarks in his paper,
describing some of the aspects of social adaptation to the new conditions that prevail in the city.

. . . The absorption problems of in-migrants in the metropolitan
cities of developing countries could fittingly form the subject of a
complete conference in itself. The present paper, therefore, will of
necessity be highly selective. I propose to review briefly two facets
of the situation that seem to me to be of crucial importance. These
are (1) the relationship of in-migration to social change in the Third
World city and (2) the problem of housing provision. I shall not here
discuss these topics in an interconnected fashion, although toward the
end of my remarks on the first I shall indicate one major implication
for housing policy as I see it.
There is ample evidence that the volume of in-migration to cities
in developing countries has accelerated markedly over the last three
decades, and in this situation important questions arise as to the quality of the rural-urban migrants in terms of their integration into the
life of the city and their contribution to its role as an innovating
organization and major growth point in national economic development.
As Abu-Lughod has pointed out, "Numbers alone should alert us to the
probability that migrants are shaping the culture of the city as much
as they are adjusting to it."
The classic sociological view of the city as an agglomeration of
large numbers of heterogeneous people in a dense, permanent settlement implies not only anonymity and dependence on impersonal relations but also tolerance, indeed encouragement, of change. It seems
to me, therefore, that one of the most vital questions that can currently
be asked in social research on the Third World city is whether (and,
if so, to what extent and in what manner) the current massive immigration of rural-type people into the cities of developing countries is
affecting the role of the city as a center of socioeconomic change as
that role has been understood in the West, at least since the Industrial
Revolution. There do seem to be growing indications that it is unsafe
to continue to embrace the rural-urban continuum as a conceptual
framework insofar as it implies a locational dichotomy of social
characteristics between city and countryside.

48

In elaboration, several examples may be cited. A case in West Africa is the Zabrama migrant to the urban areas of Ghana from Niger. He is a single man, or if he is married his wife remains in his home territory. In the urban areas he is organized into village communities according to his origin, which does not allow him to leave the social milieu of his native home. He recognizes a system of chieftainship that is a transplant of the traditional. His room, shared with perhaps five others, all from his home district, has been described as "a little regional cell." He takes little if any part in social interaction with Ghanaians, to the extent that a stand at the race course in Accra is called the "Zabrama stand" and one of the local cinemas is known as the "Zabrama cinema." A further indication from Africa concerns Xhosa in East London, South Africa. Of these Meyer has stated, ". . . they attach themselves to their own particular cultural minority, and recreate as far as possible the moral and cultural atmosphere of their own (preurban) homes."

The issue here, of course, is whether such rural characteristics can be expected to fade with the passage of time. In other words, given the present demographic and migrational circumstances, is it still possible to envisage a one-way adaptation of rural migrants to an absorptive urban culture? Can we automatically agree with Davis and Golden in any sense deeper than the obvious demographic one when they claim that "the appearance of rapid urbanization in underdeveloped areas is . . . both a sign of change already under way and an augury for future change"?

There are a growing number of those who think not, and I must confess that I tend toward them. Abu-Lughod, in a perceptive review of migrant adjustment to city life in Cairo, has been quite explicit in suggesting that, because of the high rate of rural immigration, the culture of Cairo as a whole now fails to be characterized chiefly by the anonymity, secondary contacts, and other classic features of urban life that Wirth described. The migrants are the creators of a variety of rural-type institutions in the city designed to protect them from the shock of _anomie_. Similarly, in India it appears that many of the seemingly independent and nuclear urban families are in reality primarily appendages of village joint families, with all the accustomed means for determining their true position on the scale of the rural-urban continuum; while, of the migration of the Toba Batak into Medan, Sumatra, Bruner has stated that "the cultural premises and roots of urban Batak life are to be found in village society. . . . Most urban Batak have more meaningful associations with their rural relatives in the highlands than with their non-Batak neighbors in Medan."

These and similar circumstances in cities throughout the developing world give rise to important questions of an ecological nature. As yet, relatively little is known about the new patterns of social ecology arising from the growth of rural-urban migration. One tendency becoming increasingly documented, however, is for rural migrants to group themselves within the cities according to their origins in the countryside, and this is surely of pivotal importance if social engineering is to be a goal of physical planning for the future city and if we suspect that the volume of rural-urban migration might be fundamentally altering the socioeconomic character of Third World cities. The question that arises in these circumstances is whether residential dispersion may be required in order to stimulate the absorption of in-migrants into the "urban" sector system of the city. This kind of consideration has, however, been almost completely neglected to date in writings on housing provision and notably so by those who are presently leading the way toward the acceptance of environmental improvement in situ rather than housing provision policies. In this context it is worth reiterating Catherine Bauer Wurster's injunction that the present over-all housing situation in the major cities "may have a harmful effect not only on welfare and working efficiency per se but also in the failure to provide adequate incentives for constructive social adaptation or satisfactory new values to replace traditional goals."

The same problems were outlined again with further emphasis by MARSHALL CLINARD, who discussed problems of absorption of in-migrants and stressed deviant behavior and criminality.

. . . The "urban" man is likely to become the "modern" man. It is therefore important to understand the factors and forces involved in the changes affecting this urban man. While the growth of the large cities is generally attributed to an economic "push" from the land, one should never underestimate the great significance of the "pull" factor of city living in the process. New industries develop in the large cities, more diverse occupational opportunities become available, wages are often higher, and better employment and educational opportunities are offered. Urban life offers even more than this; the attraction of "city lights" involves not only jobs and cash but mundane things such as better transportation facilities, lighting, water, and hospitals.

Many who live in isolated villages are attracted by the city's noise and glamour, the neon lights, the heterogeneity of the people, the variety of articles for sale, the lure of the cinema, bars, and dance halls, the unattached women, the "swirl of life," and the freedom from the restraints of the village. It has been pointed out that in Africa, for example, all this has a "particularly strong appeal for individuals whose mental horizon has been bounded by the bush enclosing their village." Another study even commented on the relative attractiveness of the slums of the large cities in Ghana: "What never ceases to surprise the outsider is that rural-urban migrants from green, forest-covered mountains find the city with its shantytown periphery not merely more lively than the village but visually more beautiful. They refer to buildings, neon signs and even to roads and advertisements."

Clinard went on to comment on the difficulties of absorption encountered by the migrant.

The Problem of In-Migrants. Much of the literature on absorption problems has dealt with immigrants moving from one country to another. In less developed countries there is a close parallel in the movement of persons from various tribes, linguistic groups, or regional backgrounds to the large cities. The migrant must often acquire a new local language (lingua franca) as well as, in many cases, a European language. If the city happens to be located in an area with a dominant culture that is quite different, the city itself presents ways of life, many of them modern, some European, that are markedly different from village life. In this sense much of what has been written about the absorption of immigrants into a country applies to in-migration to a city in less developed countries. One might, for example, paraphrase Eisenstadt's measures of successful absorption of an immigrant into a foreign country to apply to an in-migrant to cities in less developed countries: the extent to which new roles are learned, successful social participation in the new social organization of the city, a limited amount of deviant behavior, a limited expression of personal and group aggression, and identification with the values of the receiving community.

Migration to metropolitan cities has varying effects on persons. Some migrants are short-term, goal-oriented, or periodically employed persons who leave their families on small plots of land in rural areas and are not committed to urban living. A Kampala study showed that this migrant characteristically comes for a specific goal, such as acquiring sufficient money with which to buy more land to grow cotton. Only 20 percent of these migrant workers stay more than five years. Some stay longer but do not break their ties with the land because of the family, tenure of family land held back home, and an attachment to traditional village life. Consequently they may return to the village at periodic intervals and eventually even permanently. Others become "urbanized" in the sense that their village ties weaken; they adopt urban occupations; their income and property are largely urban; they adopt urban life-styles, bring their families to the city, and think of the city as their home.

Coming to the city, as these migrants do, from different villages and regions and from different language, religious, and caste or tribal groups, they constitute an extremely heterogeneous population, a situation that is quite different from the homogeneous village areas from which they have emigrated. In one small area of a large African city there may be represented as many as 20 or 30 tribal groups with varied cultural backgrounds. In India it may be diverse regional and caste groups; in Latin America, various Indian populations and those from diverse regions. While some enclaves of related groups manage to maintain some semblance of their former unity, even much of this may break down with increased urban migration, the larger impersonal relationships in the city, and housing pressures. Consequently there are often few common norms and values as migrants are confronted with the conflicting standards of the large city. In relation to the larger African cities, Marris has found that, as an economy develops, it diversifies more quickly in the cities than elsewhere; as it becomes more and more diversified and people make their living through various conditions, with varying rewards, degrees of security, and prestige, their patterns of life also diverge.

Family relationships acquire a different emphasis and different value according to occupation and income. Groups within society segregate—physically, into different neighborhoods; socially, into different kinds of association; psychologically, into attitudes toward life.

Frequently the migrants, particularly those without a long-term commitment, lack a sense of importance, of community, and a feeling of unity within the social structure of the larger city. The migrant becomes bewildered by the city's impersonality, the anonymity of the municipal government, and often even by the place where he is fortunate enough to find work. In general there is little to mitigate the migrant's plight unless there is a situation where social ties play an important role among tribal, regional, caste, and other groups. In a study of Kampala, for example, tribal ties among many migrants were found to persist in effective kin or "brother" relations and marriage arrangements. In general, however, the African migrant faces many problems.

For the African worker in particular, who has been adapted in childhood to work, comfort, and recreation in a comparatively small but comprehensive face-to-face group, the transition to a series of discontinuous impersonal relations—with employers, workmates, officials, landlords, policemen, traders, and prostitutes—is abrupt indeed. The craft and other skills acquired in early patterns of domestic, kinship, and neighborhood relations are often excluded, while the self-reliance and group solidarity for shared production and sustenance under a subsistence economy are little guide to the foresight, economizing, and bargaining required in the new patterns of wage income and the need to buy most goods, while unfamiliar modes of expenditure for livelihood and display are offered and even enforced.

A major problem for most migrants to large cities is shortage of money, due either to unemployment, partial employment, or the higher cost of living. Where he has employment, the migrant is often overwhelmed with the realization that in a cash economy he must pay for his housing and for almost everything he uses, even for fruit and vegetables. He has been accustomed to growing his own or buying them cheaply.

Moreover, he finds it equally hard "to realize that cheap housing usually cannot be built, even for the labor." He is faced with a break- down in the traditional security of tribal customs where he has the right, in time of need, to make demands on the tribe and the extended family. A migrant villager who finds this resource denied him may, as an alternative, resort to crime, in part because crime "may be made less discreditable by the communal doctrine of the tribal society where the disadvantaged are allowed to share in the property of the more affluent."

While urban unemployment is produced by the complex factors that bring persons to the city, the extent of this unemployment, and the seriousness of the problems faced by the unemployed migrant, are governed by the length of time the migrant is willing to stay on in the city, how he can survive without work, and the extent to which friends and relatives can offer him support. A Uganda study showed that, while the majority of a sample of unemployed had been looking for work for less than six months, one-fourth had been looking for more than a year. Some walked several miles each day seeking employment. Some rely on sporadic income from the sale of crops or livestock back in their villages, or from gifts. Even without this help many migrants stay on in chronically impoverished states, often with transient jobs, unable to increase their earning capacity or to face up to a return to the more regular and disciplined life of the rural areas from which they have come.

The city may cause particular disillusionment among those whose expectations are too high, as often items that in the city are considered necessities had been regarded as luxuries in the village. One African study found that three-fourths of urban migrants' household members felt that people worry more about money in town than they had in the village; only one-fourth achieved their expectations.

Because of the uncertain living conditions many migrants are not able, or do not wish, to bring their families with them to the city, nor can they always; if they do become established with their families there, they accommodate friends or relatives, particularly young persons, for periods of time. Food and housing accommodation for large families are very expensive, children earn little or nothing because of the shortage of suitable jobs and urban schooling facilities, and the division of labor between the sexes has little meaning in the city, where the women cannot cultivate the land. Where polygamy is traditionally the rule, it is far less common in cities, as it is impractical and costly, and even the higher status associated with multiple wives is not accorded the urban person. Most African urban migrants who come to the city without their wives must thus make the choice between the alternatives of a temporary wife who lives with him and cooks for him, a girlfriend, or visits to a prostitute for whose attention he must pay cash. The woman migrant is usually seeking a marriage partner, but she often experiences a new view of the position of women. Often she is attracted by the emancipation and sophistication of urban life, and she can usually earn an independent livelihood through casual work, trade, or prostitution. She can even own property. The authority of the husband is weakened, and this in turn separates the wife from economic and social dependence on her husband's family.

In all these ways urbanization creates situations in which there are changes in the normative standards of behavior, the social control mechanisms of the family, the village; similar traditional institutions are weakened, and new control forces are introduced. In the city the breaking of rules does not bring with it the informal censure common in the villages; often the police are the only means of controlling people's behavior. One writer has summarized these problems with reference to Liberia: "The effectiveness of tribe and family as agents of social control has always depended upon the cohesiveness of the particular unit. In the urban areas, this cohesiveness increasingly gives way to individualism and the vacuum created by the decline in family and tribal authority has only been filled by impersonal sanctions of the law." Clifford found that in Zambia the family's ability to exercise control over the activities of its members diminished and the pressures of a homogeneous community, of common family residence, and of traditional respect for age and authority, are dissipated.

The Young Migrant. Developing countries are universally characterized by large proportions of young people in the population—a situation particularly prevalent in Africa. Many thousands of youths in African countries constantly migrate to the cities; in fact, some cities consist primarily of younger persons. It is these young persons who appear to be most seriously affected by urbanization. The younger migrant is also more likely than is the older person to become committed to urban values and an urban way of life, thus cutting himself off more readily from his village ties and the traditional patterns of his family life.

Among youthful migrants the age-generation integration of traditional society declines. When migrant families move to the city much of the traditional, tribal, cultural control over the children tends to diminish; each family tends to be an isolated unit. Older boys and girls feel that they can take care of themselves. "The impotence to control their children and their lack of parental authority is a source of dismay to large numbers of urban Africans." Traditional premarital chastity comes to have little meaning; girls and women are frequently induced into prostitution or have illegitimate children. A Lagos study found that in the urban family "age loses its authority when the experience of one generation becomes irrelevant to the next." Only a quarter of the young people were found to have the same occupation as had their fathers. Group festivals of tribal life are replaced by individual beer-drinking and parties. Many youths are left with little external control over their behavior, as the criminal law, the police, and other law enforcement agencies of urban society may not be regarded as legitimate sources of authority. These factors, coupled with heterogeneity, high density, and size of the urban environment, appear to lead to the emergence of youth peer-groups exercising strong deviant influences on the activities of migrant young males.

Urban Slums and the In-Migrant. The urban migrant, whether moving singly or with his family to the city, generally finds himself forced to live in the squatter communities, shantytowns, or the stabilized slums in the older parts of the large cities of the less developed countries. The way of life in these slum communities soon resocializes him to a different life from that of his home village. In fact, the greatest impact on the new migrant comes from his slum way of life, where the physical problems pose less serious threats than do the sociological aspects that are reflected in various deviant behavior patterns such as alcoholism, illegitimacy, prostitution, delinquency, and crime. In both developed and developing countries the majority of reported crimes appear to be committed by slum-dwellers, much of it occurring in slum areas. In large cities of Ghana, for example, one-fourth of the migrant householders surveyed stated that one of the major problems of urban life was the slums, bad housing, and poor sanitation. Furthermore, a sample of urban persons tended to place the blame for crime upon rural-urban migrants and regarded the squatter, shanty slums as the seat of this criminal activity.

Too often the slum has been considered in physical terms: overcrowding, congested housing, and deficient physical amenities. These factors alone, however, have not produced slum problems, and poor housing in itself does not cause crime and other forms of deviant behavior. Even with the improved physical conditions of slum clearance, the slum way of life often continues if a similar income group is relocated there, for slum clearance brings together a new population of strangers and destroys what community feeling and informal social controls previously existed there. "Empirical evidence, in fact, is accumulating to show that improved housing does not have many of

the social benefits initially attributed to it. Yet the belief that delinquency, prostitution, alcoholism, crime, and other forms of social
pathology magically inherent in the slums will die with their demolition,
continues to persist." Actually, slum clearance is impractical in
developing countries where most personal incomes barely support life
at a tolerable level and when the urban populations are doubling and
tripling every decade. No government could hope to eradicate slums
and to prevent squatting under these conditions. Consequently physical
clearance is probably absolutely necessary only where housing and
sanitary conditions are exceptionally bad or where over-all city plans
require it.

One cannot conclude, moreover, that the poverty of the slum alone
produces the problems of the slum such as crime. Economically
deprived persons do not necessarily steal; rather, the norms permitting
and sanctioning such behavior must be found in the immediate environment and incorporated into the individual's life organization. Even
a careful study of crime in the slum areas of nineteenth-century England concluded that the crime rate of that day was not, as might be
expected, a consequence of poverty in the sense of immediate pressures
of want.

Criminality, Migration, and the Slum. Under conditions of urbanization,
migration, and the slum way of life it is not surprising that crimes
increase with development; particularly is this true of crimes against
property. Reports from numerous countries in Africa, Latin America,
and Asia reveal these increases. The President of the Ivory Coast
Supreme Court said, in fact, that the more a country develops the more
its crimes increase. The crimes are largely concentrated in and the
highest rates of increase are centered in the largest cities, and cities
like Bombay, Calcutta, Caracas, Lagos, Accra, Abidjan, and Nairobi
have a much larger share of crime and delinquency than their percentage of the population would warrant.

Increased crime presents serious problems to developing countries, as it diverts needed development resources to crime-control
measures, using additional manpower, equipment, and buildings needed
by police, courts, and prisons, and improved roads and street lighting
for greater security. Perhaps the fear generated among the population
generally for the security of their persons and their property is of
greater significance. The new migrant is not only more likely to become
involved directly in criminal activities but also to be victimized by
them. Large numbers of in-migrants are exposed to thefts and the
women to prostitution. One African study found that two-thirds of the
urban migrants believed that city life tended to corrupt persons; 12
percent indicated that crime, heavy drinking, and prostitution were
major problems of the city. A Latin American survey found that

"delinquency, crime, prostitution, mental illness, alcoholism, and the like were disproportionately common among in-migrants endeavoring to adjust to the new urban environment."

Some variations do exist in types of slum areas, and the number of in-migrants becoming involved in criminal activities may tend to be greater in one slum area than in another. The factors that account for this difference were shown in a recent study by the author and Daniel Abbott of two slum areas in an East African city, one with a high rate of deviation in the form of crime, prostitution, etc., and the other with a lower rate. The physical and economic factors were held to be constant, both groups being equally poor and living in equally poor housing. The young had similar educational and occupational backgrounds. In the area that presented serious problems there were more physical mobility, more unattached males, more prostitutes, and a larger number of places to dispose of stolen goods than in the area with fewer problems. Local markets sold stolen goods to slum-dwellers at prices considerably less than would be charged elsewhere either for new or used items. Located near the main downtown bus depot, the cheap housing and anonymity of the area attracted migrants.

The area with a high crime rate was characterized by more community acceptance of deviant norms, greater heterogeneity of the population, less organization for self-help activities, less social control over inhabitants, less stable family units, and less interest in the larger community. There was far greater diversity in tribal back-grounds than in the area of limited problems. Older adults gave less support to traditional tribal and family obligations than did those in the other area, and they had less contact with relatives in their home villages. There was greater tribal diversity in the backgrounds of close friends, and such friends were not necessarily from the local community.

There were greater differences between the two areas in terms of community structure among males older than 25 as compared with those who were younger, indicating the important role exercised by the older generation in determining the social organization of an area. Where the social organization of the older males is more unified, a greater degree of social control is exercised over the behavior of urban youths, even though the latter have more diverse contacts and partic-ipate less in local community activities.

Other adjustment problems of urban migrants to slum areas were shown in a related study made by the author and Daniel Abbott of 200 incarcerated young males, first offenders, in the same East African city, compared with a control group of the same age and social class. While both groups consisted almost entirely of migrants, migrant offenders were more likely to have moved directly to the large city from village areas and were less likely to have had a relative or fellow tribesman to help them settle and become oriented to urban life. Lacking this guidance, offenders, as new arrivals, were more likely to have come in contact with slum areas with high crime rates.

The offenders, as compared with the control group, tended to be "target workers," that is, those who had come to the city for a special purpose such as securing funds for a bride price, poll-tax payment, etc. Those workers had less education and were more likely to be unskilled. There were, however, few differences in economic pressures. Contrary to what one might expect, the offender was more likely to desire eventually to return to his village, where he had land or access to land. He did not appear to have been someone who had broken off his ties with his rural homeland, yet he did not actually return to the village as frequently as did the nonoffenders. The offenders were less likely to be influenced by social controls because they tended to move about more in the city, even though their length of time in the city was greater. They had a greater diversity of tribal friendships, less contact with kin, and less participation in social organization.

Patterns of association are closely linked to the criminal behavior of migrants. Such associations appear to be the most important distinguishing factor and indicate the role of contact with those with criminal norms when a migrant comes to the city. Offenders had more male friends who had engaged in crime and provided conditions favorable to criminal activity. The offender was more likely to be living with a woman, and there was some indication that the men may have stolen partially as a result of pressures from their girlfriends. Another study of young offenders in Accra, practically all of whom were migrants, showed that those who became delinquents were exposed and susceptible to the influence of delinquent associates. Whether manifested in stealing or in prostitution, delinquency is learned predominantly from association with other delinquents.

Professor MILLER shed some further light on the subject.

. . . I wish to comment on the widely held prejudice about crimes committed by poor people in urban areas. Statistics on crimes committed by or against poor people in rural areas are practically nonexistent throughout the world. In the United States, for example, crimes committed against black people in rural areas are traditionally unreported in the rural South, which is where most of the poor migrants to large urban areas come from. Furthermore, the very definition of crime as it is compiled in statistics is biased against poor people, especially in urban areas, simply by the way crime is defined. That is a thesis that I cannot elaborate here, but I am confident that it is true.

The real issue for a rural resident who considers migrating to
an urban area is whether his person and his property will be more or
less secure in an urban area than it was in the village or rural area.
In my opinion there is not a shred of evidence that suggests that his
kind of security is less in the city than it is in rural areas. There is
certainly no evidence of this in the United States and some evidence
to the contrary.

I believe that by far the most important cause of what we think
of as crime, especially that committed by poor people in urban areas,
is poverty and the inability to escape from poverty because of oppres-
sion and exploitation. In the United States the evidence is very clear
that, when discriminatory and oppressive practices against black
people are removed, they are then able to help themselves escape from
poverty and criminality.

The impression that crime in the slums is a social rather than
an economic derivative was further strengthened by the comments
of MANORAK LUANGKHOT from Laos.

. . . In Laos, more precisely in Vientiane, the capital city, we
have slum areas where migrants or rather immigrants from neighboring countries live, who came there for many reasons. There are
also migrants from rural areas and other regions of Laos. There they
form groups of the same background, so we have the Vietnamese slum
section, the Chinese, Indian, and Pakistani, as well as Laotians who
originally came from the same village. Contrary to what has been
said by Professor Kleiner, crimes in these areas do not exist at all.
The slum people are law-abiding, more so than the people who are
not slum-dwellers. The slum people cooperate with the local
administration. In many ways they are well organized. I am not a
sociologist, I am an engineer, and I do not know the reasons for all
this. Maybe the behavior of the slum-area people reflects the ancient
philosophy concerning the law of hospitality, and our religion as a way
of life.

Another example that I would like to point out concerning
criminality and religion is the case of Chinese immigrants to the
United States. I spent six years studying there and throughout that time
I hardly heard of any crimes committed in Chinatown, either in San
Francisco or in New York City. From my experience of dealing with
people in the cities, the population of the slum areas are the easiest
people to talk to and to work with.

THE EMERGENCE OF DUALISM

Any attempt to isolate the social factor of urbanization out
of the various topics and discussions held at the Conference would

prove both futile and misleading. Virtually all speakers acknowledge the social processes as the foundation upon which the economic, physical, and technological frameworks rest. A good example of the complexity of social-factor involvement in the economic and physical development of cities can be found in MASAHIKO HONJO's paper on dualism in the development of cities in Asia.

Dual Structure of Cities in Asia. In visiting many cities in Asia (presumably, many cities in the developing world) one's first impression is the imbalance of their development. There the contemporary age and the past coexist. The environment in which the modern city center is placed is entirely different from that of the traditional sectors where the general populace flocks together. Narrow roads, highly dense living dependent primarily on one-room dwelling houses, incomplete pipe water and sewage systems, disorderly land utilization, and the inevitable accompaniment of extreme poverty—these drawbacks are something totally apart from the modern sectors of the bright cities.

Quoting Geertz's definitions, Professor McGee of Hong Kong University characterized their economic structure as the dual one of "firm-centered economy" and "bazaar economy." The former is the sector "where trade and industry occur through a set of impersonally-defined social institutions which organize a variety of specialized occupations with respect to some particular productive or distributive end." The other is based on "the independent activities of a set of highly competitive commodity traders related to one another by means of an incredible volume of ad hoc acts of change."

The firm-centered economy is of the capital-intensive type. In it, labor becomes a commodity to be hired and dismissed by the enterprise. The bazaar economy is dependent on the utilization of the entrepreneur's family (kin), and possibilities for employment seem much greater even though productivity is much lower and the end product is a condition of shared poverty.

McGee points out, "In practical terms, the immediate consequence of the dual economy can be seen in virtually every aspect of the Southeast Asian cities' economic structure. In the labor-intensive bazaar sector hawkers, small cottage industries, underemployment, and low productivity are ubiquitous. The land-use patterns of the parts of the city in which this sector dominates are chaotic. Illegal housing, both in the interstices and on the periphery of the cities, often tends to be occupied by the people working in the bazaar sector. In the modern sector economic units are larger, people work regular hours, capital investment is on a large scale, levels of technology and productivity are high. Unemployment—not underemployment—is characteristic." He concludes, "It may be argued that this dualistic structure of the Southeast Asian city may appear to be little different from that of the Western city at a comparable stage of development, but it is in its persistence that the chief problems of Asian urbanization lie, for, above all, the continuance of the dual economy is basically the symptom of economic underdevelopment and of the relationship of these countries to the developed economies."

I consider it important to acknowledge the existence of such dual structure in attempting to solve the questions relevant to our regions. The ideas that prompted the planning so far are based on the perceptions common to the Western world and can be effective in a firm-centered economy, such as is the case with the Western world; but they cannot be put to effective use in a bazaar-centered economy. This dual structure creates independent groups in each sector, and the relations between the two sectors are independent. The modern banking institutions, for example, have little to do with the latent basic structure of the bazaar-centered economy. In a similar context, government measures designed primarily for the modern sector can have few relations with it. The problem is that in the developing world the bazaar-centered economy constitutes the greater part of the activities of the man in the street. Therefore the effectiveness of planning and the scope to be covered by it will be quite limited as far as the ordinary citizen is concerned.

Dual Structure the of Japanese Economy. In the process in which its economy was upgraded from premodern to up-to-date, Japan had to face the problem of dual structure. For this reason repeated discussions of this problem have taken place. The issue has been studied as a means of clarifying the underdeveloped character of the Japanese economy and finding out why and how the Japanese economy has made rapid progress while using its underdeveloped economy as a lever.

As regards the employment structure, it is obvious that the ratio of owner-operating business entrepreneurs and family employees is still large in proportion to wage-earners. The ratio of wage-earners stood at 60 percent in 1965 against 80 to 90 percent in the West. It might be said, therefore, that this clearly indicates the existence of premodern characteristics in Japan's employment structure. A check of the businesses employing these workers reveals that smaller businesses—an enterprise employing fewer than 300 workers is known as a small business in Japan—account for 99.8 percent and their workers account for 82.4 percent of the total. Of these, businesses employing fewer than nine persons, which might be described as those at subsistence level, are 90 percent of the total and their work force is 30 percent.

Among these varying types of businesses there are striking differences in wage and other labor conditions. There is a gap of about 60 percent between the average wages of big businesses. In small businesses wages begin to level off at 35 years of age, while in big businesses they keep going up under a seniority system until the prescribed retirement age. The differentials become far greater when welfare and health facilities are taken into account.

The relation between big and small businesses is, however, complementary to some extent. The latter, in most instances, constitute a follow-up production division of the former or a subcontract division, with paternalistic relations existing between them; yet it is always the big businesses that gain more benefits—they can pass on the risks resulting from market fluctuations to the small businesses and are able to boost their manufacture without investing in any plant outlays. One might go as far as to argue that this factor has served to support the recent rapid growth of the Japanese economy. The fact remains, however, that small businesses find themselves in a more risky economic condition at all times.

As a result, the superior labor force concentrates in big business, with the consequence that small businesses can only employ surplus labor. Labor-management relations are modernized, but not in small businesses. There is a wide gap between workers in big businesses and those in small businesses—in economic conditions as well as in ways of thinking and approaches to life. In this context, therefore, there is the contention that there is a dual structure in the Japanese labor force.

The number of workers in the small and tiny businesses that form the basic structure of the society is extremely large. In the past, farm villages in Japan from which surplus labor flowed served as the supply source, and an incomplete labor structure of underemployment or of part-time work in order to supplement the family budget was produced. These circumstances have functioned to prevent free distribution of labor in Japan to a large measure. The flow into industry of young labor and the shortage of labor arising out of the economic growth of recent years are changing this pattern, but a serious question still remains as to the labor force in middle and high age brackets who are not adaptable to the changing situation so that this dual structure will continue.

Reflection of Japan's Dual Social Structure on City Structure and Housing. These characteristics are also clear in the structure of Japanese cities. The city centers that represent the advanced sectors present an extremely modern aspect, which is further accelerated in the central business district (CBD) of big towns such as Tokyo, where Japan's central managerial functions are concentrated. Commuting white-collar workers live uptown, and the range of commuting fans out to an ever increasing degree, with the result that extensive residential areas are formed. Downtown, on the other hand, small and petty businesses are concentrated. The blue-collar workers who are employed in this sector are unable to commute from distant places due to their labor conditions, and therefore are compelled to live in a poor environment in which industrial, commercial, and residential land use is mingled.

Essentially, Japan's city planning, irrespective of such a housing environment, has been devoted to the construction of infrastructures that are determined by the higher-level planning of the whole of the city. It was consequently anticipated that dwellings and other buildings would fit into the framework of the given infrastructures through activities of the private sector, in accordance with specifications set forth in the building codes and ordinances, and that a city would be formed in the course of time.

Judging again from the viewpoint of Japan's dual structure, the housing sector might well be described as the most nonmodernistic sector in management. In order to cope with its rapid growth the Japanese economy busied itself with investment in industrial capital outlays and fundamental social infrastructures, leaving inadequate funds for housing. Most of the dwellings in Japan are either privately owned or rented houses, and the latter were left to the subsistence-level management of petty landlords, thus being kept out of the stream of the modern economy.

A check of the present stock of housing in big urban centers indicates that about 40 percent each are owner or rental dwellings, a little less than 10 percent are company housing, and about 5 percent are public housing. There has been an apparent trend toward polarization in terms of quality in each housing sector. The area per unit of newly constructed owner-houses has been rising continuously, now reaching an average of 95 square meters, while that of the newly constructed rental houses has only risen to 43 square meters. This is because wooden tenement houses of one- or two-room units have been constructed en masse in these 10 years to conform to the poor paying ability of the people in the low-income brackets. Construction has proceeded by filling up vacant lots in the yards of individual dwellings in the inner sections of cities. The number of houses built in this manner now accounts for about 30 percent of the total housing stock in Tokyo, for example, so that the housing environment has deteriorated still further. A check of housing tenure in relation to household income reveals that owner houses are polarized in the high-income bracket and rental houses in the low-income bracket.

In the case of Tokyo the public housing supply should be made available for the comparatively low-income brackets, but it is actually serving a wide range of income brackets. The result is that housing difficulties weigh even more heavily upon the low-income earners.

If one observes the relation between housing tenure and the employment of the head of a household, the circumstances in which most of the employees in small businesses rent wooden tenements built by the private sector become eminently obvious.

The housing supply is such that the lowest part of the dual structure of our society is heavily dependent on housing made available by small house-owners who are the most nonmodernistic in terms of management. Public housing should have filled this gap, but the supply is too scanty and tends to be oriented toward the upper stratum of society. This point must be fully considered. On the other hand, we have to accept the cynical reality that, in fact, the supplying power of this magnitude lies at that pole of the dual structure that we used to consider the most meager sector, and we have to devise measures to correct this situation.

Policy Theme: The Community's Social Realities. The physical structure of a town is basically the reflection of the ways of life of the community of which it is constituted. The community of the "bazaar economy" sector has its own way of life. Although it may change according to the trends of the times, it matches prevalent ways of life to a specific degree of the development of the society. Analyzing the structure of old Delhi, Fonseca points out that it is comprised of the district unit, which is known as Mohalla, where the small vocations are shared regionally and which has a district hierarchy with a council similar to that of village elders. The town is constructed with lanes, plaza, and courtyards to suit its citizens' way of life. He expresses his obvious anxiety about the fact that "politicians and planners, intent on tidying up the image of the capital, ruthlessly sweep away this rich environment, replacing it with a cultural vacuum based on Western solutions."

Sternstein surveyed the pattern of migration in Bangkok and discovered that it was conducted in fairly large groups. He surmised that each group was big enough to form a farm community and pointed out the existence of hamlet communities in a city as in a village. In this report Sternstein suggests similar points to those elucidated above.

The city's physical posture is a manifestation of activities conducted within it. The posture will naturally alter in conjunction with the changes that take place in activities. Redevelopment and other remedies will be conducted on the basis of an alteration in the situation. In the event that there is no basic change in the ways of life of people who stay in the basic part of the dual structure, it would be useless forcibly to change the form of a city by means of redevelopment.

CONCLUSIONS

Modern man is the beneficiary of a technological revolution that is the result of centuries of toil and misery. His life is one of almost infinite opportunities, and even the man in the street may live the life that has hitherto been the domain of kings.

These facts, and the impressive statistics that are often brought in to back them up, often obscure the other, less pleasant side of the coin: the fact that there are millions of people in the large cities living in abject misery, that the rates of crime are on the rise practically all over the world, and that among the well-off life is not always the better for it. Loneliness and mental stress have become household words. Suicide, as Emil Durckheim first pointed out, is one result. Personal disorientation, anomie, and social disorganization are the grounds on which modern art is laying its foundations.

It has recently been discovered that the picture is often at its worst in the rapidly developing countries where social frameworks are crumbling faster than progress can erect alternatives, and it is the social changes in these countries, therefore, that must be given top priority in planning as well as in administration.

4

SPECIAL PROBLEMS
OF URBANIZATION

The main and perhaps most influential force of urban growth in the last few decades has been the large metropolitan city. Like most other urban developments it is a fairly recent creation and one that is seemingly only in its early stages. Cities of 1 million inhabitants, almost unknown a few decades ago, are rapidly becoming commonplace in developed and developing countries alike, and futurologists are seriously contemplating urban agglomerations of 20, 30, and even 40 million people before the end of this century.

The very large, highly developed, and prosperous city, with its highly specialized economic systems, with its unique social pressures and physical construction problems, is an endless source of research and speculation, posing extremely urgent and intriguing questions for thinkers and planners alike. The participants at the Rehovot Conference understandably refrained from tackling such cities and turned their attention instead to the metropolitan cities of developing countries only. Although much of the debate on slums, housing conditions, and primacy may ultimately be true for some of the cities of the more developed countries, such cities were beyond the scope of the Conference. The primary problems raised, therefore, were not those of New York, Los Angeles, London, and Paris but rather those of the Latin American, African, and Asian metropolitan cities, cities struggling with mass migration, chronic lack of funds, and undeveloped, unbalanced economic infrastructures.

METROPOLITAN GROWTH

LOWDON WINGO introduced the subject in his paper.

. . . Few appraisals of the future of the developing countries of
the world have ignored the problems created by the rapid growth of
urban settlements. Between 1950 and 1960, while the aggregate
population of major developing areas expanded at a rate of 1.9 percent
per annum, the population of urban settlements with a population of
20,000 or more grew at 4.7 percent. Yet, when this urban population is classified by size of city into a metropolitan class of people
residing in cities with populations larger than 500,000 and a small-
city class made up of those residing in cities with populations ranging
between 20,000 and 500,000, we find that the population of the smaller
cities grew only at the rate of 3.5 percent per annum, while the
metropolitan population increased at exactly twice that rate, 7 percent.
In 1960 the metropolitan cities accounted for approximately 9 percent
(and the smaller cities for 16 percent) of the 2 billion people of the
less developed regions of the world. Moreover, with the exception of
the very large countries such as China, India, Indonesia, and Brazil,
these countries are frequently characterized by massive population
concentration in the largest city and its environs. Such cities have
become known in literature as primate cities. Caracas, Mexico D.F.,
Cairo, Santiago (Chile), Teheran, Lima are many times larger than
the second-ranking city in their countries and contain a fifth or
more of the national population and as much as half of the productive
capital of the nation. Since metropolitan cities contain vastly disproportionate shares of their countries' modern economic activities,
policies affecting the development of these larger cities have ramifica-
tions for the development effort of these nations as a whole.
  We have come to accept as fact the proposition that in the process
of economic development there is a fairly strong relationship among
levels of development, measures of social welfare, and degree of
urbanization. It is no mystery that among nations such variables as
the proportion of the male labor force gainfully employed in nonagricultural pursuits, the percentage of the total population living in urban
settlements (however defined), and per capita incomes exhibit very
strong intercorrelation; indeed, such variables are frequently used
interchangeably to describe differential levels of economic development.
  Nevertheless, the precise relationship among these phenomena
is sufficiently obscure as to leave unresolved at least two key questions: (1) How are rates of change of these variables related, and
(2) How are characteristics of these variables related? Uncertainty
about the answers to these questions has given rise to much controversy about the consequences of government programs and policies
tending to influence the way in which urbanization takes place. Some
argue that the rate of change of urbanization variables can be retarded
without affecting either the rate of growth of welfare measures like

gross domestic product (GDP) or impairing the rate of the agricultural-industrial transformation that lies at the heart of our conventional view of economic development. Others argue that a given national urban population can be distributed in different ways among cities of various sizes without any loss in welfare or in the rate of economic development. Both these questions are brought to the fore in the current controversies in a number of developing countries centering on the relative scale and rate of growth of their principal metropolitan regions.

The issue can be formulated in different ways. Are these major urban settlements "parasitic" on the economic body of the nation, depriving other regions of the country of resources and assets essential to development? Are they responsible for increasing the disparities of income among the various groups of the society?

A number of participants appeared to reply to these poignant questions in the affirmative. The disproportionately large city is frequently regarded as the source of all evil, both in the light of undeniable statistics of income diversity, social deprivation, and cultural atrophy and because of an often historical predisposition against the cities, on which JORGE HARDOY elaborated.

. . . The settlement patterns that we see in each of our nations are undoubtedly a heritage of the colonial period, which have been accented during the recent process of neocolonialism in which we are now living. The result of this, if we follow historical trends, will be the continuation of an uneven distribution of income favoring the already dynamic urban centers and some sectors of the urban population, consequently neglecting the rural population.

JOHN FRIEDMANN, however, outlined an academic analysis in favor of the large metropolitan city.

. . . Perhaps it would be useful at the outset to get an idea of the range of metropolitan city sizes, because the term "metropolis" has so many different connotations and meanings that there might be considerable misunderstanding unless we begin with a view of the actual extent of the experiences represented.

Let us take the size of the largest city in each of your countries. In Malta, the population of the largest city is 150,000; 2 million in Singapore; 850,000 for the Tel Aviv metropolitan area in Israel; Venezuela, 9.5 million; Argentina, 2.5 million; Turkey, Istanbul, 1.2 million; Belgium, 5.5 million; Korea, 1 million; Guatemala City, 250,000; Laos, 350,000; Madagascar, Mauritius, 250,000; Senegal, 650,000; 500,000 for Abidjan, the Ivory Coast; Nepal, 500,000; Chile,

3 million. The range is clear—from 150,000 or 200,000 all the way up to almost 10 million people; 10 million is roughly four times the size of Israel, while 150,000 is 1.5 percent of the largest figure.

We have seen that the growth rates in the developing countries vary from 2 percent to 11 percent. At 11 percent, the population doubles every six years or so. In order to obtain a more precise understanding of this range of values we have to know two more things: the percentage of the total national population in these metropolitan centers and the percentage rate of growth, which may vary between some 3 percent to 9 percent per year.

This is just an illustration of the range of values. Though it is extremely difficult to see anything of general value with respect to metropolitan development, I shall nevertheless ask a number of questions that I hope will help us to focus our subsequent discussions. There are four kinds of question. The first and perhaps the one that will meet with the most agreement is, Is the metropolis necessary? Do we need a large urban agglomeration? Relative to the size of the country?

The second question is very frequently asked and sometimes differently from the way I would formulate it. Is there an "optimum" size for a metropolis? I put optimum in quotation marks because we shall have to reach some sort of agreement as to what we mean by "optimum" size of a metropolis.

The third question relates to a policy issue of which this is the first indication, an issue that is frequently introduced into national discussions of policy. If it is desirable to limit the size of the metropolis, how are we to stem the flow of migrants to the metropolis? This is an operational question.

My final question is, What is the appropriate spatial framework for metropolitan development? Professor Hill was discussing the administrative and planning framework, and I ask the question in terms of the spatial framework.

We all agree that these issues are likely to be raised in your own countries, and the question is how to answer them in the context of your own countries and on the basis of such knowledge as has been accumulated over the years. I admit from the outset that we know very little about how to answer these questions precisely. I shall therefore indicate some of the points of current investigation and research and suggest what tentative conclusions have been arrived at—in no way a comprehensive or well-organized statement.

As to the first question, the most frequently used argument in favor of metropolis is that it provides external economies, that it makes production cheaper. The actual figures, however, are not clear on that point because they suggest that there are important external economies to be obtained for private business in cities of up to approximately a quarter of a million population. It becomes very problematical, then, what cities beyond that scale can offer in terms of substantial additional external economies. A quarter of a million is no imaginary figure; it probably relates to a highly advanced economy with a very high standard of living. When we use population figures we ought to ask ourselves what the income of that population is, because the question of external economies is related more to total income than to total population. Yet, since the figure is most often put in demographic terms, I shall stay within that framework and suggest that there is an upper limit of metropolitan size from an economic point of view. The size may be 250,000 or 500,000; it may even be slightly lower than 250,000 in some countries. Beyond this threshold limit the economies of scale and external economies are not likely to be important.

More important, however, for many types of enterprise, particularly for the management sector, is the possibility of contact networks of face-to-face relations in the city. This is particularly important in the case of the management sector of industrial and other business enterprise, and it takes quite different forms in different countries.

In the case of the developing countries, where the industrial input-output matrix is not highly developed and industries are not closely tied to each other, most of the face-to-face contacts that are necessary are between management of industry and the government, and it might be said that it is access to power that management is seeking by locating in a metropolitan area. This is an extremely important issue in doing business in all countries; though the form of the face-to-face contact changes, it explains the reason for the continuing growth of large cities.

The third argument for the necessity of a metropolis is that it is essential for the diffusion and generation of innovations, particularly those innovations that are required for the modernization of the country. I put diffusions first because in most cases the innovations reach the developing countries from outside, but in the process of being diffused to a country the innovations—whether they are technological, social, economic, political, or consumer innovations—become transformed and adapted to local conditions.

This process requires research in institutes, communication facilities, and so on, which are usually located in the large metropolitan centers. Also, if we look for the origin of innovations, we find that the majority of those that are important to the modernization process originate in the large metropolis.

It is my personal view that the metropolis as such is necessary for the development of a country that has only cities of small size— if we were to try to develop a country on the basis of cities no larger than 25,000 or 50,000 population.

For the sake of an intellectual exercise, ask yourself whether it is possible to have development in a country without urbanization, without cities. If your answer is that it is not, then why? That will perhaps give you a reason for the existence of cities. Or if you say it is possible without cities, then it would be interesting to hear your reasons in the discussion.

As to optimum size, there is so far no persuasive evidence that there is any particular population size that is optimum in any sense whatsoever, particularly in relation to the process of development. There are indications that the cost of urban development increases with population size up to a certain point and then begins to level off, but this only indicates the cost side of the equation; and something should also be known about the benefit side, because it is in the relation of benefits to cost that the crucial issue of optimum size lies. Thus as long as the social benefit of metropolitan growth is greater than the cost of metropolitan growth there is no reason to limit the size.

On the other hand, you might ask whether, for the particular developmental stage at which your country happens to be at the moment, the spatial structure, the distribution of population and economic activities is of the sort that is likely to facilitate the movement of the total economy to the next level of development—in other words, whether the urban structure of your country is in fact optimal in the sense of facilitating development to the next stage of economic growth. Here we shall probably arrive at quite different solutions if we spend some time later discussing them.

There are some other questions relating to the optimum size issue. First of all, the question might be put—and frankly I do not know the answer—whether the job of absorbing population might be easier and perhaps in administrative terms less costly if it occurred in the smaller centers rather than in the large cities. In other words, the large metropolis does present extraordinary problems of management; the complexity is very great. Perhaps by shifting the main burden of population absorption to the smaller centers this task might be reduced in size. That is only a possibility and your experience will be of the utmost interest.

What seems to be the most important in this whole question of optimum size, however, is that we should perhaps relate it to the question of organization rather than leaving it as a size issue alone. There are two forms of organization that seem to be relevant. The first is spatial. We say Buenos Aires has 9.5 million people and this is the largest metropolis of the countries here represented—but how is Buenos Aires organized spatially? Is it all one large cluster distributed at random, or does it break down into smaller segments?

For the pupose of illustration let me remind you of Professor Kanus's speech on the first day of the Conference when he pointed out that cities could be conceived of in terms of clusters of cities. At the time many participants thought this scheme was irrelevant to the problems of the developing countries, but let me suggest that the case of Israel is a perfect case of this kind of clustering.

The third major question is, By what methods might the flow of migrants to the metropolis be stopped—or reduced? It is a known fact that almost all countries here presented are in some measure concerned with the development of centers outside the metropolis. In political terms this raises the issue of whether the nation is not spending too much money and effort in the metropolis itself, and whether it ought not be decentralized—meaning some measure of encouraging the growth of intermediate and smaller centers.

The final question to be asked is, What is the proper spatial framework or territorial geographical framework for metropolitan development? Here I would suggest that the metropolis depends for its existence on a small number of critical regional resources, such as water supply, supply of recreational areas, areas of tourist interest, and, of course, labor force. These resources—water, food, recreation, and labor—extend substantially beyond the boundaries of the metropolis. Only think of the large distances that water has to be carried in order to supply a population of millions.

The food supply for the urban population, particularly the perishable commodities such as vegetables and fruit, usually competes for land with the metropolis and is found at some distance away, going out and merging with the general agriculture of the country. Recreational travel to points outside the metropolis is becoming increasingly important. In many countries the metropolis increasingly draws its labor from outlying communities. I would suggest, therefore, that the spatial framework for metropolitan planning should in fact be regional, and the extent of the region must be defined in terms of the resources required to sustain the development of the metropolis and provide for its welfare.

URBAN GROWTH AND THE HOUSING PROBLEM

The rapid growth of metropolitan cities has created new and special problems in practically all facets of human life and urban construction. The most pressing one is undoubtedly the chronic lack of accommodation that seems to affect any rapidly growing town.

ROBERT CROOKS was one of the lecturers who enlarged on the subject.

The Formation, Magnitude, and Growth of Transitional Settlements.
People migrating from the rural areas to the towns and cities in
developing countries are at present being accommodated in two
principal ways:

(1) by a rapid increase of living densities in central low-rental,
low-income areas, extending and intensifying slum conditions;

(2) by the invasion of vacant public or private lands, typically
in peripheral areas, with little or no provision for the long-term
improvements necessary for development.

In some cases the two forms overlap, where former migrants
already established in the urban area through the squatting process
provide rental accommodation to successive migrants.

In the Latin American experience the low-income migrant has
been found to locate in rental accommodation during the early stages
of job-seeking and adaptation to urban life. Progression from a rural
to an urban existence may have been gradual or abrupt, with the initial
accommodation in the city being found in the deteriorated areas of
the urban core or in a preestablished squatter settlement. The rent
paid by the migrant is commonly a very high percentage of his income, and this combines with the probable instability of his employment, which threatens his ability to pay rent at all, to encourage him
to seek a situation where he is not at the mercy of a landlord. Once
he is established in the urban area, a process that may take several
years, he may join an organized "invasion" of vacant land.

The United Nations Center for Housing, Building, and Planning
has been able to assemble crude but roughly comparable figures for
36 cities in developing countries around the world, which allow comparison of the population of transitional settlement areas with the
population of the urban area as a whole. Of these cities only 6 had
transitional settlement populations that were less than one-fourth
of the total urban population; half had transitional populations that
were one-third or more of the urban area populations; in 5 cities
transitional populations were in the majority.

The following examples illustrate the comparative size of these
areas.

Calcutta, India. In 1961 the population of the metropolitan
district was 6.7 million, of which 70 percent of the families were
living in one room or less. At least 2.2 million of these people were
then living in slums and uncontrolled settlements.

Manila, Philippines. More than 1.1 million people out of approximately 3 million live in slums and squatter settlements.
Squatter population alone increased from 360,000 in 1962 to 767,000
in 1968.

Turkey. An estimated 2.37 million people, or 21.8 percent of
the country's urban population, were squatters in 1965. It was

estimated in 1970 that 60 percent of the population of Ankara and 65 percent of the population of Izmir were squatters.

Dar es Salaam, United Republic of Tanzania. According to a 1968 survey, more than one-third of the population of 273,000 were living in slum and squatter conditions. At current growth rates the city population will double in less than 12 years.

Seoul, Republic of Korea. Out of a total population of about 4.6 million, it is estimated that 970,000 families live in only 440,000 dwellings. Yet the city population continues to increase by an estimated 400,000 people each year.

Guayaquil, Ecuador. Out of a total population estimated at 730,000 people, almost half, 360,000, were living in squatter settlements in 1968.

Lima, Peru. Out of a population estimated in 1968 to be 2.8 million, approximately 25 percent lived in squatter settlements.

Brazil. While all cities of over 100,000 people are expected to double in less than 12 years, favelas (slum and squatter settlements) are predicted to increase sixfold.

While population in developing countries typically grows at 2 to 3 percent per annum and many city populations grow at rates exceeding 6 percent, transitional settlements in urban areas commonly grow at rates of 12 percent and some of these settlements grow at rates in excess of 20 percent. At 12 percent population doubles in less than seven years; at 20 percent population doubles in four years. It is clear that within general conditions of rapid urbanization in developing countries, transitional urban settlements are by far the fastest growing part of urban areas.

The virulence of the problem of transitional settlements has contributed in many cases to a fruitless, negative view of the whole urbanization process, leading to the hope that if the process cannot be stopped it can be greatly slowed or deflected. On the contrary, this is not the view of the Center for Housing, Building, and Planning, where it is felt that, despite the broad measures toward rural development programs that must be undertaken and that are wholeheartedly encouraged by the Center, migration to urban areas will not only continue but will grow in force. Rural population will grow significantly in number in the years remaining to the end of this century despite rapid urbanization. What is happening, however, is that urban areas are in general growing at a far greater rate than rural areas. Rural development, population control measures, and urban development are interdependent. The process of urbanization and the development of urban attitudes are necessary to rural development rather than harmful to it.

URBAN GROWTH AND THE
SERVICES PROBLEM

Another problem parallel with that of housing is the question of the shortage of public services in large cities, which do not keep up with the rapid rates of growth.

The "pull" of the city is attributed not only to its economic merits but also to the possibility of attaining better services and living conditions, according to ROBERT SADOVE.

. . . Although urban amenities may be lacking, those that are available appear highly attractive to the migrants when compared with living conditions prevalent in rural areas.

RAANAN WEITZ had the following comments to make on this subject.

. . . Economically, the advantages attributed to the large city included agglomeration and external economies, especially the existence of a well-developed supporting structure, an expensive labor market with a larger number of skilled workers, and a high concentration of consumers. All these factors afford enterprises in the large cities a measure of efficiency not to be found in smaller settlements.

Despite the merits of the city as a supplier of services, it is evident that in many of the developing countries the process of urbanization has not substantially improved the living conditions of those who migrated to the big cities; in some cases their condition has even deteriorated.

A bleak description of the condition of migrants to cities in Africa, excerpted in Chapter 3, was given by Akin L. Mabogunje in his paper on "Urbanization Problems in Africa." Similar descriptions were made of cities in the developing countries of other continents—Asia and Latin America.

We may thus say that though the city with its services and amenities holds out hope for a better life to the individual, in many cases the facts prove differently. We find dualism within the cities themselves: areas supplied with all those services, and side by side with them the slums, where living conditions are not much better, if at all, than they are in the rural areas.

However, as EDWIN MILLS saw it, services benefit from urban location, and therefore in the long run urban development in the developing countries holds out brighter prospects for the supply of adequate services for the individual.

. . . The production of public and private services often benefits greatly from location in large urban areas. In many service activities scale economies are exhausted at employment levels that are small relative to those in manufacturing. But demand per capita is very small for many business and consumer services, and the market of a large urban area is needed to support the activity. Furthermore, many service activities benefit greatly from locations close to related activities. Lawyers need to be near courts and libraries, doctors need to be near laboratories and hospitals, and institutions that provide insurance and other services for those engaged in international trade need to be near ports. In the United States, services are the most urbanized of all sectors, and their growth has accounted for a large part of the employment growth in metropolitan areas, especially in central cities, during the last two decades. Although service employment may be relatively less important in many less developed countries than in the United States, its importance to urban growth is likely to be considerable.

In summary, the economic advantage of large urban areas is that production of goods and services can take place on a sufficiently large scale to be efficient, and yet the goods and services can be sold or consumed within a small area, thus avoiding high transportation and communication costs.

URBAN GROWTH AND THE FINANCIAL PROBLEM

Both housing and service deficiencies are largely results of the often chronic lack of public finances that affects urban growth in developing and developed countries alike, as MASAHIKO HONJO pointed out.

. . . In an over-all context the first question that has come out here is the extreme scarcity of capital accumulation. Surplus investment power for the whole of the national economy might be described in broad terms as growing parallel with the rise in the national income. Professor Duccio Turin made a computation on the formation of gross domestic capital for the whole of the world and found that 41.8 percent of the world's investment power is concentrated in the countries whose per capita gross national product (GNP) is over $2,000 and 46.1 percent in the countries where the per capita GNP stands somewhere between $700 and $2,000. It follows, therefore, that nearly 90 percent of the world's construction investment power is concentrated in the nations where the per capita GNP is over $700. The ratio of construction investment to the national income increases in proportion to the rise in the per capita GNP, and the share that could be set aside for housing investment also increases. Thus, it naturally follows that the amount that could be allocated for housing in the developing world must be extremely small. Turin notes that in developing countries construction investment is also done in forms other than monetary expenditure—such as labor—and points out that this type of investment reaches 20 to 30 percent of the total construction output. It must be pointed out that how this investment is to be mobilized is of great significance in the sense of how the urbanization of the developing world is to be sustained.

Mr. Sadove and Dr. Epstein reach depressing conclusions on further financial aspects of the physical development of cities. Far from keeping up with demographic growth, it is in fact hopelessly behind, hampered by the chronic lack of investment possibilities.

If this appears to present an extreme position, let us indulge in a small numbers game. The aim of the exercise is to illustrate that the problems of New York or even Rio are far different from those of Bombay, Lagos, or Djakarta. Institutional impediments—and perhaps insurmountable ones—at present obstruct the resurrection of New York or the creation of a better-housed Rio. However, the financial and human resources required to improve living conditions actually exist within the nation and even within the state's boundaries. Peter simply does not want to pay Paul.

In our numbers game Peter could not pay Paul even if he wanted to. Thus, the rules of the game itself may be at stake. As an example, take a city with a population of 500,000 and a per capita income of $150. At a savings rate of 10 percent, the city will generate $7.5 million in gross savings annually. At a 6 percent growth rate of population with 60 percent labor force participation, there will be 18,000 new labor force entrants and 30,000 new population each year. The annual capital cost of creating employment for the incremental work force would be $21.6 million, assuming the modest cost of $1,200 per worker. The annual cost of providing the additional population with necessary infrastructure including housing would amount to $15 million, assuming low per capita cost rate of $500. Thus, some $31.6 million would be annually required compared to total gross savings of only $7.5 million. These comparisons cover only the costs of providing employment and infrastructure for the annual increase in the city's population. Excluded from this calculation are the costs of maintaining and replacing existing public facilities and services and the high capital requirements of supplying infrastructure to remedy the overwhelming deficiencies. Yet they are indeed a fact of life.

If the gap between the needed costs and available savings is $24 million, then not even the most stringent fiscal policy could force the rate of taxation to the point where it would exceed total savings generated by the community. Almost half of their income has to be saved to reach this level. Furthermore, the 30 percent of the population with high incomes, who generate the largest part of the savings, would be heard from when it comes to investments for additional amenities.

Let us continue with the numbers game to penetrate further into the dilemma by testing the sensitivity of the key variables. Keeping per capita income at $150 and increasing the savings rate to 15 percent, our city would generate savings of $11.25 million, and at 20 percent the amount would be $15 million. Both of these figures still fall short of requirements.

Of course, in the total cost of the infrastructure requirement the larger part of the investment arises from the creation of new job opportunities. If this cost component could be reduced from a generally accepted medium-level estimate of $1,200 to a low estimate of $700, then the $21.6 million requirement (assuming 6 percent population increase and 60 percent labor participation) would be reduced to $12.6 million—a figure that alone would still be in excess of the total gross savings that could be generated at all but the relatively high 20 percent rate.

The level of infrastructure costs could also result in a substantial change in the calculation. If the per capita cost of providing infrastructure could be reduced from $500 to $100, the total cost needed to accommodate the new population would amount to $3 million instead of $15 million. But even with these adjustments the total amount of $24.6 million necessary for both job creation and infrastructure would still exceed savings at the high level of 20 percent.

JOSE D. EPSTEIN carried this topic further.

. . . The financial dimensions of the urban problem are staggering. Let me try to project this little numbers game to the Latin American continent. Using the minimum figure of $100 per capita for a partial solution for basic urban infrastructure, Latin America's urban population would require some $12.5 billion of investment.

A calculation that we ourselves have been able to help reach for one of the cities of one of our member governments, Medilina in Colombia, appears to me somewhat more realistic. Medilina is a somewhat typical city, and for those of you who know it no explanation is needed. It is an atypical city in the sense that it is a fast-growing but sound city with excellent financial management, and it is one of the best entrepreneurs in Colombia, possibly even in all Latin America. The minimum urban requirement for Medilina, without housing, turns out to be $300 million, for a city with a population of slightly less than a million people. That works out at about $300 per capita.

From this research, which we have financed, this comes to a total requirement on the order of $37.5 billion to finance the urban infrastructure needs of major Latin American cities. That is about one-third of the area's total gross national product before housing. The magnitude of this investment would therefore absorb the area's domestic savings for more than two years. That is, we would have to devote all of the resources to urban development only. Can we afford to do this?

If external resources were to be used for this purpose, the total external flows to the region for some 17 years would have to be devoted to nothing but financing urban infrastructure—before housing or any other financing in the country.

URBAN GROWTH AND ENVIRONMENTAL PROBLEMS

While the physical development of cities cannot keep up with the march of urbanization, another physical property, environmental decay, is racing ahead at an ever increasing pace. Relatively recent phenomena, environmental deterioration and pollution, are rapidly becoming among the worst ailments of modern society in developed and developing countries alike. Broadly speaking, it is a product of the Industrial Revolution and the demographic explosion, and the city, being likewise a product of these two, often plays decisive roles in its promotion.

ROBERT BOOTE treated the subject in his paper "Impacts of Urbanization on the Environment."

. . . Human needs and the level of fulfillment at which they are sought will vary considerably between and within nations. Attitudes differ greatly. The two-thirds of mankind living in the developing countries and those in the slums of any area may be less concerned with the quality of the environment than with their struggle for the necessities of life. To a hungry man the first priority is food, and economic progress—narrowly construed—becomes his primary goal. Overriding demands in most of the world's swelling cities are for clean piped water, drainage, better dwellings, and basic social services.

The acquisition of higher material standards, however, need not be at the expense of the environment. One of the main contributions to the well-being of peoples in the developing countries could be to help them appreciate that modern planning and technology enable the quality to be enhanced without increasing the cost of development and may often result in long-term economies. Yet Western "tools" require careful adaptation to the conditions of the developing nations, who should realize anew that their values and cultural patterns are vital to the implementation of a grand design for the future of this planet.

The Background. Throughout history human settlements have evolved in close relationship to topography and resources. Until a few centuries ago, settlement patterns were mainly determined by agriculture, fishing and mining, water, and defense. Towns and villages developed as business and market centers to serve the hinterland. In Europe, from the time of the Renaissance, the rich built large dwellings in the countryside and moved between town and country. Most of this urbanization developed on a scale and at a rate of change that enabled it to be harmonized with the natural environment.

With the advent of the Industrial Revolution and accelerated population growth the situation changed dramatically. Urban centers grew and new ones multiplied. About 1,000 cities of over 100,000 population have developed in the past two centuries. Many of these are densely populated and lack the facilities to satisfy even the barest needs and aspirations. This vast concentration of population continues. It is primarily based on the movement of people from farms to cities, which accelerates in developing countries and which is encouraged by governments in developed areas to get the immediate benefits of intensive productivity. Yet increasingly this concentration results from the total growth of population, which is often greater in urban than in rural areas.

The rate of urbanization is relatively faster in the still largely rural developing countries. These, too, have the most rapid increase in population. Here the city acts as a magnet, appearing to offer escape from the subsistence level and drudgery of rural life. It also provides the opportunity to raise living standards and the possibility of greater social mobility.

The developed countries are already facing a second phenomenon— the drift from the cities to the suburbs. Here the aim is often to seek relief from the pressures of urban life while keeping some of its advantages—to gain the best blend of town and country. This movement usually hastens the decay of city centers and intensifies pressures on the surrounding countryside, and the spread of great cities on coastlines and in strategically placed lowlands becomes more and more obvious.

These trends are widespread. Their continuance may imperil the capacity of the environment to provide man with the means for survival—food, clothing, shelter. Yet, on the assumption that we shall survive—that no major war, pandemic, or other large-scale disasters occur—there remains the further great threat of insidious mediocrity or squalor in our surroundings and the loss of qualities essential to a full life.

Pressures. There is little of today's environment that does not reflect the interaction of man and nature over the centuries. In Europe this interaction may have given rise to a more diverse and attractive landscape, although in many places beautiful landscapes have been mutilated or lost and many natural systems, such as river basins, have been despoiled.

Urban expansion encroaches on rural land and requires ever greater areas. The material needs of town-dwellers lead to demands for greater productivity from agriculture and to more pressure on the better soils. One of the increasing forms of intensification is monoculture in agriculture and forestry, which is sometimes accompanied by degradation and erosion of soil. Conditions develop that lead to more and more use of chemicals for fertilizers and in order to control pests. Often fundamental ecological balances, which have adapted themselves over centuries to traditional systems of agriculture, are disturbed and become unstable.

The mechanization and chemicalization of agriculture require better roads to make areas more accessible and to achieve speedy transport between farms and towns. Water supply, drainage, electrical power with its pylons and telephones with their poles, are rendered necessary. Farm buildings take on an industrialized aspect and often lose their harmony with the landscape. These changes clearly affect the amenity of the landscape as well as the total area left in "natural" conditions.

But the city, like a huge life force, also has its own "entrails" or infrastructure. Roads and railways link cities and ports; power lines and communications make a wirescape across the countryside; pipelines convey oil, petrol, and gas; and massive power stations dominate the skyline. The land is pockmarked with holes as minerals are gouged out to provide the raw materials for the physical structure of urban life. Activities located outside the cities include obnoxious trades, airports, reservoirs, and mental institutions, which in developed countries such as England and Holland may occupy another 10-20 percent of the land surface. Thus the countryside surrounding the towns increasingly becomes less rural.

The total area of land taken for towns and cities is not at present as important as its quality and location. Greater efforts should therefore be made to ensure that developments take full account of prevailing weather conditions and the availability of water and drainage channels and use low-grade land. Nevertheless, despite the best planning and landscaping, towns must always have some impact on the environment.

Many urban areas in developed and developing countries alike are now characterized by sprawl. They lack coherence in form and function. The social cost of all this, in terms of services and facilities, of minimizing pollution and coping with transportation and congestion, increases. Slums concentrate in definable geographical districts to become ghettos with unhealthy, debasing social conditions. Unplanned suburbs spread into transition zones—areas where rural land has effectively gone and refuse tips, car cemeteries, hoarding, and petrol stations proliferate. All these pressures not only make a visible impact on the environment but may lead to indifference and acceptance as people become inured to squalor.

Pollution is today's great threat. It takes a variety of forms: the dereliction of land (so common in Europe and North America), with spoil tips like pyramids in Britain, vast wastes such as the lignite mines in Czechoslovakia, and the open-cast coal disfigurements of the Appalachians in the U.S. The bulk and complexity of the refuse to be disposed of from the cities rise to special difficulties of land use and contribute to water pollution. Many of the rivers flowing in or near urban areas are open sewers. As well as creating hazards for human health they destroy vital ecosystems. And what goes into the rivers usually fouls the seas, which are becoming dangerously contaminated. Air pollution—from old and new sources—causes ill-health in Calcutta and Ankara, in Frankfurt and Tokyo, and in many American cities.

As there are more and more of us and less and less unspoiled land and water, no country can afford to continue these wastes and failures. Everywhere growth is largely unplanned, unrelated to society's needs and long-term values, and insensitive to long-term ecological factors. We need to recognize that the environment—town and country alike—is now largely man-made, and we must take full responsibility for its condition and its capacity to meet the needs of future generations.

DAVID AMIRAN concurred and added some further observations to the over-all picture.

. . . We should look at environment as a system that in nature is balanced, which means that the components—soil, air, and all the other factors—are balanced in such a way that the processes modifying them are cooperating at volumes and speeds to which the factors can maintain a running adaptation.

This has been essentially so in most rural agricultural environments throughout the ages until very recent times, when we introduced the widespread use of pesticides and all the other paraphernalia of modern agriculture.

This balance has been basically changed in the cities, especially in the large cities of our age, together with our powerful modern technologies. Here man is inducing inputs that, in their power and their speed, are far beyond the power of assimilation by the environmental systems, and therefore we obtain the whole range of malfunctions of the pollution type with which we are only too well acquainted.

For obvious reasons quantity is breeding quality, because the more people you cram into the limited confines of one city the more powerful the effect of these malfunctions will be. In 1971, and taking into account recent trends all over the world, urbanization is growing very rapidly. I would refer to an earlier comment by Dr. Weitz on future plans of settlements in which the cities are the essential parts and the rural places and villages are the minor, less important components—which I believe is an important fact of life. Cities have to make very great efforts to create an acceptable environmental balance and to prevent cumulative degrees of environmental maladaptation.

Unfortunately an increasing proportion of urban populations are concentrating in and migrating into the super-large cities. These are growing much faster than the entire city populations, and the people who migrate to these cities are motivated by the lack of any reasonable outlook for a better life in the places they are leaving and by expectations that they, at least, place on city life and hope to see fulfilled there.

Most of them, in the very large cities, do swell the ranks of the lower-level income group; many of them swell the growing large urban slums, which we see in the world's cities. Indirectly this process seems to be even more powerful and faster in the developing countries than in those that are already developed. Cities, with overloads both of slum populations and of deteriorating quarters, which are also growing as the cities expand and add new modern quarters, are not well fitted to invest the vast means needed to counteract the deterioration of environment in urban localities. The alternatives seem clear, and I am quite in agreement with what Professor Boote said: We are looking at either the short-range or the long-term value and we shall be presented with the long-term bill for not taking care of our short-range problems in environmental quality.

A number of other speakers raised this subject, all with the same convictions and all coming to the same conclusions. EIICHI ISOMURA said:

 . . . As precedence must be given to the protection of life, there is a need to regulate or control the growth of economy in order to safeguard life. The theory of priority for the economy should make way for the theory of precedence to survival. The Japanese economy has continued to develop under a conservative party administration for many years, and it is a fact that phenomena of environmental pollution have appeared. The public as well as the opposition parties have begun to urge that priority be given to life as a matter of course. At first it was possible to look upon the notion of economic priority versus life security as a discipline of enterprise versus citizen and of conservatism versus reformism. Today, however, it is accepted ipso facto that priority be given to life security and to the protection of the environment.

GABRIELE PESCATORE added his views:

. . . Territory and its organization are one of the basic themes of "Progetto 80." First, the urgency of appropriate measures for soil conservation and adaptation is acknowledged, for protection of natural resources, for defense against air and water pollution, for establishing natural parks and reserves, for preserving archeological and cultural assets. In the absence of detailed rules, territorial transformation would, under the pressure of industry and consequent urbanization, still follow the pattern of logical choices prompted by immediate economic convenience. Unfortunately, this type of expansion has already caused some severe damage to urban and economic structures and still more to natural beauty and cultural assets. Life in congested urban centers is becoming more and more unhealthy and uneasy; there is the risk of decay in the relationship between man and his environment, with urban disorder and degeneration of the natural platform. One of the most urgent measures is reeducating man to a feeling for nature and esthetic taste—and the latter was a characteristic that Italy centuries ago diffused in abundance throughout the world.

ROBERT WEAVER, looking to the future, assessed the difficulties involved.

. . . It has been estimated that the urban population will increase fivefold over the next generation. Already overloaded urban facilities are occasioning widespread pollution, and future population growth will accentuate the situation. The industrialized nations articulate mounting concern for ecology, but they also share with mankind everywhere a pressing need to consider the total urban environment. We need not only to eradicate air and water pollution but also to provide our inhabitants with opportunities to develop and utilize their full potential at the same time that they modify the stresses and strains to which they cannot adjust. Although problems of pollution have lower priority in developing countries than do matters of employment, housing, health, nutrition, public facilities, and social services, these nations too must recognize that economic development and environmental protection must be pursued simultaneously.

ROBERT J. CROOKS, examining the imminent problems of transitional housing, painted the bleakest and most pessimistic picture.

Environmental Characteristics of Transitional Urban Settlements. The apparent homogeneity of transitional settlements—the low quality of housing and community facilities—conceals a wide range of deficiencies and an even wider range of outlook. In addition, conditions in these settlements are usually undergoing a process either of gradual improvement or of deterioration and are seldom stable.

Most often, however, the degree of environmental deprivation is severe. Families establishing themselves in these areas will commonly begin their existence there at the meanest of subsistence levels. Access to water will be difficult, irregular, and expensive, with the water itself in all probability being contaminated.

Inadequate or, more likely, nonexistent sewage and garbage disposal services will have provided fertile conditions for the breeding of vermin and pestilence. The living accommodations will be overcrowded, lack privacy, and be very hot in summer and cold and wet in winter. The surrounding areas will suffer from a high density of population and lack open space and ready access to transportation to other parts of the urban area. Fire will be a constant and devastating hazard. Access to normal community facilities such as health, education, and recreation facilities will be difficult or impossible. Sickness and infant mortality will be high and life expectancy short.

Whatever the story of the individual transitional settlement, be it newly formed or many generations old, it is probable that the majority of its population will now be young newcomers to the urban area, motivated by the opportunities that seemed to exist in the city. The incomes of these people as a whole are so low and unsteady that they are beyond the reach of conventional institutional assistance mechanisms such as publicly assisted low-cost or low-rental housing and financial and credit mechanisms that would allow participation in the officially recognized housing market.

The nature of the environmental conditions of any area is to influence the behavior and social attitudes of the inhabitants. In the case of transitional settlements, their inhabitants lack the economic mobility to escape for any significant period from their microenvironment, which exerts a correspondingly strong influence on them, in some cases creating frustration and dissatisfaction with their inability to participate more fully in urban life. It is apparent that the continued growth of these areas in their present form could lead toward deep social problems and unrest of a magnitude that may act substantially to counteract the potential benefits of the development process.

Considering the present magnitude and rate of growth of transitional urban settlements in developing countries, the environment of these areas increasingly determines the environmental quality of the cities of which they are a part. It appears that about one-third of most urban populations in developing countries now suffer environmental degradation in transitional settlements. Who can argue that he is well if one-third of his body is ailing?

CONCLUSIONS

While humanity seems destined to an urban existence, and cities of 30-40 million are foreseeable in the near future, the precarious equilibrium between man and his environment is at stake.

It has now become clear that the main and worst culprit is the large metropolitan city, an entity that is completely unnatural and as yet unassimilated in an organic way in the surrounding landscape.

Unless urgent steps are taken to solve the inherent problems of the large metropolitan city, the delicate balance is likely to be upset and to turn the very epitome of progress into a mouldering garbage heap.

5

FORECASTS
FOR THE FUTURE

Whether discussing the past or analyzing the present, attention at the Rehovot Conference was naturally devoted mainly to
the future—a future that at best is largely an educated guess but
that nonetheless is already featured prominently on drawing boards
and in textbooks.

One of the main interests of participants at the Conference
was the ever intriguing question: What will the future hold? Although there was no one conclusive opinion about it, various trends
began to emerge out of the voluminous and often confusing demographic data.

KINGSLEY DAVIS pitted the recent past and the future against
various demographic pointers and presented an elaborate picture.

FUTURE RATES OF URBAN GROWTH

. . . Among the phenomena associated with economic modernization, none is more dramatic than the revolutionary shift in the location of people. Once spread out over the land, the population of
industrial societies is now concentrated in large urban complexes.
Some 75 percent of the American population, for instance, lives on
approximately 1 percent of the land, at an average density more than
200 times that of the remaining 25 percent.

The World's "Urban Fraction" and Its Future Growth. Let us start
with the world as a whole and, in so doing, focus first on the rise in
the "urban fraction," the proportion of the population living in urban
places or in cities above a certain size. The term "city" in our study
means places of 100,000 or more, delimited in the majority of instances

as the "urbanized area" or "urban agglomeration" rather than the political city or city proper.

According to our 1970 projections, 24 percent of the world's people live in cities, 39 percent are urban, and 61 percent are rural (Table 1). Thus the earth is not yet highly urbanized. It has reached about the point that the United States had reached in 1910. For all its vaunted technology, the human species is still devoting most of its energy to meeting the elementary needs for food and natural fiber. Yet the urban percentage today, modest as it is, is very recent. Prior to 1850, no country, no matter how advanced, had as large a proportion urban as the whole world does today. The transition to a fully urbanized world (that is, one as urbanized as the United States or Britain is today) may be complete in less than a century.

Many people think that the rise in the percentage urban is unusually rapid at the present time. This impression seems to be based mainly on confusion between an increase in this percentage and the growth of cities. The evidence is not conclusive, but it suggests that, if there has been any acceleration in the last two or three decades, it has been very slight. The remarkable thing is how consistent the rate of rise in the percentage urban and the percentage in cities has been, as Table 2 shows.

These findings are not without interest. One would expect the rate of change in the urban fraction to be slowing down, because the pattern of change in individual countries seems always to be a logistic type of curve with the inflection point coming early in the transition. In the United States, for instance, the most rapid gain came between 1830 and 1870, when the percentage urban was rising from 8.8 to 25.7 and the percentage in cities of 100,000+ was moving from 1.6 to 10.7 — all well under the world proportions in 1950. If, then, the rate of rise

TABLE 1

Percent of World Population in
Rural, Urban, and City Categories, 1950-70

| | Percentage | | Relative Change |
	1950	1970	(percent)
World Total	100.0	100.0	
Rural	71.8	61.4	-14.4
Urban	28.2	38.6	36.6
Cities 100,000+	16.2	23.8	46.7
Cities 1,000,000+	7.3	12.4	20.2

TABLE 2

Historical Change in Urban and City Proportions, 1800-1970

Year	Percentage of World's Population	
	Urban	In Cities 100,000+
1800	3.0	1.7
1850	6.4	2.3
1900	13.6	5.5
1950	28.2	16.2
1970B	38.6	23.8
	Relative Change per Decade (percent)	
1800-1850	16.4	6.2
1850-1900	16.3	19.0
1900-1950	15.7	24.1
1950-70B	16.9	21.1

in the urban proportion in the world population is not slowing down, a stepped-up developmental pressure affecting the world as a whole is possibly at work at the present time. I shall come back to this question again, after considering the future implications of the present trend.

There are two ways of projecting the future rise in the world's urban percentage. One is to assume that the percentage will continue to rise at the same rate as it manifested in 1950-70. The other is to assume that it will change from its current level just as the percentage changed, from the same level, in the past history of an individual country that has already gone through the urban transition. The United States affords a good model for the latter case, not only because its rate of change in the urban fraction has been about average for the advanced countries but also because the rate was closely similar to the recent world rate when the United States' urban fraction stood at the same level as the whole world's.

According to the first method of projection—a straight extrapopulation of the 1950-70 rate—it would take only 17 years after 1970 for the world's population to be 50 percent urban, and 61 years for it to be 100 percent urban. For the proportion of the population in cities to rise to 50 percent would take 39 years, and for it to rise to 100 percent would take 75 years. Half the human species would be living in cities of over a million in 53 years, and all mankind would be living in them within 79 years!

Projecting the world's future urban fraction on the basis of the historical change in the fraction in the United States yields a less spectacular estimate; but it still shows the earth to be 50 percent urban in 29 years, and to have 50 percent in cities in 45 years. Comparison of the two methods is easier if we confine ourselves to the short run and to two specific dates, 1985 and 2000. This is done in Table 3. Up to 1985, the two methods yield essentially similar results. By 2000, however, the American model shows the world somewhat less urbanized but nevertheless with a majority of human beings living in urban places and nearly a third in cities of a million or more.

The Past and Projected Future Growth of the Absolute Urban and City Population. So far I have been talking exclusively in terms of proportions. Additional information is obtained by shifting to absolute figures. The urban fraction is of the type $\frac{a}{a+b}$, where a is the urban (or city) population and b is the rural (or noncity) population. Whether the value of the fraction rises or falls does not depend on either a or b alone but solely on their rate. If the urban and rural population both have zero growth over a given period, the proportion will remain fixed. It will also remain fixed if both populations double. It follows that changes in the proportion urban tell us nothing about changes in the urban or rural population considered separately. In modern history a rise in the proportion urban has generally been accompanied by a growth in the urban population, but this is not an inherent requirement and the relation between the change in the fraction and the change in

TABLE 3

Projected Percentage Distribution of
World Population in Year 2000

	Estimated Percentage	1985		2000	
		Constant Rate	American Model	Constant Rate	American Model
World Total	100.0	100.0	100.0	100.0	100.0
Rural	61.4	52.9	53.7	44.2	46.4
Urban	38.6	47.1	46.3	55.8	53.6
Cities 100,000+	23.8	30.6	30.3	37.9	40.0
Cities 1,000,000+	12.4	17.5	15.9	23.6	26.5

the urban population has been far from uniform. The growth of the town and city population can continue indefinitely after the urban fraction has stabilized itself.

In contrast to the urban proportion, the recent growth of the absolute town and city population has been spectacular, as Table 4 shows. In two decades the entire urban population rose by 98 percent, the city population rose by 113 percent, and the population in cities of a million or more rose by 147 percent. Over half a billion people were added to the earth's urban population, and over a fourth of a billion were added to cities of over a million.

Furthermore, the world's urban population grew much faster recently than it ever did before (Table 5). The rate of growth in 1950-70 was 1.6 times the previous rate for the city population.

The rate of growth in the absolute urban population in 1950-70 was more than twice the rate of rise in the urban fraction. Why the difference? The explanation is to be found in the rural population. If the rural population had remained fixed, the proportional increase in the urban percentage would have been identical with the proportional increase in the number of urban inhabitants. In fact, however, the world's rural population has also been expanding—at a rate that is about a fourth of the town and city rate but still enough to double the number of rural inhabitants in 64 years. Of major significance is the fact that the greatest acceleration in the rate of absolute population growth in the last two decades compared with the first half of the century occurred with respect to the rural population.

Clearly, then, an important conclusion emerges. The accelerated growth of cities in the world since 1950 is not due to an acceleration in the shift from rural to city residence. It is due, rather, to an acceleration in the growth of the world's total population. This

TABLE 4

Growth of Rural, Urban, and Total Population, 1950-70B

	Population (millions)		Increase	
	1950	1970B	Absolute	Percent
World Total	2,502	3,628	1,126	45.0
Rural	1,796	2,229	433	24.1
Urban	706	1,399	693	98.1
Cities 100,000+	406	864	458	112.8
Cities 1,000,000+	182	448	267	146.8

stepped-up general population growth has affected both the cities and the countryside, but it has affected the countryside more. Had the world's population not grown at all between 1950 and 1970, but had the urban fraction changed as it actually did, the number of people living in urban places in 1970 would be only two-thirds the number found.

The reduced rate of growth (16.9 percent per decade) would have been substantially lower than the rate of growth of the absolute urban population during the half century from 1900 to 1950 (25.8 percent per decade). On the same assumptions, the rural population would have decreased. Instead of having a rise of 11.4 percent per decade, it would have fallen by 7.5 percent per decade. This would have been much lower than the half century prior to 1950, when the rural population increased by 4.7 percent every 10 years.

Given the unprecedented general population growth, the future increase in the absolute population of cities and towns appears fantastic, regardless of which of our two projections of the urban fraction is used. The figures are shown in Table 6. By the constant-rate projection, the urban population at the end of the century will exceed the entire population of the world today; by either model, the population in cities of a million or more will exceed or equal today's urban population.

TABLE 5

Historical Growth of World's Urban and
Rural Populations, 1850-1970B

Population (millions)	World Total	Rural	Urban	Cities 100,000+
1850	1,262	1,181	81	29
1900	1,650	1,426	224	91
1950	2,520	1,796	706	406
1970B	3,628	2,229	1,399	864
Growth Per Decade (percent)				
1850-1900	5.5	3.8	22.7	25.6
1900-1950	8.7	4.7	25.8	34.9
1950-70B	20.4	11.4	40.8	45.9

TABLE 6

Projected World Population
in Rural-Urban Categories, 1985 and 2000

	Actual Population (millions)	Projected Population (millions)			
		1985		2000	
		Constant Rate	American Model	Constant Rate	American Model
World Total	3,628	4,794	4,537	6,335	5,478
Rural	2,229	2,535	2,436	2,797	2,539
Urban	1,399	2,259	2,102	3,538	2,938
Cities 100,000+	864	1,465	1,376	2,399	2,191
Cities 1,000,000+	448	838	721	1,497	1,449

On the basis of these figures, the mundane need of finding accommodation for the masses of people flocking into the cities assumes ominous proportions, as put by MARSHALL CLINARD, who focuses on cities in developing countries.

. . . The urbanization process in the less developed countries differs markedly from that of the more developed nations. These differences directly or indirectly affect the course of their urbanization. One specific example is the greater tendency for the urban populations in the less developed countries to become increasingly concentrated in the large, or largest (primate), cities of 250,000 to a million or more inhabitants. In 1960, 49 percent of the populations of developed countries lived in large cities, an increase of only 3 percent since 1940, while in the less developed it was already 43 percent. Since 1960, large cities of less developed countries have been growing at phenomenal rates. Cities like Caracas, Manila, Addis Ababa, Accra, Abidjan, Nairobi, and Kinshasa have doubled, or even trebled in size; Greater Djakarta grew from 53,000 in 1930 to 2,080,000 in 1958 and to 4,500,000 in 1970.

ALARCON MAGNO HERRERA was one of the many who also attempted a forecast of future growth.

. . . Other "emerging" cities have also grown rapidly, increasing in the short span of two decades—the number of large cities of Latin

America. At the same time, the total population residing in this category of cities has risen. In 1960, Latin America had 9 cities of over 1 million inhabitants; in 1970 there were 15 in this category; in 1980 there will be 26. Latin America is rapidly becoming a sub-continent of cities and markedly of large cities, as indicated in Table 7.

PROBLEMS AND ISSUES OF THE FUTURE

Most participants, however, pointed out what they considered to be the grave problems that most countries will face in the near future. Robert E. Boote and Robert C. Weaver have addressed themselves to environmental problems. DENIS JOHN DWYER was directly concerned with slums.

. . . Spontaneous settlement has become a major element in the urban form of cities of the developing world during the last 30 years. About one-quarter of the population of Manila and Djakarta live in spontaneous settlements; in Hong Kong, despite the fact that the formation of such settlements has been brought under effective control, the current figure is 11 percent of the urban population. Comparable figures elsewhere are 20 percent for Caracas, 33 percent for Mexico City, and almost 50 percent for Ankara. And, undoubtedly, this situation will soon become much worse. Turner has estimated, for example, that by 1990 4.5 million out of Lima's anticipated population of 6 million will be living in barriadas. He has also pointed out that growth rates of such settlements are now reaching 12 percent annually in several countries, for example, Mexico, Turkey, the Philippines, and Peru, or in many cases double those of city growth rates as a whole.

TABLE 7

Urban Population in Latin America, 1960, 1970, 1980
(in millions of inhabitants)

Year	Population in Cities of 20,000 to 100,000	Population in Cities of 100,000 to 1,000,000	Population in Cities of over 1,000,000
1960	21	18	28
1970	47	25	48
1980	108	33	75

EDMUNDO FLORES addressed himself vehemently to the
problems at hand, viewing the future in the light of the present.

. . . In 1969, on the occasion of a conference on Agrarian Reform
held in the Philippines, I visited the perplexing countries of Southeast
Asia, then making what might be termed a professional pilgrimage to
Calcutta, since I was driven by the feeling that an economist concerned
with food should also be familiar with hunger.

Calcutta affords the opportunity to see large-scale misery in
its full harshness. At night its broad sidewalks become public dormi-
tories, heaped with more than 600,000 emaciated men, women, old
people, and children, as in Mexico vacationists pack the beaches of
Acapulco during Holy Week. The poor of Calcutta lack the most elementary belongings, owning neither pillow, mattress, nor blanket;
their bodies stink and are covered by soiled rags. At dawn, before
the city awakens, carts collect the corpses of those who have died in
the night.

I, at once, realized that the misery of Calcutta was quite familiar
to me. Hungry, ragged human beings were no novelty, since they are
a standard part of the rural and urban landscape in Mexico, Bolivia,
Peru, and Brazil, countries I know well. What moved me in Calcutta
was the overwhelming proportions of its misery. I then remembered
Lincoln Steffens and decided to paraphrase him. I bought postcards
showing Bengal tigers and the Taj Mahal, and wrote "I have been to
the future and it doesn't work," and mailed them to friends in Latin
America.

The probability that within 30 years social conditions in Latin
America will resemble those of Calcutta today is not far-fetched.
Only profound changes in Latin America's economic and social structures could prevent this; and, judging from the past, it is more probable that Latin Americans will arrive at the Malthusian impasse of
Calcutta than that they will effect the necessarily painful and exacting
transformations to avoid sinking into the waiting abyss.

According to United Nations estimates, the population of Latin
America in the year 2000 will be 640 million persons. Ceteris paribus,
the migration from country to city will continue with ever growing
intensity until the bulk of the population is concentrated in urban areas
which, with certain differences of local color, will become a Dantesque
replica of present-day Calcutta.

To forestall this nightmare, two options are open to us—both of
them seemingly distasteful to the ruling elite, local and foreign. One
is the proposal of Robert S. McNamara, president of the World Bank,
in his recent address to the Board of Governors, in Copenhagen:

There are thousands of clinical facilities to be established;
hundreds of thousands of staff workers to be recruited,
trained and organized in the administration of the vast national programs; hundreds of millions of families to be informed and served; and well over one billion births to be
averted in the developing world alone, if, for example, by
the year 2000 the present birth rate of 40 per 1,000 population were to be reduced to 20 per 1,000. What we must
understand is that even if an average family size of two
children per couple is achieved, the population will continue to grow for an additional 65 or 70 years and the ultimate stabilized level will be far greater than at the time
the two per couple is achieved.

This proposal was rejected by the Latin American delegates
with florid indignation. Though I am myself indifferent to the moral
and religious considerations that moved most of the delegates to reject birth control, I must admit that I find it extremely difficult to
envisage the lame, contraceptive world that would ensue from
McNamara's modest proposal. Besides dispensing family-planning
instructions, what else would governments do?

The other option is to incorporate Latin America rapidly into
the twentieth century by introducing such basic structural reforms as
effective and massive land reform, followed by the swift modernization
of agriculture, public works construction, progressive taxation, education at all levels, and industrialization at unprecedented rates. Only
such policies, which entail momentous shifts of income and power,
would exorcise the ghost of Calcutta and would allow the economic
growth rates of the 1960-70 decade, which were less than 2 percent
yearly per capita, to double. This growth rate would create the necessary new jobs to use productively the 60 percent of the labor force
now unemployed or engaged in unproductive services that tends to
concentrate in the cities.

The main issues facing planners and thinkers, however, are
to find ways and means by which the trends of the future can be
harnessed and controlled for the maximum benefit of man. LLOYD
RODWIN outlined some of these issues in his paper.

Urbanization and Regional and National Development Policy: Problems
and Issues. In the next three decades the world's population is expected to reach 6 billion. Of this total, approximately 6 out of every
10 persons will probably be living in cities in the year 2000, as compared to 4 out of 10 in 1960. The figures are guesstimates since we
do not know whether urban population will simply double or perhaps

even triple during this period. It grew 25 percent a decade from 1920 to 1950 and then jumped to 40 percent from 1950 to 1960. The exact figures hardly matter since the order of magnitude of growth is so large we are forced to resort to ingenious comparisons to establish the scale of the tasks that confront us. Ernest Weissmann, for example, has emphasized that in the last five decades of the twentieth century, we will have to provide a tolerable urban environment "for thirteen times as many people as in the previous 150 years; to do so, the rate of construction in the next fifty years must average almost 40 times that of the past." Others, citing the increasingly poor quality of current service levels for power, water, sewerage, housing, and education, contend that the situation is all the more serious because in the past generation we have "used up" most of the existing capacity of urban infrastructure. Still others add that new regional centers will also be required in many countries because the growing markets for intermediate and basic goods make it feasible to develop new fabrication activities that are likely to be established in different regions and different centers. A notable example is the development of Ciudad Guayana in Venezuela.

This complex array of needs and pressures creates formidable problems, which in many respects offset some of the alluring prospects of economic growth and rising standards of living. Ideally we would like the new cities and the bigger cities to reflect the varying regional development needs and goals of the different nations. But this is hardly likely unless nations can decide wisely a number of critical questions concerning urbanization, such as

(1) how much to invest in infrastructure;

(2) where urban growth should be encouraged (relative emphasis on existing big cities, smaller towns, or new towns);

(3) what growth patterns to encourage (especially scale and density);

(4) what performance standards should the development patterns satisfy, particularly of density, transportation, and accessibility, community facilities and municipal and commercial services;

(5) what trade-offs might be desirable in reconciling such diverse goals as efficiency, growth, amenity, and welfare; and

(6) what mechanisms, or changes in mechanisms, would help to improve the way these decisions are made.

Unfortunately all too little is known about these matters. Although governments are constantly making decisions that affect urban and regional development, and although the United Nations and other international and national technical assistance agencies are being increasingly asked for advice and assistance, the amount of intellectual capital to provide helpful guidance is very meager. The main reasons for this state of affairs are limited experience (urban and regional patterns were rarely the result of explicit policy decisions in the past) and the lack of an ongoing program of research and of training in this field. The situation is changing, however. Today, urban growth strate gies are being improvised in many parts of the world, and governments in effect, are learning in the process of doing. This process might be aided, however, by well-designed research projects that could help nations to assess, and to inform others about, significant urbanization policies and experience—both positive and negative.

JORGE E. HARDOY attempted an over-all forecast of the future in the light of present conditions.

. . . During the postwar decades, new aspects of the process of development have attracted the attention of an increasing number of people:

(1) the rapid growth of the world's population and especially of the population in developing countries, which already has and will continue having an impact on their settlement patterns and on the growth of some of the largest metropolitan areas and cities;

(2) the growing awareness, by most sectors of the population of the tremendous disparities that exist between the modern areas and the depressed areas, between the rich and the poor of each country

(3) the recognition that local governments have not the political and economic power to solve the urban problems, as urbanization is essentially the consequence of decisions undertaken by the higher levels of government and by the private sector;

(4) objections against living conditions in the cities; and

(5) the underdeveloped technology employed in the construction of cities and in the improvement of the basic facilities for urban life.

What is not yet clear to most people and even most professionals and leaders in government is

(1) that we are moving rapidly toward models of human agglo-merations that in size, form, internal structure, and functions have no historical precedents;

(2) that such cities will have to be planned and built with new approaches and technologies and will require different institutions to solve the many problems that they will pose;

(3) that the situation of such human agglomerations will be aggravated because they are centers and areas of a national spatial structure that, due to historical and political reasons, does not serve adequately the needs of developing nations; and

(4) that there are no quick solutions to most of the pressing ur-ban problems, as they depend on the values adopted by societies and, therefore, of the use made of resources.

Behind these ideas are problems of regional imbalance that many governments are trying to solve, and a lot of talk about the city as "a crucible for change and economic progress," of the social costs of excessive metropolitanism, of optimum size and minimum size. The truth is that we know very little about the behavior of urban systems at regional, national, and international levels, or about how to anticipate urbanization in order to maximize its advantages and decrease its disadvantages, or how economic policies affect the regional social structure and how this structure is changing.

Most urbanization policies attempted are related to the interest of some national governments to counterbalance the concentration of economic activities, population, and institutions in one center or in one area. This was the reason mentioned by Turkey, Brazil, and Pakistan when they decided to create new capital cities, by Venezuela, with the promotion of Ciudad Guayana, or by Cuba in recent years. It is also implicit in Japan's effort to develop the rich resources of the northern region of Hokkaido, despite its rigorous climate, while controlling the growth of Tokyo and Osaka, and in the continuous efforts of Italy to develop the southern provinces, and in the recommendations included in India's Third Five-Year Plan (1961-66), calling for the promotion of dispersed industrial and economic development while avoiding large and congested cities and its emphasis on small-town urbanization. Other countries have moved in these directions for decades. The need to curb the growth of Moscow was announced in the Third Five-Year Plan of the Soviet Union (1938-42), and, through its new towns program, thousands of cities, towns, and urban settlements of different sizes and functions have been established since the beginning of Soviet rule. At present, "the growth of towns in the Soviet Union is kept within bounds and in step with the national plan by regulating the factors of urbanization." Cuba, since the mid-1960s, has successfully curbed the growth of Havana and promoted the concentration of productive investments and population in the province of Oriente and in selected centers and areas throughout the island.

Such are the forces that determine the dynamics of rapid urbanization and the characteristics of cities in developing countries under a capitalist economy that without regional plans that define the functions and size of the most sensible settlement pattern, it doesn't make much sense to plan the directions of city growth and promote functional zoning, land densities, and the like, all aspects that are not controllable at city level. We have lost too much time, effort, and money trying to promote local or metropolitan master plans that have proved to be of little or no value because they couldn't be related to the orientation of unplanned economies and they didn't receive adequate support from supra-local levels of government. As a result of rapid urbanization, the cities and towns in developing countries lack an adequate economic basis. Furthermore, the economic and social systems of developing countries lack integration and show the characteristics of the transitional stage toward industrialization with its collorary of unemployment, underemployment, constant shifts in the distribution of the population, slums and marginal settlements, poor services, low or inadequate technology, and social tensions.

The most oft-repeated word in recent literature dealing with problems of urbanization is "crisis." What do we mean by a "crisis?" Implicit in the word is the existence of a disease, but who is affected by the disease, the cities or the urban social systems that leave their impact on them? Which is the crucial decision, to produce a different city or to change society? The construction of cities does not mean using billions of dollars, but using improved technologies. National societies that can do that, and there are not many that can, will continue eroding every type of city they design if they don't develop a coherent relationship between the social groups living in them. We should be aware then that different sociopolitical systems develop or can develop different urban systems, and these will serve a country or a region better or worse depending on the use governments are making of the factors that determine the functions of such systems. We should also be aware that different sociopolitical systems are reflected in different urban ecologies. Social mobility loses its meaning in a context where urban land and housing have a social meaning. Health and education are matters of national policy, and full employment and the redistribution of incomes are key objectives of a planned economy.

EDMUNDO FLORES also views future trends broadly, analyzing possible development.

The Cities of the Future. By extrapolation of present trends, it is possible to predict the emergence of two radically different types of cities in the coming 20 to 30 years. Each of these types of city will be the result of political and economic forces that will move in opposite directions. To be conventional, the first type can be called Utopia; and the second Disutopia. Utopia is used in this paper only as a point of reference, a placebo, so to speak, designed to emphasize contrast, and frankly I feel uncertain about it since it is essentially alien to my own experience. Perhaps the cities of Western Europe will evolve into something resembling this model, but I do not think that American cities will fit into either one of my two prototypes. The rules of the game will be as follows:

Utopia and environs.

(1) The political organization will tend toward egalitarianism. There will be disparities in power, income, and wealth, but these will not be significant.

(2) The population explosion will be under control, and there will be stationary or slightly declining rates of growth.

(3) In the labor front, conditions approaching full employment under widespread automation and vestiges of featherbedding will prevail. The week's work will be limited to two or three days at most. The remaining time will be spent mostly in games and idleness. Research and creative activities will be wide open to consenting adults. Drug consumption and the like will be as common as the use of coffee and tobacco is today.

(4) The rural-urban migrations set in motion by the wide income gap between country and town will have disappeared and will be considered as remote as, say, the enclosure movement.

(5) Today's industry produces, as Kenneth Boulding puts it, goods and "bads." The bads are the contaminants. Environmental disruption will be minimized by the discovery and widespread use of refined "clean" industrial processes and by the minimization of the bads. Regulatory city plans and urban planning will have a function in the 50-60 million population megalopolis and will make living conditions from tolerable to pleasant.

(6) Cities will be dispersed, partly to minimize the risk of bombardments and partly because it will be possible to substitute messages for personal travel. In addition the development of the self-sufficient autonomous housing unit, free from service connections, will help dispersion. The quantity of garbage and refuse produced by these cities will be huge, but most of it will be recycled. These types of urban arrangement will fit into Aldons Huxley's Utopias—whether Brave New World or Island.

Disutopia. The opposite model—about which I feel more confident—rests on the facile and fantastic assumption that the present political and economic organization, with minor alterations, will prevail well into the future in most present-day underdeveloped countries. The rules of the game will be these:

(1) Politically not all the significant groups in the community will enjoy effective representation to bargain in favor of their group interests. Consequently, there will be wide disparities, which will tend to perpetuate themselves, in the distribution of power, income, and wealth.

(2) The population explosion will continue unchecked. The high birth rates will be reinforced by a decline in mortality rates. Eventually population growth will decelerated by Malthusian checks: plagues, riots, famine, etc. These calamities will have an effect that may be thought of as retroactive birth control.

(3) The blatant disparity between rural and urban conditions, its diffusion and exaggeration by the mass media, will feed and add momentum to rural-urban migrations. Urban population will double every 15 years and rural population around every 30 years.

(4) The need to fight unemployment on the spot, and the urge to satisfy the growing demand for cheap goods and services exerted by the growing populace, will lead to desperate efforts to accelerate industrialization, without concern for antipollution measures, except if these already are present in the current productive techniques and do not increase costs or lower demand for labor inputs.

(5) The unregulated use of cheap obsolete transportation, cars, Diesel engines, etc., will accentuate environmental disruptions.

Given these assumptions, the frightening emergence of cities like Calcutta is foreseeable. But these Calcuttas will be much bigger, their architecture will be amorphous, and their regulatory urban plans will lack viability and will be inoperant, as many such plans already are today. These cities will look like foggy, interminable spreads of drab housing, slums of the lowest imaginable quality, crossed by perpetually congested speedways.

Besides, as in the Middle Ages, there will be walled-up urban enclaves where the rich and powerful will live and play in safety and comfort. This type of urban enclave is, in fact, already beginning to emerge. Where smog is not intense, in Manila or Mexico City, one finds this type of exclusive, segregated, expensive residential area.

In conclusion, the future city of the underdeveloped countries will resemble the setting of George Orwell's 1984 unless the developmental policies outlined above are put into effect. But to apply such policies will require great changes in the power structure, social valuations, and goals pursued in the economy and policy. To regulate the rates of population growth, accelerate economic growth, and avoid getting more entangled into the Malthusian impasse, vastly more sophisticated nets of communications and control will be essential.

Yet, for all the deep concern and uncertainty expressed, a number of speakers were fundamentally optimistic about the chances of urban recovery in developed and developing countries alike. The participants from Japan, in particular, viewed the future hopefully, and MASAHIKO HONJO said,

. . . In spite of all pessimistic forecasts, the fact remains that we shall have to cope directly with the realities of urban development. The boost in production centered on industry has indisputably been sustained by urban development and has in its turn ensured an ever larger market for farm produce, with the consequence that it has sustained the whole of the economy. Perhaps the paper of T. Fujii at the Pacific Conference on Urban Growth in Hawaii, 1968, was one of the earliest to discuss urban concentration positively, though there previously had been some hesitation in the matter of supporting it. Fujii's paper made a deep impression on the participants. He put forward propositions in positive support of the role of development of big cities and contended that "urban growth based on capital accumulation will encourage the growth of the nation in the long run."

Commenting on Professor Isomura's paper, EDWIN MILLS remarked,

. . . In many developing countries, especially those that have been developing rapidly, one should expect to find, and indeed, should welcome very rapid growth of the largest cities, unless the government adopts extremely harsh measures to prevent that concentration of activity. I take it that that is exactly what has happened in Japan. Japan has certainly been one of the most rapidly growing countries throughout the entire postwar period. I do not know details, but I am sure that in many underdeveloped countries, probably also in Japan, if governments adopt harsh policies to prevent the concentration of people and economic activity in large cities, they can achieve their aim, but only at the cost of slowing down the rate of economic development. The moral that I draw from Professor Isomura's paper is that, in a country like Japan, the government should worry less about the growth in the Tokyo–Osaka regions and a good deal more about improving the undesirable by-products of such growth. There is no doubt that extremely rapid growth in very large cities in a country like Japan, or in any other country, does have most undesirable by-products. That is not to say that it should not be done. The growth may be worth the cost. But it is to say that something has to be done about the undesirable by-products in the form of pollution, congestion, etc. I believe that the Japanese have recently become extremely aware of the environmental results that their very rapid growth and highly concentrated development is causing, and they are now in their efficient fashion setting right those results. I have no doubt whatsoever that within the next decade we will see some very dramatic improvements in public policies to improve the environment in Japan. As Japan has been an extremely rapidly growing economy— firstly, these undesirable by-products emerge very quickly, and, secondly, the resources are available to do something about them. All it really requires is for the public sector to organize itself and begin to adopt appropriate policies. The point I wish to make is that in Japan, and probably also in other countries, the appropriate policies are not to say that pollution is terrible, so stop urbanization, but to say instead, if it is true, that, since urbanization is most desirable and important in promoting economic development, it is up to the government to solve the problem of the undesirable by-products of urbanization. None of them are inevitable results of urbanization. A wealthy country, like Japan or the United States, has an enormous spectrum of possible solutions, and the public and the private sectors can do a great deal. The combination of public and private action to be taken depends on the institutions of the society in question.

The same is true of congestion. Congestion results mainly not from large cities, but rather from concentrated cities. One can either have cities that are somewhat less concentrated, or, through the development of varied transportation systems, one can even develop a concentrated city in which congestion, although it is present, is relatively unimportant. It seems to me that those are the issues on which it would be most productive for public policy to concentrate in a relatively wealthy society like Japan, and not to worry so much about the major metropolitan areas.

Relevant to the above, Dr. SHEFER of Israel made the observation that,

The Urbanization Process Is a Consequence of "Push," Not "Pull." We should concentrate on the problem of how to shelter, feed, and take care of the people rather than how to control the population. In this regard, I also maintain that the pattern of urbanization that emerges, that cities grow and they grow larger, indicates there are some market mechanisms, some efficiency inherent in large cities. The studies we conducted in the U.S. on developed countries showed that the standard of living in larger cities is higher than it is in smaller cities. Also, it shows that large cities enjoy economies of scale in localization economies.

All indications show that large cities are beneficial and desirable, and I think that, if this is agreed, we should learn to study the ways by which we can so arrange development that it does not detract from environmental qualities and other elements of living and working situations.

Many of the participants, however, in predicting the future of urbanization in developing countries, were far less optimistic. WALTER SEDWITZ said,

. . . Therefore, with the large cities already overcrowded, with the potential for rural-urban migration still large, and with the total population continuing to grow rapidly, a maintenance of current trends in urbanization together with slow development can only lead to severe declines in average urban living standards and to increased congestion. By the year 2000, about 60 percent of the Latin American population may be urban and 47 percent may reside in cities of at least 500,000 inhabitants. Some experts feel that a situation of this kind will be due in part to the fact that, since the attraction of a primate city is already so great, improvements in its environment may very well be offset by additional migration so stimulated.

ROBERT SADOVE expressed the gravest doubts as to the foreseeable future.

. . . What appears to be the outlook for this trend toward continued rapid urbanization? What are the conditions under which it is taking place? Despite average per capita income and productivity differentials between urban and rural areas, unemployment in developing urban centers is high and getting higher due to increased rural-urban migration. It appears an almost universal phenomenon in developing countries that the investment required to employ the potential labor force productively has plainly outstripped the means available. The position here is bleak, with registered unemployment growing rapidly to rates well in excess of 10 percent of the labor force in many cities, rates that need to be multiplied by two or three in some of the cases investigated in order to make an account of underemployment or unrecorded unemployment (including those who have involuntarily dropped out of the active labor force for want of opportunity). The Organization of American States estimates indicate that for Latin America the average officially registered unemployment rate doubled between 1950 and 1965 to well over 10 percent and the rise has continued since. For some individual countries and cities, the situation is much worse.

In such circumstances, it is not surprising that the living conditions of low-income groups in the cities have worsened substantially, in contrast to the over-all average growth in income per head. With increasing unemployment, inequality in income distribution appears to have intensified. Nowhere are the results more obvious than in the growth of shantytowns, often without minimal services of water supply, sewerage, or electricity and accounting for a rapidly increasing proportion of the total population of many of the large cities. As noted earlier, with the major exception of India, urban populations are typically growing at over 4 percent per annum. Squatter settlements in the major cities investigated appear to be growing much faster — usually at more than double this annual rate and sometimes even at over 20 percent. Such settlements frequently now account for more than one-quarter of the total population of the large cities. Average rates of occupancy per room are appallingly high in many of these cities. The case of Calcutta, where more than two-thirds of families are reported as living in one-room dwellings, is familiar; but only slightly less drastic conditions prevail in many other cities of Asia, Africa, and Latin America. In the squatter settlements of Nairobi or Dakar, occupancy rates reach about six per room. Except in Latin

America, few towns outside the major metropolitan area have water supply or drainage for the great majority of the population.

Projections for the years ahead, unfortunately, give no basis for optimism of any early or automatic relief to these problems. Past demographic trends preclude any early reduction in over-all population growth or the growth of the labor force. Total population appears likely to grow in the next decade at much the same rate as in the 1960s. The rate of increase in the labor force may be somewhat below that for the over-all population due to lower participation in the labor force by people in the working age group. There are few grounds, however, for expecting the work force rate of increase to be significantly less, if at all, than in the 1960s.

It is difficult to avoid concluding that the deterioration of urban conditions underway in the 1960s will be further accentuated in the 1970s and 1980s unless determined action is taken along new lines to counter or accommodate current trends. To cope with the existing deficiencies of major urban centers in the context of the natural population growth rates—often exceeding 3 percent and at times reaching as high as 3.5 percent—would be difficult enough. In the context of continuing heavy migration from the countryside, the urban problem threatens to become explosive.

Attention should be drawn to the existing ratios between rural and urban population. In many parts of Africa and Asia over 80 percent of the population is rural. In such cases, migration to the towns of even a small proportion of the natural increase in rural population will produce a large increase in urban population. For instance, a country with an 85 percent rural population would undergo an urban rate of increase of 5.3 percent as contrasted with a 3.2 percent growth rate, where the existing rural/urban ratio is 60/40.

The implications are serious. The poorer developing countries where the rural percentage is at present very high will have to deal with the more rapid rates of urban growth, yet these are the countries that have fewer resources to cope with the urbanization problem.

CONCLUSIONS

When the various forecasts and projections for the future are summarized and condensed, the prevailing mood at the Rehovot Conference was found to be one of great concern and apprehension. True, various delegates expressed optimistic views, based primarily on the success of particular projects, but the over-all mood of most participants was that the future is not to be taken lightly. Urban trends are likely to continue at ever growing rates and, with them, bring problems of a magnitude hitherto unknown.

While slums, transitional housing, and unemployment will, in all probability, continue to be the first and foremost concerns of the developing countries, pollution and environmental decay are catching up as the main problems of those countries that, by the end of the century, will have managed to escape the status of "undeveloped."

6

URBANIZATION AND
THE PRODUCTION
SYSTEM

Though urbanization in the developing countries is not necessarily a result of economic development, the development of economic sectors, nevertheless, affects the rate of urbanization
considerably. The development of agriculture and industry adds
impetus to migration from rural to urban areas; new urban centers
emerge and the existing ones tend to expand.

The effect of economic development on urbanization was
widely dealt with by a number of speakers—both scientists and
policy-makers.

AGRICULTURE AND URBANIZATION

Comprehensive studies on the relations between agricultural
development and urbanization were presented by Dr. Marion
Clawson and Professor Gerald Wibberley; each speaker studied the
subject from a different point of view, and one study complements
the other.

The Process in the Developing World. According to MARION
CLAWSON, agricultural development affects urbanization, but
urban growth is equally basic to agricultural development. In his
paper, he analyzed the subject from many aspects.

. . . One need not assert that either agriculture or urban growth
is more important than the other, nor need one argue that either must
precede the other; national economic growth and health require
mutual development and interaction.

Urbanization is proceeding rapidly around the world today, in
economically developed and underdeveloped countries alike.

Migration from rural to urban areas is an old process in the economically developed countries. In such countries, cities grew during the nineteenth century (and earlier) as well as in modern times, as industry and other economic development offered employment opportunities, which drew young people from rural areas. With temporary exceptions, such migrants found employment. The fact that city growth was often moderate or slow permitted a fairly close adjustment between labor force and job opportunity. One should not minimize the extent of the social adjustment required of such migrants, nor should one imply that all was perfect in such urban growth.

The rapid growth of cities in the economically less developed countries, especially since World War II, has often been rather different in character. In a great many cases, this rapid migration of people from rural areas and small towns to the larger cities has proceeded faster than the growth of employment in the cities. Substantial unemployment developed in the larger cities of many less economically developed countries; while this has often seemed extreme, even wasteful, it has often merely replaced latent unemployment in the agricultural areas. While housing conditions in the slums of the rapidly growing cities of the economically less developed countries have been very bad, by modern standards, yet often they have been no worse, and have perhaps been better, than housing conditions in rural areas. One may deplore some aspects of the rapid growth of cities in the economically less developed countries, yet growth of such cities is almost certainly a necessary part of economic development. The migration of many young people to the cities may create some problems, but it also creates opportunities.

The Urban Impact on Agriculture. The rapid growth of cities in the economically less developed countries has several major effects on agriculture.

First of all, the growth of the cities provides a market for the agricultural products of the farming areas. In traditional agriculture, the farmers produce primarily for their own consumption; in many countries, as much as 7 percent or more of total agricultural output does not leave the village where it is produced. Each farmer produces that range of crops that it is physically possible to grow and that is needed to feed his family, and his consumption is largely limited to the products he can produce on his farm. There is limited trade, which may be highly important in providing the farmer with industrial and other products but which does not involve a major portion of his output. Under these circumstances, there can be relatively little specialization, either by broad regions of the country or by farmers within any region. As the cities grow, their populations require food and other agricultural commodities, which must move into the cities either from the country's own hinterland or from abroad. A cash market for agricultural commodities grows up, expanding at least as fast as the city population grows and often somewhat faster if average incomes in the city permit some upgrading of average diets. Farmers find it possible, and often profitable, to increase their output in order to have a salable surplus.

This development of a larger market, as cities grow, has numerous impacts on the nature of agriculture. It begins a process of commercialization of agriculture. The farmer now produces more for cash sale instead of primarily for family consumption. He is now more concerned with prices of salable commodities and with costs of needed inputs than he was previously. As he begins to produce commodities for sale, he is likely to begin to specialize somewhat; in time, he is likely to begin to buy some agricultural commodities that he cannot produce efficiently but that he needs for family consumption. The whole nature of agriculture changes under the impact of a growing urban market for farm output.

Urbanization affects agricultural areas in other ways. As the cities grow, they offer attractions for rural people, especially for the young. The attraction is not merely a better job, higher pay, more dignified, and perhaps easier work. It is also for a different style of life—more excitement, more interaction with other people, often other people of different backgrounds, and many kinds of social activities. Educational opportunities are often better in the cities. The possibility of economic, social, or political advancement in the cities may be much greater, at least for the abler and more energetic. It can be argued, and often proven, that the attraction of the city is in part an illusion, that some migrants are not, in fact, better off than they would have been had they stayed in the rural area of origin. But, where migration from rural areas to cities is persistent and relatively large, obviously the stream of migrants is not convinced of the equality of life in rural and urban areas.

A constant pull of young people away from rural areas exerts a major effect on the farms and the rural areas. If the relative volume of migrants is not too large, it may actually facilitate agricultural adjustments and progress. For instance, migration of one son to the city may remove the necessity of dividing the father's farm between the sons, thus avoiding land fragmentation. But a constant competition for labor force may require major adjustments in farming operations; a shift from labor-using to capital-using methods of production, for instance, may now be profitable.

When rural poor people migrate to a city, whether in an economically developed or in an economically less developed country, they often acquire a political power they lacked in the rural areas. In the countryside, the population is often too dispersed to make concerted political action possible. When the same people are concentrated in a city, they are able to act together in a political way and to force concessions from governments. One may decry the actions of urban poor, which sometimes include rioting, but one must confess that such actions obtain consideration of their problems and needs, which was unattainable in the countryside.

The growth of cities is usually associated with some degree of industrial development in the economically less developed countries. Such industries can often supply agriculture with its needed inputs of fertilizer, machinery, chemicals, and so on. As agriculture commercializes, the volume and the range of such inputs increase, and their use becomes more sensitive to their relative prices. The cities have both an opportunity for profitable business and an obligation to national development to provide such inputs on reasonable terms. Likewise, the developing agriculture requires many services of marketing, transportation, storage, financing, insurance, and the like, which the city can supply, often profitably. Modernization of agriculture in an economically less developed country is highly dependent on an infrastructure that almost certainly must be urban in its location.

The Role of Agriculture in Developing Countries. If an economically undeveloped country is to move forward satisfactorily in its economic development, agriculture must play a major role. Agriculture is expected to perform several important functions in a developing country.

First of all, agriculture should provide an ample supply of food for the population of the country, and more particularly for the growing city population in a developing country. This does not preclude some international trade in agricultural commodities, of course, but a country that seeks economic development, while it is forced to spend a substantial share of its scarce foreign exchange in importing foods of the kinds grown within the country, labors under an unnecessary handicap. While disparities in diets for a substantial part of the lower-income population seem a regrettable but unavoidable aspect of life in nearly every country, no country today will permit starvation or massive food shortages. Unless the workingmen of the cities can buy adequate food at prices that are reasonable in relation to their earnings, there will be serious unrest, and economic development is likely to be jeopardized. Agriculture's first and basic task, therefore, is to feed the people of the country.

But agriculture must provide employment opportunity for most of the rural young people. Although there may be a continuing stream of migration from rural areas to cities, which is an essential part of economic development, nevertheless urban growth in most economically undeveloped countries cannot provide employment for all the surplus rural young people. In a country where only 10 percent or 20 percent of the people live in the cities, urban employment— whether in industry or in trade—cannot possibly expand fast enough to absorb all the surplus young people—the 80 percent or 90 percent of the rural population, especially if the rate of natural increase is high. Even where agriculture already has an ample, or even an excessive, labor supply, so that many rural people are not now fully and productively employed, it will still have to absorb more workers, at least for a few decades. Later, urban growth may be larger, in part because the urban base will be larger, so that the surplus of young people from rural areas might then all be absorbed in the cities; and, still later, as the economy evolves, migration may reach a volume that actually reduces the population of rural areas. The latter has happened in many economically advanced countries; in the United States, for example, nearly half of all the counties lost popu- lation during the 1940s, the 1950s and 1960s. But, for the years immediately ahead, agriculture must provide employment opportuni- ties for more workers in many economically advancing countries. Such additional workers will produce something even in a generously manned agriculture; and employment at socially acceptable work is a social necessity.

Farm production, farm people, and associated rural and small- town population must provide the market for much or most of the economic output of the cities in the economically advancing countries. The development of industry and services in such countries is not easy; with some exceptions, it will be difficult to export successfully the output of such emerging industry and services. The market will lie within the country, primarily; and, since most of the people are rural and agricultural, it is only with them that a market for the products of the city can be found. The urban manufacturer in an economically advancing country has a great stake in successful agri- cultural development, for that is where most of his potential customers work and live. As, or if, agricultural incomes rise, farm people will increase their consumption of many items of living, and this also provides a market for the output of urban industry. "Import substi- tution" means, above all, providing production and consumption goods for farm and rural people.

In many economically advancing countries, agriculture must provide a part, sometimes a very large part, of the savings out of which capital investment can be made. This will often be difficult; farm incomes are usually low, savings small; and agriculture itself is likely both to need capital and to reward additional capital highly. Nevertheless, capital accumulation within the urban sectors may also be difficult. Some savings do occur among farmers; there is evidence that in some countries the agricultural savings could be higher if profitable and secure investment channels were open to farmers. The very size of the agricultural sector in many low-income countries makes such savings critical. One difficult task of economic development is to stimulate and mobilize savings from the agricultural sector and to invest them as productively as possible in the nation's economy. In many developing countries, agriculture must provide a substantial part of the foreign exchange with which the country can purchase needed goods and services for investment and for consumption.

Coordination of Agricultural Development and Urban Growth. Agricultural development and urban growth in an economically advancing country are closely interrelated and must be considered jointly. Agriculture has several indispensable roles to play, which we have described briefly; but city growth is also an indispensable part of economic development. Each can be a vital and productive part of the country's total development; and each, unfortunately, may fail to achieve its potential.

In many economically advancing countries, especially the smaller ones, there is one main city, often the capital and the chief port as well as the center of most industry and trade. There will also generally be some smaller cities, regionally important; and still smaller cities or towns, important as local trade centers. Each type of city has important roles to play; while there may be some competition and rivalry among them, there are also important complementary relationships.

The integration of agricultural and urban development should take place at a local, regional, and national scale in economically advancing countries. The interplay between farm and city for markets of agricultural commodities, for markets of urban-produced farm supplies, for employment of rural people, and for social services and activities, exists at all levels of urban development. The urban or national planner must learn to include agriculture in his calculations; but, likewise, the agricultural planner must consider the city not only as a market for agricultural products but also as a competitor for agricultural workers and as a source of needed agricultural inputs. The precise nature of this interplay will vary from one country to another, and even among regions of larger countries, differing at different stages in economic development of the same country or region; and the way that agriculture and urban growth can best be interrelated in each country will depend on many factors peculiar to each country. There is no single way to achieve the desired goals but each country must work out its arrangements in a manner most suitable to its political, social, and cultural structure and tradition. It is essential that agriculture and urban growth be considered as complementary and interrelated, not as competitive and separate.

One aspect of agriculture as a form of production and as a way of life demands special attention from national planners; this is the prestige or social regard with which farming and associated service activities are held by the total population, including the government bureaucracy. In most countries today, but more particularly in the economically less developed ones, farmers are held in lower social esteem than are urban workers of equal intelligence and skill. Similarly, professional workers and government employees concerned with agriculture are held in lower esteem than are similar workers concerned with other economic and social problems. The ambitious farm youth frequently seeks to leave farming for a city occupation, not only because its economic reward may be greater but also because its social prestige will be greater; and the young man seeking university education frequently takes agriculture because the field of his choice is, for some reason, closed to him. In all too many countries, agriculture is a field of economic activity of second or lower rank, socially speaking. Such an attitude greatly impedes agricultural development and greatly complicates a coordinated development of agriculture and of urban centers. National planners and leaders must adopt measures to increase the social standing and the public regard for agriculture at both farming and professional levels, if agriculture is to advance as much as is economically possible.

Urbanization and Agriculture in Developed Countries. While Dr. Clawson, in his study, concentrated on relations between agricultural development and urbanization in the developing world, GERALD WIBBERLEY dealt mainly with developed areas such as North America and Western Europe, and the lessons to be learnt for the developing ones.

. . . These are countries where all the persons who live in urban areas, or are in the process of moving to them are, in general, fully fed by highly developed agricultural structures that have relatively few difficulties in producing enough food for all their people.

Professor Wibberley went on to describe the features of such countries and the nature of urbanization there.

. . . The food surpluses that result from these developed systems of agriculture make it possible to feed the populations of areas of the world where less than 7 percent of the population is directly employed in food production. This has resulted from a whole complex of agro-industrial forces. Methods of production are sophisticated and are geared to local soils and local climates. The farms and horticultural holdings lie within well-developed rural/urban infrastructures that cater to a large number of needs—markets for food and its processing, services to farmers and farms of a financial and technical nature, and usually a good system of minor roads that are usable at all times of the year. All farmers are literate and because the countryside has moved over entirely from the horse to the tractor and car, the mobility of people and supplies on and off the farm is very great. This type of modern agriculture is essentially capital and labor intensive, but land use may be either intensive or extensive. The incomes received by food producers are high, but still relatively lower than incomes outside agriculture. The agricultural system may use few people directly, but it is very interested in the quantity and quality of land available for food production use because it has many choices to use the land either intensively or extensively.

Modern agriculture, therefore, in terms of urbanization, has certain characteristics. It competes against urban growth for land but mainly for the high-quality areas: that is, the special soils and favorable microclimate. It is interested in good location in relation to markets, but the location is measured by communications and their quality to thriving urban areas rather than by close physical proximity. With its large surplus of food to sell, it needs good major and minor roads, transport facilities, financial arrangements, bulking and grading terminals, and so on. It also needs a ready outlet for its surplus people because it continues to increase productivity per man, and at the same time it has to compete for its people with non-agricultural jobs in urban areas. Its competition with urban growth for land area, though selective, tends to be close to the major towns because the latter have usually been sited, in the past, in the areas of land with high natural fertility. In other words, land prices around towns are often high because of high returns for both urban and agricultural use.

There is a general retreat of commercial agricultural production from urban areas as the latter increase. The nature of the retreat of agriculture from the growing urban area is, however, different between country and country and from area to area. In depends on the following:

(1) Where there is over-all abundance of land in a modern community and particularly if there are weak land-use planning controls, actual land dereliction can be found close to the edge of the urban area or in between urban developments.

(2) If, however, land is thought to be short for food-production purposes and particularly where the land is inherently good and in

situations where there are financial advantages in holding land, active farming use will stay close to the changing edge of the urban area.

(3) Tax systems and other physical and financial benefits or disadvantages in holding agriculture land will again very much determine the nature of land use close to urban areas. If land taxation is based on existing use, there is an incentive to keep cultivated land close to the edge of the built-up area. If, however, the tax system is based in any way on the prospective new use of the land, that is, that urban growth casts its shadow before it, then land dereliction can occur through tax delinquency.

(4) Modern agriculture shows tremendous mobility in goods, services, and people. It moves people and things off the farm and out of the village, but it also moves industrial inputs like fertilizers and chemicals and farm services and even farm workers back easily on to the farm. This means that although there are relatively few people engaged directly in food production, these people can live at some distance from the land on which they work. It also means that the increasing number and specialized nature of personnel used in providing services to farms do not have to live locally but can live in towns and even in cities and yet move quickly on to farms to provide necessary services. All this means that the rural settlement pattern of the past has little direct relevance to the agricultural needs of the present or the future.

(5) The theory, and in particular the practice, of land-use planning has a great influence on the structure and use of agriculture on rural/urban fringes. It is affected by the pattern of urbanization, the density of development, the degree of planning control in practice on all land uses, and whether or not there is any conscious grading of the better-quality food-producing land in planning practice.

(6) There is growing concern in developed societies, particularly among urban people, as to the uses that they want from their rural areas. Most people want agricultural activities to take place close to the urban fringe. It is interesting that housing areas for the higher-income groups contain people who seem to be rather more concerned that the traditional farming scene around them should change as little as possible. People who are farming close to new urban areas built for the lower-income classes do not seem to have such deliberate physical and emotional pressures.

(7) The confusion and conflict as to what people want from their countryside extend over wider areas than the urban/rural fringe, and many of the opposing points of view are held very strongly by individuals and by organizations, which are well run and very vocal. For example, certain groups of people in developed countries want a technically modern and economically viable food production industry

in order to get good yet cheap food, and there are powerful bodies working on the government in all modern countries to secure this end. Other groups are preservationists in rural matters and seem to want to maintain the appearance and (almost) the practices of the countryside that they knew when they were young. There is also a strong group of persons who are fond of the rural settlement pattern even though it has lost much of its importance to modern farming. The third group of urban persons are basically interested in natural fauna and flora and in biologically rich habitats. These people are concerned with preserving traditional forms of farming or creating new forms of farming that do maintain a wide range of species of fauna and flora.

Modern urbanization also is accompanied by a stress on outdoor recreation. There has been a large change from passive indoor recreational activity in the early 1950s through to more active outdoor pursuits, and, as modern agriculture is linked with these new attitudes and new means of private mobility, obviously rural areas are under constant use by urban people for recreation.

Lastly, there is the emphasis on the countryside being available for peace and solitude, and this is where less fertile agricultural areas and particularly the mountains are needed.

Modern agriculture and urbanization are, therefore, full of actual potential conflict and confusion. Not only is there the direct conflict of urban growth over food-producing land of different qualities but also there are great pressures on agricultural land to provide for many other old and new non-food-producing uses and desires. The planning of modern agriculture to satisfy all these urban activities will be a very hard thing to do without considerable deterioration of the environment generally. There is, however, the very big advantage in that modern agriculture and modern urban growth have lessened the gaps that have been present for centuries between country and town. These gaps were nearly always to the detriment of the countryside and the country person. There were the gaps in education and particularly in the standards and quantities available of all physical and social services, in job opportunities, and in general mobility. There was also a big contrast in the physical appearance of country and town people and their attitudes to their work and to their lives. These have now changed so that in modern societies there is no reason why either urban youth or rural youth should be deprived of fairly similar opportunities in living.

Urbanization and Agriculture in Turkey. The impact of agricultural development on the process of urbanization was clearly demonstrated by YILMAZ GURER in his paper on "Urbanization in Turkey." Dr. Gurer illustrated and demonstrated the process that Dr. Clawson referred to in his paper, "Urbanization in Agriculture and the Development of Other Economic Activities."

. . . The reason for migration from rural area cities is—detachment from the land. Western experts emphasize the population increase, while they are analyzing urbanization or population concentration in cities. Yet detachment from the land should be taken as the main factor for urbanization. It is not important whether the population concentration is in cities or in rural areas. The reason for detachment from the land is mechanization, the polarization in land ownership and the transition to intensive agriculture.

The commission on Turkey's urbanization problems of the Ankara Chamber of Architects explained the internal and external factors of urbanization in Turkey. The three internal factors were:

(1) Detachment from land caused by mechanization: When mechanization in agriculture takes place, the labor force is discharged. It is calculated that a tractor displaces 10 agricultural workers.

(2) Polarization in land ownership: It is observed that in places where most of the owners have farms of less than 200 acres, one-fourth of the land is lost in 25 years. Transition to modern agriculture is possible by large land ownership. Thus, the peasant who has lost his land migrates to the city.

(3) Transition to intensive agriculture: The labor force is displaced even if there is no mechanization in intensive agriculture. Thus, in the production of goods like tobacco and hazel nuts in small establishments, some of the members of the family are displaced.

If the population increase is added to these three basic factors, the flow of population form rural areas to cities can be explained easily.

Among the external factors is the necessity of integration, especially with the Western bloc, where conditions of foreign aid are feasible. Integration with the outside world during World War II induced Turkey to transfer its main development choices (1) from agriculture to industry; (2) from development based on internal resources to development based on external sources; (3) from railway to highway policy; (4) from development led by the public sector to development led by a mixed economy.

In fact, there has been a structural change in agriculture in Turkey. It is clear that this change will cause rapid urbanization if rural and urban areas are accepted as an integrated whole, and it is emphasized that, unless there is no sectoral change in the rural areas, there will not be any sectoral changes in cities.

Agriculture in Turkey has been undermechanized in comparison with mechanization in industrialized countries. Yet, due to the economic policy adopted after World War II, mechanization in agriculture increased rapidly until 1955. The decrease in the rate of mechanization since 1955 has been due to limited sources of foreign exchange.

The table below shows the area of cultivated land per tractor in the years 1935-60.

Years	Cultivated land/tractor (ha.)	Index
1935	8,263.3	100.0
1940	7,637.3	92.4
1945	6,958.5	82.4
1950	595.0	7.2
1955	351.6	4.2
1960	363.3	4.4

A tractor displaces 10 agricultural laborers, so that increase in land cultivated by the tractor caused a decrease in the density of rural population. It is obvious that modernization in agriculture makes it impossible to keep the population in rural areas. Opening up new lands to agriculture has also proved that the population cannot be kept in rural areas. An experiment was tried in 1950-60, when all kinds of land were opened to agriculture, and the result was a decrease of productivity.

Years	Cultivated land (100 ha.)
1950	14,542
1952	17,361
1954	19,616
1956	22,453
1958	22,768
1960	23,227

In contrast to 14,542,000 hectares of agricultural land in 1950, the area has reached 23,227,000 hectares in 1960. Since this growth has taken place at the cost of forests and meadows, while, on the other hand, marginal lands have been opened up to agriculture, it has led to decreased productivity, which is the cause of detachment from the land.

Though there are no further areas left to be opened up to cultivation, it is actually necessary to turn some cultivable land into meadows. Under such circumstances, increased productivity in agriculture is only possible by introducing modern technology. It has already been mentioned that the introduction of modern technology in agriculture will lead to the detachment of agricultural labor from the land.

Polarization in land ownership, which is one of the internal factors, is reflected in the rapid decrease of small land ownership, increase in large land ownership, division of farms into smaller plots through inheritance processes, and, as a result, the appearance of a new group of wage laborers in agriculture who have recently lost their land.

The table below indicates the increase in the average size of farms.

Years	Average Size of Farms (acres)	Index of Size
1948	848	100
1949	875	103
1950	944	111
1951	1,011	119
1952	1,113	131

People thus detached from the land migrate to the cities in order to earn their living. On the other hand, it is difficult to assert that cities are able to absorb this incoming stream.

"Town Pull" and "Village Push." While, according to Dr. Gurer, the main reason for rural-urban migration is detachment from the land, JEAN CANAUX attributed this process mainly to "town pull."

. . . Historically speaking, all classical processes of organization of urbanization were of the town-pull type and not of the village-push type. That was the type of urbanization in England in the second half of the eighteenth century, that was a type of urbanization in France, during say, the thirties and the forties and probably fifties of the nineteenth century, and to a large extent also that of the United States.

The village-push motive stems from the accumulated frustration of village life, either as the result of labor productivity being close to zero or of frustration, a sense of hopelessness in view of economic exploitation, as in the existing conditions in Latin America.

Economically speaking the fundamental difference between the two is that the town-pull motivation operates by creating economic opportunities that drain away productive manpower from the village by offering a higher rate of remuneration, though the pay may even be substantial in the village itself.

It is usually occupations that are not in high demand by town dwellers (such as the hard nonskilled physical labor in postwar Germany, heavily supplemented by temporary labor from other parts of Europe) that probably provides the most classic type of town-pull urbanization. Britain also had that kind of town-pull urbanization, which had to be supplemented by the importation of people from the West Indies. The same process is now taking place in Eastern Europe—in Hungary, Poland, and Czechoslovakia. This kind of urbanizational process, apart from sociological and ecological considerations, is essential as a part of economic development.

On the other hand, the village-push urbanization does not take place because of the opportunities offered within the normal course of development of the urban economy. When this occurs, the city takes in people without absorbing them and without developing its economic and municipal infrastructures, which thus deteriorate through this type of urbanization; it makes for a kind of infrastructural disequilibrium when economic opportunities are not in demand by the city itself. Instead of working at a series of jobs requiring manpower in industry, in services, or in transportation, the immigrants develop a wide range of unnecessary trades as hawkers and petty retailers whose nonaccounting contribution to the national product is virtually zero.

This has been a typical urbanization process in many developing countries and is a type of urbanization that should be avoided. How can it be avoided? First by preventing the push effect of the village, by providing further means of earning a living, and by opening up economic opportunities within the villages, channeling more capital to agricultural development than has been done in many countries.

History indicates that no industrial revolution in the past has taken place without having been preceded by agricultural revolutions. This was the case in England in the eighteenth century, and in the United States as well as Western Europe. It was not by chance that it happened that way. Without agricultural growth and an increase in agricultural productivity, no capital accumulation and no surplus food provision could be made available for industrialization. The infrastructural setup of the economy would thus have produced an imbalance in industry instead of that type of industry that grew up in Western Europe.

Consequently, modernization of agriculture is among the most important preconditions for smooth urbanization.

E. YALAN agreed that industrialization should not be embarked upon without the proper agricultural basis. He further elaborated the subject, stressing that, even after both industrialization and intensification of agriculture, overurbanization can and should be avoided. He gave an example from Israel.

124

. . . If you have a son who has graduated in electronics, there is no need for him to be pushed to, or pulled by, the city, because there can be employment for him in rural areas, on condition that the farmers do not only produce food and fiber, but also deal with processing, marketing, and credits, by an evolutionary process of local cooperation that progresses to regional cooperation. I am not talking about dreams; I am talking about things that are actually taking place in Israel.

The importance of cities as markets for agricultural products, which was stressed by Dr. Marion Clawson, was criticized by Professor FINKEL, who based his criticism on experience in some of the developing countries where the cities are surrounded by rural areas that cannot offer sufficient agricultural products to these cities. He also argued that industrialization and urbanization can only start after the peasants have reached a certain level of development.

. . . A great many underdeveloped countries are in tropical regions. It is well known that tropical agriculture has not been strong on food crops, market vegetables, and so on. Let us examine what crops are grown in the hinterland of these countries. I have very recently come back from a very large city on the Ivory Coast, Abidjan, which is a beautiful example of urbanization. It is one of the most beautiful cities I have ever seen, but it is located on the coast, as are all major capitals of the West African countries. It is surrounded by forests, which are not particularly good food-producing areas. Foods produced in the forest are the starchy tubers that provide a certain amount of fuel but form a very poor diet and have a very small commercial market in the cities. It is much farther north, in the hinterland, in very remote areas of the savannah, that food is properly produced. Foods produced in the forest, which is the hinterland of most of the African capitals are industrial crops like copra or palm oil, cocoa, coffee, and things that are not even bought in the cities but that are exported.

In the Middle East, the hinterland around Teheran is certainly not a food-producing region. It is a very bleak desert. There is area beyond the northern mountains of the Caspian range and another where I also recently worked—about 1,200 to 1,500 kilometers south of Teheran, over terrible roads—that are food-producing areas.

For these developing countries we cannot take the model of a thriving industrial city in America or England, surrounded by crop gardens, producing asparagus and brussel sprouts and all sorts of high-cash-value luxury vegetables, which are brought fresh into town daily by huge trucks. You cannot draw any sort of parallel between the examples of the United States and England and those in the countries mentioned and many others that time does not permit me to give.

At which point do we begin to reach the symbiosis? When agriculture in rural areas reaches a certain minimum income level for a farm family—which some people call the takeoff point—and there are some savings left for improvements, with each successive improvement, a certain amount of the labor force will be released and will be able to go to the towns.

As long as the agriculture and the rural population are 40, 50, 60, 70, and, in some countries, close to 80 and 90 percent of the total working force, nothing will move industrially and no real urban development will take place until this majority—anywhere from two-thirds or three-quarters of the working population—has enough income to buy some of the products of the cities.

Any city in a developing country that bases its industry on exports entirely may find itself in a very precarious economic position because of world control of prices beyond its control, competition, synthetic substitutes marketed instead of natural products. Industries must be based firstly on domestic consumption and only then on export. If 7 percent of the country is rural population, they may well be sophisticated farmers, with a significant effect on the market. If, however, 50, 60, and 70 percent of the population are agricultural with no purchasing power, then industry will not be firmly based and will have nothing to depend upon.

The economic situation of the rural population is not improved by reducing its numbers. It is only improved if it is reduced for negative reasons. When the Indians in Brazil, Bolivia, and Peru move to the cities, this adds nothing to the agricultural situation of the country. There are 3 or 4 million natives there, and the fact that some of them leave and become an impossible burden on cities like Lima and La Paz adds nothing to the development of those rural regions.

Comments made by Y. ABT highlighted the different opinions expressed in the discussion on agricultural development and urbanization: Whether agricultural development should precede urbanization and industrialization or whether urbanization is the real incentive for agricultural development. What comes first, the chicken or the egg? Mr. Abt outlined his opinion on the subject.

. . . I am in favor of agrarian reform and development as a first phase. Yet, if we are talking about 1971 in developing countries, I do not think that we can glibly say, Change structures in rural areas, raise yields, and only then enter upon the process of urbanization. I do not think it is realistic. Take meat, for instance, one of the commodities that at this moment is extremely scarce. Only a few years ago, we could think globally in terms of having meat from an extensive ranching system, whether it be in Argentina, in Uruguay, in Brazil, or in countries in Africa. Today, production has not met rising demand, and many of us who are engaged in project planning abroad find that the same commodity will only be available to consumers everywhere if, and only if, there is a radical structure change in the system of production of that commodity.

If we take the classic situation, for instance, of Uruguay's meat problem, it is now clear to the planning authorities of this country that is so dependent on meat exports that there will only be a radical change in accelerated production, if not only tremendous changes in production systems for meat itself are introduced but also if processing facilities are brought into the areas of production.

You can produce grain and ship it to the port. You do not need to process it in any way. If we are talking about higher-value agricultural products, and that is what will bring in income—not the grain alone—then we have to think in terms of completely different structural and spatial methods.

For that reason, in our programing, in our work, and in our policies, we must bring elements of industrialization and urbanization into the agricultural areas. I can give one other example. Four or five years ago, everybody was talking about a shocking situation of overproduction in sugar. The latest FAO (Food and Agricultural Organization—U.N.) figures indicate there is going to be a sugar deficit because of so-called inefficient factories. Today, if factories are to be built, they will have to be much larger than they were five or six years ago.

Therefore, we have to think in terms of combined agricultural and industrial development. It seems obvious that if we wish to meet commodity targets, that is the road we shall have to take.

This view coincided with the opinion expressed by Dr. Clawson and others that agricultural development is essential to urbanization and industrialization; but, at the same time, urban growth is vital and hastens the process of agricultural development.

INDUSTRY AND URBANIZATION

The Conference did not deal specifically with the relationship between industrialization and urbanization, but the subject was discussed both in the plenary sessions and in all three working groups. Some of the papers and many of the speakers and discussants referred to this subject, stressing the role of industrial development in the process of urbanization and the types of industries that should be developed.

The Reciprocal Impact. EDWIN S. MILLS criticized the view that there is a direct correlation between the rate of urbanization and the percentage of labor force in industry.

. . . Those who believe that many less developed countries are overurbanized base their contention on the alleged relationship between urbanization and industrialization. Several writers have correlated the percentage of the population that is urban with the percentage of the labor force employed in industry. Sample data are values of the two variables from a variety of developed and less developed countries during the 1950s and 1960s. It has been found that many less developed countries lie above the average relationship, or regression line, between the two variables. Many people have concluded that such countries are more urbanized than is justified by their levels of industrialization and that overurbanization produces parasitic urban areas that become pockets of misery.

The first criticism of such studies is somewhat technical. The correlation methods employed measure the straight-line relationship between the variables. But, even if one believed that urbanization and industrialization should be closely related, the relationship should not be expected to be a straight line. A more plausible form for the relationship would be a logistic or S-shaped curve. Countries with little industrial employment should be expected to have some urban areas because urban areas perform functions other than providing places for industrial activity. Until industrial employment reaches a substantial level, it would probably have relatively little effect on the extent of urbanization. Likewise, countries with very large industrial sectors should be expected to have some rural population, because agriculture and other activities take place in rural areas. When industrial employment reaches a high level, it will probably have relatively little further effect on urbanization, but, in the middle range of levels of industrial employment, it may have a substantial effect on urbanization.

The conclusion that little-industrialized countries are, therefore, overurbanized reflects the mistaken assumption that the true relationship is a straight line. Such studies provide no evidence of overurbanization.

It cannot be doubted that urbanization is related to industrialization in the broadest sense. Rapid urbanization in Europe and North America during the nineteenth century was undoubtedly spurred by the rapid industrialization of the times. But the relationship has never been very close. In the United States, whose data I know best, urbanization was substantial before the period of rapid industrialization that began about 1840. More important, urbanization has proceeded rapidly since 1920, although the percentage of the labor force that is in manufacturing is almost the same now as it was in 1920. Likewise, urbanization and industrialization are not highly correlated in Europe. Sovani has shown that the correlation between urbanization and industrialization is only about 0.40 in Western Europe and North America, whereas it is about 0.85 in the less developed countries.

In fact, there is no strong reason to expect urbanization and industrialization to be closely related, and I am at a loss to know why so much attention has been paid to the issue. Urban areas have many functions, of which industrial production is only one, although it is an important one.

Despite this, Professor Mills agreed that urbanization is linked to economic development and industrialization.

. . . But, if the sizes of large urban areas are not closely related to development, what are they related to? How should appropriate sizes and functions of the largest urban areas be judged in less developed countries? It is clearly possible to concentrate too much of a country's economic activity in one or a few urban areas. How can one find out what kinds and amounts of economic activities should take place in large urban areas?

The first thing to say on this issue is that we do not know much about it. We know relatively little about the kinds and amounts of activities that should be carried on in urban areas in the sense that it is most efficient to locate them there.

The first purpose of this section is to suggest that urban specialists turn their attention to the above issues. I believe they should stop looking for simple regularities between urbanization or primacy and measures of economic development. Instead, they should study the kinds of things that are best done in large urban areas and the kinds of things best done elsewhere. The second purpose of the section is to suggest a general framework for approaching the issues.

The basic economic function of urban areas is to facilitate production and exchange of goods and services by proximate locations of a variety of activities. Manufacturing tends to be carried on in urban areas because it is subject to important scale economies that make it economical to produce in large volume in a single plant. This, in turn, makes it advantageous to locate in the same area workers' residences, suppliers of inputs to the manufacturing industry, buyers of its outputs, and suppliers of goods and services for workers and their families. A complex of manufacturing and more or less closely related activities constitutes the core of many urban areas.

In the paper presented by YILMAS GURER, Professor Mills's opinion was clearly shared. Dr. Gurer argued that urbanization in Turkey is to a large degree a "demographic urbanization," and thus it is not always accompanied by industrialization.

. . . In Turkey there is a marked disparity between rate of urbanization and rate of industrialization. Yet, industrialization is the only means of achieving rational urbanization.

The migrants to the city experience many social hardships and face economic setbacks. Since job opportunities in industry can only be created by large investments, many newcomers to the city cannot secure their living easily.

The table below shows that, in 1960, in cities of over 100,000 population, industrialization lagged behind urbanization. The 1960 population indexes have been compared with the labor indexes—labor in this case being the work force employed in workshops under the jurisdiction of the Labor Law.

Province	Labor Index	Urbanization Index
Ankara	232	224
Eskisehir	123	170
Istanbul	149	149
Bursa	102	148
Konya	167	190
Kayseri	180	160
Izmir	121	160
Adana	159	196
Gaziantep	66	175

Due to the slow rate of industrialization, urbanization in Turkey is "demographic urbanization," a characteristic also observed in other developing countries. Although Western experts term this type of urbanization "overurbanization," we believe that this term can lead to misunderstanding and it is better to call this type of urbanization "pseudourbanization," to express the fact that the increases in economic and social functions do not parallel the rapid increase in population.

The incoming groups try to earn their living by nonproductive work because of the slow rate of increase of industrialization in cities. The recent increase in the services sector has been effected by the increase in the number of people occupied in such jobs. Yet the contribution of such jobs to the economy of the country is very limited. Therefore, a new category must be added to the services sector, because inclusion of servants, street peddlers, and porters in the same category as workers in the large transportation companies, in the communications sector, etc., opens the way for mistakes.

According to a study conducted by Professor Ibrahim Yasa in the gecekondu areas of Ankara, only 27 percent of the 1,000 heads of families in Ankara gecekondus are artisans and skilled workers.

The fact that urbanization increases the ratio of the work force in sectors that contribute relatively less to the national economy is a positive process, because the development of consumption tendencies of the urban population will stimulate production. On the other hand, unless they are backed by industrialization, employment opportunities created in the service sector in order to increase employment in the short term are bound to face a lack of further development opportunities, particularly in feudal countries.

A similar view was expressed by Robert Weaver, who stressed the fact that "in the less developed countries people are being crowded together in cities without an industrial base to provide employment."

Despite the many cases of urbanization without industrialization, it may be taken that industrialization affects the spatial organization and location of urban centers, as well as the rate of urbanization.

In his paper, AKIN L. MABOGUNJE described how the pattern of industry and its location affects urban development in Africa.

. . . One major factor affecting urbanization in Africa is the pattern of industrial development. The major principle that has guided this development in most African countries is that of import substitution. According to this, instead of importing final consumer goods, a country now imports the machinery, the skilled personnel, and very often the semiprocessed raw materials needed to produce these goods locally. An important feature of this form of industrialization is its high capital-labor ratio. It is estimated that for this form of industrialization it costs between $10,000 to $15,000 of invested capital to employ one factory hand. This fact means that, although many African countries have increased their industrial capacity over the last two decades, the extent to which this has meant an expanded employment market has been very limited. Ewing noted, for instance, that, as of 1960, total African employment in mining and manufacturing was no more than 1.5 million.

Within each country, the pattern of distribution of this industrial labor force is noteworthy. Because of the strong import orientation of the production processes, the most economic location for most of the industries has been the port city. This type of city is also very often the national capital and the headquarters of commercial houses, religious and social organizations, and various public institutions. One of the most striking features of urbanization in Africa since 1950 is thus the very remarkable rate of growth of these port cities. Lagos, for instance, grew from nearly a quarter of a million in 1950 to about 1.5 million in 1970; Abidjan from 69,000 in 1950 to 500,000 by 1968; Kinshasa from 191,000 in 1950 to 508,000 in 1966; and Dar-es-Salaam from 99,000 in 1952 to 273,000 in 1967. Each of these cities has grown so rapidly ahead of all other urban centers in the country as to constitute a veritable primate city, attracting to itself a disproportionate section of the talents and resources in the country.

In his paper "Urban Policies in Latin America," Dr. Walter Sedwitz described the evolution of urban development there. Cities in Latin America were, according to Sedwitz, originally located for trade, communications, or military purposes; later on, industries needing markets settled in these urban areas and further contributed to the growth of the cities. This process produced urbanization oriented mainly toward the coastal periphery. However, industry could not absorb all those who migrated to these cities in search of a better life; thus, the migrants found employment in sectors where productivity and wages are low.

Types of Industries and Urbanization. The type of industries to be developed in the growing urban centers and in the developing countries and how to bring these industries into these areas was the theme of comments made by JACQUES R. BOUDEVILLE.

. . . Towns without industries mean overpopulation in the towns. This means that industry is needed. The important question is what type of industry and how is it to be introduced?

Mostly it can only come from outside, so that there must first be a harbor, a coastal town, which can organize industry in connection with foreign countries.

Thus, in the first instance, you only have industries that are linked with foreign markets. These markets then create the industries inside the country, in a little village at first. These villages are rural central places. Typically they lie on the border of the forest in the savannah and serve as the first commercial centers within the rural areas.

These first commercial centers gather what is available through cultivation, and bring it to the central "growth ball." This growth ball is an industrialized center. In its first stages it is what is called an agricultural complex, where the transformation of agricultural products takes place. All this is always dominated by the market outside the country.

Then there is what I call the "development ball," where real industrialization begins. Here, there may be industries like construction material, cement, petrol itinerary distillation, etc. Later you may have textiles, iron, and so on, until you arrive at the top with the elaborate industries like the automotive industry and others. We know then that, if we wish to set up an iron plant before having the other basic industries, we cannot expect real, sound development. Each time you ascend a little higher in the scale of development, you must have greater diversification of industry.

The developing countries have, of course, to start with basic industries such as agricultural industries, repair industries, mechanical workshops, and so on. Only later, with development, may one think of the more complex industries that require both capital and know-how.

Another speaker who discussed types of industries suitable for developing countries was JORGE E. HARDOY. He stressed the point that industries aimed at import substitution will in many cases not be able to compete on world markets.

. . . Industrialization requires capital and technology and skills that are often not available and that cannot be rapidly created. Industrialized products will face strong competition in quality and prices in world markets and will be limited to their national markets, thus reducing output, purchasing power, or both. Furthermore, industrialization in developing countries must also acknowledge several world realities: (1) import substitution requires large inflows of capital goods, which affect the balance of payments, trade, and, consequently, the supply of foreign investments and loans; (2) industrialization, based on import substitution on a national scale, will soon reach saturation point in the domestic markets for the reasons explained above despite initial saving of foreign exchange; and (3) for complex reasons, but mostly because of poor skills and technology, only a few developing countries can seriously attempt to industrialize on the basis of imported raw materials.

Without losing sight of their national objectives and values, therefore, developing countries will have to plan and implement regional strategies of international scope. Difficult as they are, because of both internal and external pressures in each country, a way out of underdevelopment in many areas of the world lies in coordination and complementing, not in isolation and competition.

To sum up this section on the link between industrial development and urbanization and industrialization, it may be said that
the direct correlation between urbanization and industrialization
that existed in the developed countries in the past does not always
exist now.

Urbanization in developing countries now, in many cases,
is the result of the attraction or the "pull" of the city in the hope
of a better life there. Therefore, it is not always accompanied
by industrialization; people moving to towns and cities are employed
to a large extent in nonproductive work, which does not contribute
to the country's economy.

To overcome this, industrial development should be initiated.
However, this should be planned with great care, taking into
consideration the various limitations, such as lack of skills and
capital, on the one hand, and the competition of world markets,
on the other. The choice of industries should thus be made with
great care and with preference for simple industries such as the
transformation of agricultural raw materials, production of
building materials, and so on. The more sophisticated industries
should come only later, after the process of industrialization has
gained momentum.

CONCLUSIONS

This chapter on the link between economic development and
urbanization may be summed up by drawing the following conclusions:

The process of urbanization in the developing countries is
to a large extent not the result of economic development. In many
cases rural-urban migration takes place not because of new economic opportunities in the city but mainly due to the hope of the
migrants for a better and easier life in town. This is the basic
difference between the process of urbanization in the developing
countries and the developed countries, where urbanization was
mainly the result of economic development and new employment
opportunities in town.

Despite this, there is no doubt that economic development
such as modernization of agriculture, on the one hand, and the
development of manufacturing in the city, on the other, hastens
the process of rural-urban migration, thus, contributing to the
growth of cities.

Agricultural development—namely, increased productivity,
mechanization, intensification, and land reform—causes a decrease
in labor demand in the rural areas, thus increasing migration to

134

the city. This process is accelerated by the development of industry in the city and the growing demand for labor there.

Urban growth has a major impact on the development of agriculture, industry, and services. As regards agriculture, the city provides markets for agricultural products, thus increasing demand. It attracts people from the rural areas, which contributes to the increase in productivity and mechanization on the part of those who stay in agriculture.

The city with its industries and services supplies agricultural inputs (fertilizer, chemicals, etc.) and various other services needed for agriculture such as marketing, storage, etc., thus impelling the modernization of agriculture.

As regards industry, the process of urbanization increases demand for manufacturing goods, on the one hand, and the supply of labor for the manufacturing plants, on the other. Manufacturing, which is subject to scale economies, needs the big city to produce in large volume at a single plant.

It must be admitted that, in many of the developing countries, migrants to cities do not enjoy better amenities than they had in their native village. Urban development, which was a blessing in many developed countries and brought about economic and social progress, is different in the developing world. It is essential, therefore, that the process of urbanization there should be controlled and adjusted to the prospects of economic development.

We have seen how economic development affects urbanization, which must, therefore, be regarded as part of the development process, and any policy or strategy should take this element into consideration.

Only a clear policy followed by appropriate means and methods can direct the urbanization into the desired channels, thus avoiding its negative tendencies.

This policy should take all the elements concerned into account: economic, social, physical, organizational, and political.

In this chapter the development policies of these aspects will be examined—all of which were raised and discussed at the Conference.

The need for a comprehensive approach to development was clearly formulated by WALTER SEDWITZ in his paper "Urban Policies in Latin America."

. . . Since a large number of the factors that affect urban growth are beyond the influence of any one city, many of its problems must be solved by other, higher levels of government. The widespread recognition of this fact has lead to pleas for a national urbanization policy or strategy. The provision of urban infrastructure is a powerful means through which the national government can attain its objectives. Urban infrastructure must, therefore, be related to employment opportunities; to the growth prospects of different areas; to the cost of providing such facilities in various cities; to agricultural development and food production; to industrial location; to mineral resources; to the feasibility of establishing new centers based on government services, transport and communication facilities, or tourist potential; to locally available materials and skills; to the balance of payments, both on current and on capital account; to macroeconomic variables such as saving, inflation, and, generally, economic growth and development.

NATHANIEL LICHFIELD, in his paper "Economic Growth and Urbanization," discussed in detail the need for a comprehensive approach to development, analyzed the experience gained in this matter in developed countries, and drew conclusions for the developing countries.

. . . What conclusions can be drawn for developing countries from this review of practice in developed countries, and of economic theory in relation to economic growth and urbanization? In brief, the answer must be that there is clearly no apparent and standardized approach. Perhaps the situation is best expressed in a conclusion from a recent U.N. review of the field, which also recognizes that there is no general prescription: "The situation in each country clearly must be examined in the light of its own stage of development and urbanization and its national factor endowment. Policies best suited to national objectives in type, place and time can only be devised in the full knowledge of alternative costs and benefits. This calls for information and analysis at a level of magnitude not yet even considered in this field of investigation."

This approach might be called a strategy for urbanization. Given this approach—for the policies to be implemented in any particular country, it is necessary to have some integration of national, regional, and local planning, for otherwise there can be no coordination between the socioeconomic and the physical urbanization dimensions. Such an approach could clearly best be made within the framework of comprehensive planning at all levels. By this is meant planning that is carried out at the national, regional, and local level, with a comprehensive approach to the meaning of development in its economic, social, and physical terms. This includes the planning process, which is geared to the needs and possibilities of action through development and where the implementation process is as important as the planning process itself and the use of physical development for community development is as important as both.

Comprehensive planning on these lines for a country as a whole is difficult to conceptualize and even more difficult to carry out in practice. It is probably true that only a few countries in the world have even attempted it (perhaps Ireland, Holland, Puerto Rico, Poland, France), although there are notable examples of such comprehensive planning in particular regions (TVA, Damodar, Volta, Guayana). This reality has led to the counterreaction against comprehensive planning both in concept, where the impracticability is stressed, and from experience, leading to an emphasis on the desirability for satisfactory short-term projects that will produce a contribution toward the advancement of the theory.

Even such a move to abandon comprehensive planning should, however, not undermine the attempt to introduce a comprehensive planning approach. In this, it is important to recognize the inter-relatedness of all the themes in comprehensive planning so that none is ignored even if it cannot be fully taken into account. With this in mind, some general principles might be formulated for fostering the contribution of urbanization to economic growth in developing countries:

(1) Learn from, without necessarily following the experience in, the urbanization and economic growth of developed countries that have some comparability in location, scale, and socioeconomic goals. Such experience will indicate the paths that should not be followed and those that might be, including data as to the nature of the legal and institutional framework and institutions that are necessary for the purpose. Two things might be of particular importance. First, the very concept of "urban" changes in the postindustrial society, for no longer need it be a location and a standard of living (urban as opposed to rural) but only a location. Second, there is the realization in developed countries that the pursuit of economic growth in the past, by which was normally meant the expansion of wealth and profit in the private sector, has been achieved at a great sacrifice of social and environmental goals, leading to the ironic situation that the very goals of economic growth in the developed countries are now under serious attack. Thus one question arises in the developing countries: Should economic growth be pursued within the constraints affecting social values and the environment, or would it be better to maximize economic growth without the constraints and provide for later generations to contribute the cost of remedying past mistakes?

(2) Recognize the lessons that can be learned from current practice in developed countries that are using their knowledge of the past and contemporary tools to formulate regional development policies of a comprehensive nature that in themselves are a microcosm of the requirements in developing countries. This arises since every country has its underdeveloped as well as its developed regions, and the relation of the two within a country is not dissimilar from that between a developing and developed country. Furthermore, such underdeveloped regions provide a large array of diversity and thus provide workshop examples that can be applied to many differing situations in the developing countries (examples are the resource frontiers in Russia and Canada; rural depopulation and decline in Ireland and Whales; modern industrial expansion in southern Italy).

(3) Recognize that society in any developing country is in the
process of rapid change in all its aspects: economic, social, political,
institutional. Thus, perhaps, the most essential need for the comprehensive planning policies of any such country is an understanding of
the trends, nature, and dynamics of these interrelated changes. What
is needed is "understanding of the relation between economic development and urbanization and of the process by which urban growth helps
to transform a nation's economic and cultural life as an essential
base from which practical development policies can be formulated."
It is perhaps in the failure to assess these interrelationships and
control them that the biggest weakness of ongoing development planning
in the developing countries is seen, of which the most vivid and visual
evidence is the shantytowns around cities. The rate of migration
from the land to the cities, accompanied by the upturn in natural
increase through improved health, is not met by sufficient job opportunities for the newly urbanized population. This means that the
members of the new urban population have no income base for urban
living and are pushed, therefore, into the low-wage and low-condition
marginal service trades. They expect urban services that cannot be
provided for them by the urban center to which they have been attracted, because of its low economic base and perhaps because of the
time lag in institutional reforms that would recognize the need for
the expansion of its financial resources. It is clearly here that an
urbanization policy is needed that aims at some better balance between
the sizes of towns and their location, parallel to a policy for the rural
areas and aimed at increasing their economic viability.

In the search for such a contribution, some comprehensive theory
is needed on the lines pioneered by Friedmann, which specifically
tries to link the stages in socioeconomic advancement of a country
and the stage of its urbanization, with the opening up of regional
centers as poles for the regional development of the underdeveloped
areas of the country. It might be argued that this is in a sense
following the urbanization path of a developed country, but the
probability exists that the path will be made much easier and pleasanter
through the use of a better understanding of the social sciences,
urbanization, and comprehensive planning than was available to those
who were responsible for the economic growth and urbanization of
the developing countries of the last century.

SOCIOECONOMIC POLICY FOR URBANIZATION

The impact of economic and social development on the
process of urbanization and the development strategy to be followed
here was extensively discussed and also demonstrated by a number
of case studies from developing countries.

Government Intervention in Economic Development. Some speakers stressed the role of central government in economic development and thus in the process of urbanization. This was clearly expressed by JORGE E. HARDOY in his statement at the Conference.

. . . One of the lessons of Japan and of many of the Eastern European countries—the socialist countries—is the role of the central government in development. These countries would not have moved from a semiindustrial and a preindustrial stage to an industrial stage without the intervention of the national government.

A laissez-faire attitude has been quite traditional in the political history of many of our developing countries, and it has never helped a developing country to become a developed country. In my opinion, the laissez-faire attitude we frequently see in our type of countries will never help an underdeveloped city to become a developed city.

National decisions in the key aspects of urbanization offer more guarantees for the over-all harmonious development of a city if they are made at the national level than if they are made at the local level.

LLOYD RODWIN suggested that planners should focus first on the identification of goals in relation to development, that only afterward can the development policy be clearly formulated.

. . . One of the basic shibboleths in the field of planning is the notion that one must intervene in the field because one is going to improve on the traditional solutions, provide better solutions than those traditionally provided by the market economy.

An essential feature of this is the conventional wisdom of planners, which specifies that one has to identify goals and then devise efficient means by which they can be achieved as well as implementation and feedback mechanisms by which this process can be operated. All this presupposes a kind of quasi-rational faith, which I think may be a necessary illusion, an important heroic myth by which planners must live, but which in no way describes the behavior of planners or the way things actually take place.

All my experience leads me to believe that it is very difficult to formulate goals in advance and subsequently to develop programs of implementation. I might even try to be paradoxical on this subject and say you can usually formulate your goals better in the middle and sometimes toward the end of a process rather than at the beginning.

Look at the goals formulated in the early period of the century when the emphasis was on providing a decent sanitary basis for migrants from abroad. Then housing was built to meet a housing shortage, or to provide employment for people, or to provide housing that would get rid of slums. Later on, it was necessary not to deal only with the new stock of housing but also with the existing stock of housing, with issues of urban development and so on. So that it is not just housing that we are concerned with. We have to be concerned with community facilities and with people. Now, we are wondering whether we should build housing altogether. Maybe, we should just give people the money and let them build their own housing.

As an illustration of the way that ideas in housing have changed over time, and are likely to change more in the future, I suggest that this whole question of oversimplification of the notion of goals is wrong. Another aspect that is typically oversimplified is the notion that you are dealing with one goal, whereas in the field you are constantly concerned with a complex of goals.

A similar view was expressed by Dr. Amir, who stressed the need for making a choice between different strategies—deciding which is better and which is more important.

Industrialization: The Key to Sound Urbanization. In his paper, YILMAS GURER gave this outline of the policy and strategy of economic development as related to urbanization:

. . . Urbanization means the establishment of certain human relations in space. Approached as such, it is a process that is directly linked with the goal of development. When urbanization develops in a certain way, it creates certain human relations. Development, on the other hand, is the cause for the appearance of different human relations at different levels.

In order to achieve development, the size of industries must be increased. "Development" means rapid industrialization; therefore, the implementation of industrialization and the allocation of resources to this end are the main conditions for rational urbanization.

While emphasizing that the main obstacle to urbanization is low industrialization, one should also mention that urbanization creates a favorable environment for industrialization:

(1) Although this method of development is not exactly approved of today, urbanization creates a positive potential for development through the performance of urban functions. During the process of creation of urban productive functions, certain housing and infra-structural, unproductive but necessary, investments should, in the future, meet with approval.

(2) Sociocultural qualities achieved by city dwellers create a favorable atmosphere for development. The fact that millions of people live together leads them to achieve certain levels of organization. Urbanization facilities encourage the exchange of ideas and commodities. Last but not least, the urbanized population has a greater chance of seeking and recognizing human and civic rights, which leads

to the exertion of pressure on administration and institutions by socio-political means, thus encouraging them to take more favorable steps toward development.

(3) Assuming that those who remain in rural areas work more efficiently—even when those who migrate to the cities work less efficiently—the general level of production will increase.

Planned urbanization, in the cheapest, most productive way, affects the development rate of the country positively.

The population in the cities of Turkey today has already reached the size required for industrialization. The problem confronting Turkey is its inability to conduct urbanization as an orderly, rational process because of the slow rate of industrialization. National development plans, parallel to the evaluation of resources and needs of the country, should also take the process of urbanization into consideration.

In his address to the Conference, Gurer highlighted several other points regarding development policy.

. . . In the developing countries, economic and productive activities are concentrated in one region of the territory, while the economic and social infrastructure of the remainder is comparatively weak. In countries like Turkey as well as in the Latin American countries, all economic activity as well as the infrastructure are always concentrated in one or two metropolises. The other parts or regions of the country lag behind; there is less infrastructure, less social super-structure, and very little economic or industrial activity.

The influence exerted by metropolis-type cities on the development of surrounding areas should be raised to the maximum. Here we have a slightly contradictory idea, but I would like to stress it. In my opinion, much has been done in Israel during the last ten years for countryside improvement, but we are well aware that in the last ten years Tel Aviv has doubled its population and its importance. This does not seem to be a drawback for Israel, but it does seem a fault for some African, Asian, or South American countries to have very active metropolises where there is intensive economic, social, and political life and that are comparable to second and third-rank metropolises of the highly developed countries; but generally without adequate plans for taking advantage of the organized resources of this kind of metropolis. Efforts should be made to establish relative balance in the spatial distribution of the towns, which means that urban planning should be integrated with national-scale planning; for countries that have no national-scale planning scheme, urbanization programs on a national scale should be considered.

The static functions of agglomerations in urbanization plans should also be taken into account, but without losing sight of the aspirations of urban dynamism. That means that town planning should never be a rigid system that cannot be changed. On the contrary, since city life is flexible and active, the guidelines of work to be done should be flexible and subject to revision with the expansion or urban activity.

The Planning of Services. RAM C. MALHOTRA spoke of stagnation in the sphere of development in the developing countries and of the need for a clear policy aimed at social justice.

. . . In the 1950s we used to talk about the revolution of rising expectations. I was asked if there really was a revolution of rising expectations in a country with a 5 or 10 percent literacy rate. The expression was probably premature then, but the idea has been there and has reached simmering point. People in the rural areas want the facilities that city people have. For them it is not just that the developing countries are more conscious of the United Nations or of the world as a whole; they are becoming more and more conscious of the widening gulf between the developed and the developing parts, the rich and the poor we talk about. Similarly, in a nation with an economy, there is a growing dichotomy; the gulf is growing wider because there is a greater awareness and the people are demanding, "Why do you have all these facilities and why can't we have good plain drinking water?" We have, therefore, to plan for growth, for growth plus change. It is not simple growth. Growth is bad, when you have reached a certain size, but for the developing countries the growth is needed where there has been no growth, where there has been stagnation. Consequently, when we talk about these things, we have to keep them clearly in mind.

The situation also demands a policy of social justice. It is not simply economic planning, or socioeconomic development; it is giving the people their due share proportionately, or at least equitably. This is a real issue we have to face in the developing countries.

The importance of social aspects in development and the need for a comprehensive interdisciplinary approach were stressed by A. MICHAEL.

. . . Greater emphasis should perhaps be put on the social level in addition to the plans made on an economic basis. For, indeed, if the plan is based on existing social stratification, an abrupt or too rapid change in the economic arena may be hindered by resistance on the social level. In this respect, little can be learned from experience because circumstances are different from place to place and from time to time, from country to country and even in the same country. At the various stages of economic progress, the interaction of social and economic factors may be different. . . . Social considerations would have to be taken into account, and in this respect using imagination is indeed called for: imagination in the sense of coordinating the various factors, the interdisciplinary approach, and more important perhaps, the vital necessity to develop the methodological tools necessary for implementing such an approach. Once an approach of this nature can be devised, and some rudimentary beginnings are already apparent in some centers of study in this country, I believe the time will be ripe for a few test cases to attempt to see if the comprehensive model can effectively be worked out.

The Israeli Experience. ARIE SHACHAR spoke of the new towns in Israel and how, through special government measures, they were industrialized and became economically viable.

. . . The second major instrument for the implementation of the urbanization policy was the inducement of economic development, through financial incentives for investment in industry or through direct public investment in the physical infrastructure for industrial development and by improving human resources, mainly through vocational training programs.

The economic development of the new towns could not be based, to any large extent, on providing central services. The central authorities, facing a severe crisis of unemployment in a large number of new towns, launched a massive industrialization program. The establishment of industry in the development towns frequently encountered the well-known problems of industrial growth in small towns, such as the necessity to internalize the entire cost of production not benefiting from any of the external economies of large places; remoteness from the markets; the acute shortage of trained manpower; the lack of managerial and technical expertise. To overcome some of these obstacles, the government provided generous investment credits, amounting in several instances to almost the total sum of the capital investment. The financial incentives provided tax exemptions for several years after the beginning of operation, with subsidies to equalize higher production factors (like water costs) because of location in a remote area.

The financial incentives were regulated by the law for the Encouragement of Capital Investments (1950, with amendments in 1954 and 1967), which specified geographic and economic criteria for eligibility for the various financial incentives. The geographic criterion was applied by assigning degrees of priority to the various regions of the country. The priority degree was higher the farther a region was from the metropolitan areas of the coastal plain. The central part of the coastal plain, between the major cities of Israel,

144

Tel Aviv and Haifa, was not given any priority. The types and the amount of the financial incentives were determined by the location of a development town within one of the priority areas. The economic criterion for determining eligibility for financial investment was defined, somewhat loosely, by the law as those enterprises that contribute, positively, to the balance of payments by export of import substitutes, that provide ample employment, and that ensure the continuous production of commodities defined as essential. The broad definitions of the economic criteria ensured the approval of almost all industrial projects.

On the discussion about the basic issue of economic efficiency and social equity as major goals of regional development, two points should be emphasized. First, although the provision of employment was defined by the law as only one criterion for eligibility to receive financial incentives, it played a decisive role in all the implementation processes. This fact illustrates the inclination of the central authorities toward social equity—by providing employment to the inhabitants of the new towns—rather than toward economic efficiency. With the stabilization of the Israeli society and economy, a stronger emphasis on efficiency has been emerging in recent years. A second characteristic of the financial incentives concerned the spatial context of evaluation for the industrial projects: They were evaluated within the framework of the national economy. Very seldom did the decision to establish an industrial enterprise take into account alternative regional or local locations, thus local specialization of industry based on relative locational advantages was hindered. This situation caused great difficulties in developing the linkage effects, which are essential to self-sustained growth.

Other forms of government support to the industrial development of the new towns were direct public investments in building the transportation network, developing the physical infrastructure of the industrial quarters, and providing land for industrial plants at a nominal price.

Summarizing policy measures concerning the establishment of a sound economic base for the new development towns through industrial development, one should mention that the industry in the development towns claimed between 35 and 45 percent of the total investment in industry in Israel during the last decade. Toward the end of the 1960s, the annual public investments in the industry of the development towns amounted to about IL 200 million (about $60 million). In 1967, the development towns accounted for 12.7 percent of the total industrial employment in Israel, and the share of the development towns within industrial employment and production has been growing steadily from year to year, thus increasing their contribution to the growth of the national economy.

The Italian Experience. A detailed account of the government policy
in developing services and infrastructure as part of national
development and urbanization in southern Italy was given by
GABRIELE PESCATORE. In the first part of his paper, Professor
Pescatore described the specific problem of the Italian economy—
the coexistence of two different economic systems: the northern
and central parts of the country, which are quite highly industrialized and economically developed, and the southern parts, which
are underdeveloped and share some features of developing countries.

The Cassa per il Mezzogiorno (Fund for the South), founded
in 1950, was entrusted with the task of stimulating the socioeconomic development of the South in order to narrow the gap
between the southern and central-northern parts of the country.
A fundamental part of the scheme was the regulation of urban
development. The scheme was aimed at the creation of "systems
of towns," known also as "metropolitan systems," to ensure balanced
development of the urban centers. The strategy adopted included
the development of infrastructure, services, and fundamental
economic activities such as agriculture and industry.

On the measures adopted for the development of infrastructure
and services, Pescatore wrote,

. . . A specific policy is necessary for large infrastructure—
particularly in the transportation and water supply sectors—and for
community services, when setting up metropolitan systems. The
transportation policy shall first of all aim at improving the road and
rail networks with a logical graduation as to whether the connections
are between metropolitan systems, or internal within one system.
Schematically, Italian transportation should be adjusted to two types
of infrastructural networks: primary and metropolitan.

In addition to the improvement of road and rail networks, freight
traffic will require the creation of specialized collection and distribution centers, which are important for the rational channeling of
traffic. Territorially, such centers should initially be formed inter-
regionally and should coincide with the large transportation terminals,
especially ports. Subsequently, more distribution centers can be
created within each system, commensurate with the metropolitan
structures. As to air transport, the goal is to establish one terminal
for international traffic in each of the metropolitan systems.

Particular attention has been paid to the formulation of basic
requirements, such as a foundation for all transportation plans: Each
means of transport shall be utilized so as to maximize its capacity
and speciality and to minimize territorial encumbrance; moreover,
it should be operated in strict correlation with the other means, in

order to maximize the rapidity and profitability of the combined transportation flows.

Another sector where infrastructure plays a paramount role is that of water supply. The water problems are particularly severe in the "Mezzogiorno," where climate and geography make water resources extermely scarce in certain areas. In the last 20 years, much has been done in the South toward solving this problem: 32 dams have been, or are being, erected for large storage with an aggregate capacity of over 2 billion cubic meters (more than 1.6 million acre/ feet), for multipurpose uses. Drinking-water supplies have first priority, and projects constructed for this purpose include nearly 1,400 tapping structures for an aggregate capacity of 42,000 litres/ second (almost 1 billion gallons per day), 14,000 kilometers (9,187 miles) of water mains, and over 2,700 water reservoirs and towers for 1.5 million cubic meters (nearly 400 million gallons). A total of 1,400 communities, with a population of 8.4 million, have been served.

The scarcity of a fundamental requisite such as water, and the simultaneous development of several productive activities, have already made vigilant control of water storage and distribution essential in the "Mezzogiorno." In future, the help of the most advanced techniques for applying systems analysis to the problem of optimum utilization of water resources will permit more effective planning for its multipurpose uses (potable, agriculture, industrial), which require even more thorough coordination. Particular activities are also envisaged for desalinization of sea and brackish waters, and for water rehabilitation in purification and recycling plants.

Within metropolitan systems, particular importance is attributed to such services as structures for schools, scientific research, and sanitation. For the first, a specific policy is envisaged for university location (part of the present large universities and the erection of 20 new minor centers with 15,000 to 20,000 students each), planning for 1 million students by 1980, double the present university population. As to scientific research, vast activities should be promoted within universities, which are the natural center of research, as well as providing guidance to nonuniversity scientific bodies entrusted with plans for directed research.

With regard to sanitation, a study is currently under way for the establishment of a national health service. A network of local health units should be created, each serving some 50,000 people—with the exception of those located within the metropolitan systems or in scarcely populated territories. In the framework of an integrated sanitation policy, local health units should be entrusted with prevention, diagnosis, treatment, and rehabilitation tasks and with supervision and coordination of authority over all basic sanitary activities. The development of local health units, while diffusing efficient prophylaxis,

should curb the present tendency toward increased hospitalization
and reduce bed-place requirements, so that a ratio of 6 bed-places
for a population of 1,000 may be sufficient. The hospital network
should be augmented by improved extrahospital services for treating
chronic and convalescent patients.

As regards fundamental economic activities, Pescatore
wrote,

. . . Another aspect of the policy for establishing the metropolitan
system is the development and reshaping of economic activities (in
agriculture, industry, and tourist promotion) considered to be strategic
for territorial and productive organization.
The "Mezzogiorno" is particularly interesting in this aspect,
because in the last few years a certain number of "integrated development areas" there have been defined as holding out promising possibilities in the three economic sectors and are already enjoying
substantial endowments of public works and services. In those areas,
designed as attraction poles of future metropolitan systems, the Cassa
has been operating for many years with investments in infrastructure
and incentives to productive initiatives. Cassa's agricultural inputs
have included comprehensive public works for drainage, irrigation,
water course and slope regulation, and reforestation in mountain
watersheds, while contributions have been granted toward private
land improvement and agricultural produce processing and storing.
Particular attention has been given to land-use transformation with
irrigation (some 500,00 hectares, or 1.25 million acres, were made
irrigable through 1970), directed toward the expansion in the near
future of intensive farming in the southern plains over an acreage of
between 800,000 and 1 million hectares (2 to 2.5 million acres),
mostly for fruit, vegetables, vineyards, and critus groves.
In industry, Cassa's activities to date have been directed, on the
one hand, to endowing areas specifically appropriate for industrial
development (the so-called industrial areas and nuclei), with basic
infrastructure, and, on the other hand, to encouraging productive
initiatives for constructing, expanding, and modernizing industrial
projects by means of cheap loans, capital grants, fiscal and tariff
reductions, etc. In future, such incentives should be better graduated
than in the past in order to foster employment and project location
in better selected sites. Concurrently, a counterincentive method
should be applied discriminating against initiatives proposing investments in areas already saturated and congested.
A most efficient tool for giving additional incentive to industry,
already utilized and to be recommended, is the so-called contrat-
tazione programmatica (in-plan bargaining), by which the

Interministerial Committee for Economic Planning on a case-by-case basis establishes the extent of benefits to be granted both for initiatives of larger size and for those technically connected with the investment blocks. At the same time, the Cassa will continue to equip the areas of industrial agglomeration with specific infrastructure.

Cassa's activities for tourist promotion should take the form, as in the past, of endowing the areas of greater potentiality (tourist-attractive districts) with infrastructure and in extending cheap credit and capital grants as incentives to hotel projects and allied initiatives.

The above case studies clearly show how development policy is vital to a positive process of urbanization. The planned development of economic activities, infrastructure, and services ensure that urbanization is not only a demographic process but also is accompanied by economic progress, improved living conditions, and better services for the individual. Furthermore, as seen in the Italian experience, a clear development policy may help to bring about a more balanced process of urbanization characterized by the development of the smaller and medium-sized urban centers rather than the development of only a few large, congested urban concentrations.

PHYSICAL PLANNING POLICIES

A clear policy of physical planning is just as important as an economic policy for ensuring desirable urban development. Within the context of physical planning are included land reform, land-use patterns, some elements of infrastructure and environmental planning. Physical planning is obviously part and parcel of social and economic planning and should be regard as such, and RAM C. MALHOTRA elaborated this point:

. . . With the realization of the need for integrated sectoral, regional, and physical planning, it becomes obvious that it must be a combination, a coordinated effort of the three aspects, sector, regional, and physical planning, and must also take the needs of psychological planning into consideration. There is a need to set up a suitable commission for the coordination not only of the formulation of integrated comprehensive plans, but more important for the implementation of such plans. A plan, after all, is only as good as its implementation. It is, therefore, basically in this area that we hope to profit from an exchange of experience.

Land Reform for Urbanization. EDMUNDO FLORES, in his paper, stressed the role of land reform and community development in the urbanization process.

. . . Massive and rapid redistribution of productive lands in countries where land ownership is heavily concentrated in the hands of a very small number of landlords, as is generally the case in Latin America, will surely arrest, for 10 to 20 years at least, the inordinate flow from country to town, as has been the experience of Mexico and Bolivia.

An important by-product of a land reform program is the emergence and growth of smaller urban centers, which absorb rural immigrants and partially deflect migration toward the big metropolis.

By the same token, programs for community development in rural areas will be geared to make people stay there. Educational programs, however, will have to train the young for industrial-urban work because, due to development, a small fraction of the labor force will earn its living in farming.

The importance of land reform and especially the need for a clear policy and legislation regarding ownership of land for future urban development was raised by JORGE E. HARDOY.

. . . Short of the socialization of all urban and suburban land, which few countries will be ready to adopt, governments favoring the free enterprise system must realize that leaving the private builder alone to provide housing and land with adequate location, design, and characteristics for those who urgently need them has led to disastrous results. The answer of the free market system for the lower-income sectors is to expect a descending filtration that will make housing available for them as soon as the units occupied by the higher-income sectors are emptied because they have acquired or rented better housing. Unfair as the procedure is, the process fails because in developing countries housing is never sufficiently available and the cost is too high.

The answer of the free market system of land demand is to promote new subdivisions. Such fragmentation makes the provision of services and community equipment impossible, creates appalling living conditions, destroys the natural environment, and frequently uses excellent agricultural land. Faced with the apathy of governments, the people have sometimes reacted with strength and ingenuity, invading public and private lands, organizing their communities, and building their own houses with materials that cannot last. It is correct to assume that this system can reduce building costs, but, on the other hand, the same man or woman, with some basic training, can

150

contribute more to the general production effort if he is employed according to his real capacity and potential.

To make things worse, most governments own none or very little urban land in relation to needs. To start land banks in these conditions would be extremely difficult. Besides, developing countries do not have the funds to acquire enough land at reasonable prices. Drastic solutions are necessary, and they cannot be delayed. I think that some of the developing countries can provide key elements to an understanding of the process and to finding solutions.

The knowledge of experience gained in those countries and the development of systematic guidelines for understanding and comparison should not postpone the need for immediate action. When they act, governments should bear in mind that at the root of the present urban situation in developing countries are erroneous concepts about land, homeownership, and inheritance. The tools we insist on employing, such as master plans, zoning, subdivision regulations, and the rest, are useless if other preconditions are not given. Urban land is the basic ingredient in any local policy of urban development and its socialization; although it will not bring the desired solution over night, it will provide the responsible authorities with the necessary element to control the physical growth of cities, to define land use, to maximize the investments in urban services, to incorporate industrialization into the housing industry, and to change a traditional urban ecology based on socioeconomic and/or ethnic discrimination.

The legal aspect of land use was also mentioned by YILMAS GURER.

. . . The legal and public system of land tenure, which is an indispensable condition of urban expansion, should be given prime consideration. A policy of utilization of the soil constitutes an efficient instrument for the nationalization of urbanization.

Land-Use Controls. JOHN FRIEDMANN, in his paper on the implementation of urban-regional policies, went into detail on the measures applied to carry out urban-regional policies. In his opinion, the measures are physical land-use controls, directed migration, direct public investments, and financial location incentives. On the measures of physical land-use control, Friedmann wrote,

. . . Land-use zoning applied to regions on a national scale has been tried in a number of European countries, but not, to my knowledge, in any of the newly industrializing nations. A typical example is the Danish Zoning Plan, which uses a four-part division of the country: urban and industrial development areas; areas potentially attractive for urban and industrial development; landscapes of recreational and cultural values; and agricultural areas. A more elaborate classification emerges from the further subdivision of these categories and from stipulation of patterns of spatial juxtaposition.

Conceptually, Denmark's zoning plan appears to be a useful device for focusing public attention on critical problem areas. Unless it acquires the force of law, however, it will remain a technical document for guiding the public decision-making process. Its staying power, consequently, will be weak; each new government may feel at liberty to replace the plan with zoning concepts of its own. Moreover, urban experience suggests that land-use zoning is at best a procedure for slowing down the processes of changing land occupancy. Essentially a negative instrument intended to prevent certain undesirable actions from occurring, it generates no positive action of its own.

Despite these obvious shortcomings, a simple zoning plan that is easy to administer (through a system of licensing, for example) may be a useful complement to other more positive measures, especially in areas of relatively dense settlement. For the capital region of Chile, Friedmann and Necochea have proposed the designation of agroindustrial corridors and tourist zones for the purpose of excluding manufacturing activities from these areas. The creation of an Environmental Protection District to control urban population was also suggested. These measures, however, have not been enacted. Due to the agenda of priorities in the newly industrializing countries, the political appeal of regional zoning legislation is likely to remain low.

> Friedmann argued that all the measures suggested will not produce significant results unless "a set of complementary measures is brought to bear in a coordinated and focussed way on a limited geographic area."
> LESLIE B. GINSBURG discussed the allocation of land for development and mentioned the possibility of purchase of land as a means of controlling physical planning and preventing speculation.

. . . In most countries, and in rapidly developing countries even more so, the actual purchase of land in advance of development can be the key to the success of physical planning controls. The availability of land at the right place and at the right price, as well as the right time, can well be the overwhelming factor in any planning program that involves more than economic allocations. The more precise a plan, the less likelihood of its implementation if the land is not available within the terms mentioned above. Even with a flexible structure plan, where even the lines of the infrastructure can vary, without state intervention through a land agency there will be speculation. As a result, the poorer people will have to squat outside the plan, and all the aims and objects of the plan will go by the board.

To obtain legal sanction for expropriation of land in and on the fringe of existing urban areas is very difficult everywhere, and, even when such sanctions are given, expropriation laws usually, though not always, include such heavy compensation clauses that the developing authority—be it a municipality, an ad hoc agency, or the state—cannot afford to spend large portions of their annual budget in this way. For this reason, it is always easier and cheaper to allocate land for development that is in rural areas and attracts only agricultural value rather than development value. Here again every political group tends to debate the issue in opposite ways according to who its supporters are. For this general reason, however, it is considered cheaper to make allocations for new development in "new towns," but again this depends on the subsidies and budgeting arrangements for the infrastructure.

The value of the land will sometimes be recouped in the form of local taxation, but this is very rare in the case of land for low-cost housing and is an argument that should not have to be resorted to in putting forward a form of new town or city, rather than expansion of an existing urban area. Nor are systems of "betterment levy" likely to succeed; even in the most efficient tax-collecting countries like Britain, it was not found practicable to work out this method, and in newly developing countries some form of land purchase and allocation is an absolute priority for any urbanization growth strategy.

All those who referred to the subject of physical planning stressed its importance in development policy, maintaining that there is no hope of implementing economic and social policy if it is not accompanied by a physical plan. Such issues as land reform, land ownership, land use, and zoning should be part of a comprehensive approach toward development policy.

POLITICAL ASPECTS OF DEVELOPMENT AND URBANIZATION POLICY-MAKING

The importance of the political factor in urbanization and development was clearly stated by JONES OFORI-ATTA.

. . . In reading through a number of the papers that aimed at analyzing problems of urbanization, I constantly came to the conclusion that two factors are responsible—the economic pull and the social push. As a politician, I happen to know that there is another factor operating, and that is political pull. Some of us represent rural constituencies, and, when you are elected, no sooner have you been installed in office than you find a number of people rushing to your door and asking for a job; they voted for you, and you are supposed to find them a job. The embarrassing thing is that, as soon as you find a job for one, ten of them appear the next day, so perhaps in the analysis of this problem the political pull has to be understood, too.

Discussing the issue of rural-urban relations, TOM CARROL also referred to the question of political power. Carrol focused his comments on the importance of this factor in regard to rural communities and rural-urban relations.

. . . I am somewhat surprised that in a meeting on urbanization and development there is so little discussion on the political or power element, though perhaps it is also strange that I, coming from a development bank, should take up this particular issue.

Instead of talking about economics, let me just try to raise a few issues related to this power structure. It seems that one of the essential features that underlies some of the discussions of these urban-rural relationships is that urbanization is inevitable. We are talking about its relative balance and relative ways.

Throughout the underdeveloped world there is a strand of exploitation of the cultivator. I think that we have to recognize that. The cultivator, that is the peasant, who really works the land, is doubly exploited. He is exploited by the landlords, by the administrators, particularly in feudalistic landlord-type countries. He is exploited by the market system, which is not operating in his favor, and let us be quite clear about it: He is exploited by the city, in the sense that practically all the agricultural surplus is taken away from him in some form.

I feel that the attempts that have been made by governments to return some of this surplus that has been taken away through taxation, through welfare measures, through other ways now coming into being, are really a very poor substitute for strengthening the capacity of rural areas, particularly on the level of the cultivator, to retain and develop this surplus. I think we have to face the fact that its consequences are highly political, for it has to do with the power structure. Peasants are powerless. This is a proposition in most countries, and if you want to speak of more balanced development you have to face this fact and deal with it.

I would like to remind you that what we see in Israel—and this is one of the most important and interesting things that I have learned here—that even in the phase of development where the population was 40 to 50 percent agricultural, the cultivators had a great deal more power than in any other country. From the very beginning, there has been a different power structure here, where the agricultural areas, for historical and other reasons, have been given power. This was embedded in the ideology. While this cannot be repeated in exactly the same way, I think there is something here that must be learned, for its consequences for the developing world lie not only in the political realm, but also in the way it is carried out.

The second thing one learns here is the way that this power has been translated into a special economic and social organization in the countryside. Israel teaches another very important lesson here: on the political organization of rural government, of rural councils, of the special organization of settlements and, lately, of the industrial-rural linkages that bring jobs to the countryside, of the agricultural/industrial complexes that are growing up, and of the social and economic infrastructure that is directed to rural areas. This is a very important lesson.

Finally, I would like to make some general propositions on this basis.

(1) For a balanced rural development, which we all seem to require, and this is true at the lower level as well as at the higher level of the development spectrum, rural areas should be given substantially greater power to organize, to apply their own technology, their own methods of development, and to help direct their own destiny.

The most important way to confer this power quickly is to give local communities decision-making powers, which means strengthening local governments—of cooperative organizations, of peasant syndicates, and of unions where this is relevant.

(2) In countries where there are feudal conditions for land-lordism, which means the exploitation of the cultivator to a very high degree, agrarian reform in a massive and drastic sense is a pre-requisite for development. This depends fundamentally on the power base that has consciously to be conferred on rural communities.

The most detailed analysis of the political factor in urbanization was given by JOHN FRIEDMANN in his paper on the "Implementation of Urban-Regional Development Policies." Friedmann illustrated his arguments with examples from various continents and countries where political considerations were responsible for the urbanization and development policy.

. . . A rudimentary pattern of urbanization and regional development will tend to maintain itself. Such a pattern may be established quite early in a country's history. Subsequent flows of controlling decisions, innovation diffusion, migration, and economic location will tend to reinforce this pattern, so that, whatever happens, the future will look very much like the past. This is the most probable outcome, and policy changes may require decades and even generations of sustained, counterintuitive effort to alter the network of spatial relationships in a significant way. . . .

Let me give a simple illustration. Suppose that the capital city of a country has established primacy over all other cities by a factor of 5 to 1, so that the largest city has five times the population of the next three largest cities combined. This, for example, is the case of Lima, Peru. The most probable pattern of future population migration will be one that will tend to maintain this ratio in the distribution of urban population. If, for some reason, the national government should decide to reduce the primacy of the capital to a ratio of, say, 3 to 1, it would have to adopt policies that would accelerate migration toward the smaller cities, while decreasing the flow of population to the primary city. This change in the direction of migration would represent a significant departure from the normal, system-maintaining migration pattern. In order to accomplish its objective, the government would, therefore, have to sustain its commitment to this policy over a period of several decades. Furthermore, the policy change would have to be sufficiently bold in conception to ensure that nonplanned, random events, such as changes in industrial technology, would not cancel any possible gains achieved through application of the policy.

The difficulties of sustaining major policy commitments should not be underestimated. If the period of desirable commitment should last for several decades, it must clearly cut across several periods of governmental change. It must become a suprapolitical policy, capable of receiving endorsement from more than one political regime. Few policies are ever likely to enjoy such support. Experience suggests that policies of this sort must conform to certain requirements in order to increase the probabilities of their survival.

The first requirement for a suprapolitical policy is that it must be simple in concept and dramatic in its implications. Such a policy will set the popular imagination on fire and will tend to be elevated to a national commitment. Examples readily come to mind:

> the conquest of the desert (Israel);
> the harnessing of a major river basin (Ghana, Egypt);
> the building of new towns (England);
> the building of a new national capital (Turkey, Brazil, Pakistan);
> the reclamation of new land from the sea (Holland);
> the construction of a transcontinental transport system (USA);
> the creation of a major industrial growth pole (Venezuela).

These historical examples have at least one important characteristic in common: They refer to projects whose primary impact is physical. Their appeal derives from man's emotional attachment to the land and from his pride in physical construction. If the projects are sufficiently large to become national in scope and to project an image of man pitting himself against the insensate forces of nature (deserts, rivers, the sea) or, alternately, raising the symbol-laden towers of a city to heaven, they stand a good chance of mobilizing national support.

Irrational motives are powerful incentives to action. Support for building the new capital of Brazil was mobilized, in part, because of the "almost mystical feeling that the city-bred Brazilian has for the interior," a feeling that the great wealth of the country is locked up there, far away from the coastal region, where 90 percent of the people live.

A "mystical" belief of a different order was the inspiration of Islamabad, the new capital of Pakistan. "The capital of a country is the focus and center of the people's ambitions and desires," wrote General Ayub Khan, former President of Pakistan. "It is wrong to put them in an existing city. The city must have a color and character of its own, and that character is the sum total of the aspirations, the life and the ambitions of the people of the whole of Pakistan. With the two provinces of Pakistan, separated as they are from each other, you had to bring the people on to a common platform. The thing to do was to take them to a new place altogether."

Yet another epic theme—that man should dominate nature—lies at the root of much regional planning in the Soviet Union, where it has been used for more than a generation as a basis for sustaining policy commitments. In a textbook for school children published in 1929, the authors summon up truly poetic feelings that reach far beyond a purely rational examination of costs and benefits. They write, "We must discover and conquer the country in which we live. It is a tremendous country, but not yet entirely ours. Our steppe will truly become ours only when we come with columns of tractors and plows to break the thousand-year-old virgin soil. On a far-flung front we must wage war. We must burrow into the earth, break rocks, dig mines, construct houses. We must take from the earth. . . ."

The appeal to protean feelings, however, is not without its hidden costs. For the ultimate objective is not a physical artifact (a flowering desert, a new capital city, a transcontinental railroad, the conquest of the steppe) but some specific improvement in the national "welfare" as expressed in social or economic terms, such as an increase in production, improved social patterns, or national integration. The physical project, although intended as a means toward these ends, often replaces the ultimate objective and assumes the character of

157

an end in its own right. The desert must be irrigated, the dam must be built, the land must be reclaimed, the highway must be built, the steppe must be made fertile—regardless of the costs imposed or even the ultimate (and sometimes doubtful) benefits. The project—like the moonshot—becomes a national obsession. A man must be placed on the moon; he will be placed. Alternatives to the man on the moon are not explored; alternative uses for the resources are not studied or seriously contemplated. The irrationality of the original appeal (which, I would claim, ensures a sustained national commitment to the undertaking) may also lead to a perversion of the ultimate objectives of the project expressed in welfare terms, as the unforeseen consequences of the project spill over to effect other areas of national life. Projects of this kind can be a country's ruin.

The very fact of national commitment suggests that the project will not be abandoned even if negative consequences should materialize. The project is undertaken, as it were, on trust in the "principle of the hidden hand" that any problem that might arise in the course of its implementation will somehow call forth an adequate, creative response. Impending ruin joined to promises of untold benefits (however vague) may call forth extraordinary efforts to avoid it. But the danger of ruin is always present in major national undertakings, and policy planners should be aware of it.

The second requirement is that a policy, in order to enjoy long-term commitment, must be embodied in new institutions capable of outlasting periodic changes in government. Three forms of institutionalization may be tried.

The first is legal and may be illustrated by the provision in the Brazilian Constitution of fixed percentage of national revenues that must be applied each year to the development of particular regions. This provision is mandatory on all governments (so long as it remains a part of the Constitution); it has the disadvantage of being excessively rigid and unrelated to the actual cost of realistic economic opportunities for investment. The total amount thus set aside may be either too small or too large and can easily lead to a serious misallocation of national resources.

The second form of institutionalization is administrative. This may be illustrated by the proposed regionalization of public administration and development efforts in France—that is, shifting the gravity of decision-making power from the Paris region. To the extent that regionalization is successful, this reorganization of the French administrative appartus will be difficult to reverse. The obstacles to regionalization have proved to be formidable, however. Institutionalization by administrative decree may be too weak an instrument to bring about substantial changes in the probable distribution of development benefits among the different parts of a country.

The third form of institutionalization is corporate. An example would be the creation of the Guayana Corporation of Venezuela. This corporate authority has ample financial resources; it has gradually built a political basis of support in the region of its primary impact; and it has managed to draw to it superior technical skills and leadership abilities. Its principal drawback has been the acquisition of too much power, a problem that has already been discussed. There is no question, however, about the effectiveness of this type of institutional arrangement. By now, the Guayana Corporation is the largest single enterprise in Venezuela. In the future, its power may be restricted, but its existence is reasonably assured for a long time to come.

Finally, long-term policy commitments require that the policy in question quickly produce visible results. A policy is most vulnerable during the first few years of its application. If results are not timely, those opposing it will easily be able to persuade the government to abandon it in favor of something more desirable in alternatives. Yet, frequent changes in policy for spatial development are counterproductive. Usually, they involve changes in objectives as well. Where this happens, the results of one policy will be counteracted by the results of alternative policies and so will tend to cancel each other out.

The requirement of quick and visible argues, once again, for works of physical construction. A dam is visible; the building of a new capital is visible; a new subway is visible. The effects of physical construction such as increased employment, higher incomes, more efficient administration, more efficient mass transit, are not visible. These intended effects of policy are captured only in statistics. In many cases, they are difficult to attribute directly to the policy, because of intervening variables. Whereas physical construction is impressive, statistics are not. Indeed, quite aside from the possibility of measurement, there is a deep-seated folk prejudice (not altogether unjustified) against statistical measurement. As everyone knows, statistics can easily deceive. Moreover, the effects of a given policy may take years to register results that are statistically significant. The instruments of measurement tend to be insensitive to minor variations in the phenomena observed. Where a visible product is a feasible alternative to people-oriented programs that have a certain intangible quality about them, the physical project tends to be chosen.

For instance, a land redistribution scheme that leads to the quick reallocation of property to a landless peasantry is likely to be much more popular than a slower-working policy that seeks to encourage cooperative unions, technical advice, production credit, and new marketing procedures as elements of a land reform program. Such a program will almost certainly be slower in its impact, and the total amount of land passing to the peasants will be smaller than if intangible people-oriented measures are set aside in favor of quick and massive land redistribution. That the former would lead to more permanent beneficial results than the latter is not in question. Politicians, no less than the public, are more interested in the symbolic gesture. Although willing to allocate millions of dollars for a quick scheme of redistribution, they may withhold support from a more elaborate and complex program of reform whose results would be more gradual and, in any event, less visible and dramatic.

The sunken costs in the original investment may make the policy, once initiated, irreversible. President Kubitschek insisted on speeding up the building of Brasilia so that succeeding governments might find it impossible to back off from the original decision. A tremendous effort was, therefore, launched to complete the physical infrastructure of the city under his administration. The potential monstrosity of having a brand-new ghost capital remain unoccupied would force subsequent governments to make the city work. Adversity would thus call forth its own solutions.

CONCLUSIONS

Summing up the different view expressed in relation to development policy, we should stress a number of points.

The approach to development should be of a comprehensive nature and embrace all elements: economic, social, physical, and environmental. Central governments should play a decisive role in formulating policy for socioeconomic development and in the identification of the main goals ahead.

Policy for economic and social development was illustrated by case studies from a number of countries, in all of which governments played an important role in the encouragement of the economic development through direct public investments in industry, services, infrastructure, and training programs as well as through other financial incentives.

The measures applied in specific regions stimulated the economic growth of those areas and contributed to a more balanced process of urbanization.

Physical planning—land reform for urbanization, land use, land tenure, and the legal aspects of land use—was regarded as no less vital than economic measures. Expropriation and purchase of land for urban development were mentioned as possibilities for ensuring balanced urban growth.

In many cases, political considerations play an important role in fixing development goals. Countries may decide on specific development projects that gain popularity although they may appear to be irrational economically. Policy-makers and planners should, therefore, be aware of this, and the strategy of development should be carefully studied and analyzed before any final decisions are taken.

.

8

STRATEGIES FOR
URBANIZATION

A well-defined urbanization strategy through which policy-makers and development planners may direct the dispersal of population in a predetermined pattern is a major problem that hinges on centralization or decentralization of the urbanization process. The debate on this subject touches on many facets of the development process—on spatial distribution of the population in its national space, on the centralization or decentralization of the mechanism influencing development, and, in particular, on the centralization or decentralization of the administration and institutional setup of the various governmental agencies.

THE NEED FOR A CLEAR STRATEGY

The need for a clear strategy in the development process and its influence on urbanization was taken up energetically from the outset at the opening of the Conference. In his opening remarks, LLOYD RODWIN said,

. . . The point I wish to emphasize is that this trend toward the formulation of a national policy or strategy for development is occurring precisely in the period of history when it is most important to reverse the centralization of power in order to transform that pattern. It is a curious phenomenon in a way because, in the past century and a half, in the case of the United States, for example, the whole aim has been to give the central government more power to promote programs of welfare and development. Even in countries with more centralized political institutions, the emergence of a national policy for urban and regional development is a novel exercise, despite the centralization of power in national organs.

Throughout the world, for a whole complex of reasons, the power at the center is bogged down; never perhaps in history has there been so much mass apathy to the problem of apoplexy at the center and anemia at the edges. It is vitally important, therefore, that, despite the fact that we have arrived at that historic era when we are on the verge of crystallizing or promoting a national policy for urban and regional development, we must at the same time find ways of decentralizing national power and giving more power at local and regional levels.

The need for a clear-cut strategy from this point of view was stressed by many participants. An example of conflicting view and undecided strategy was described by EIICHI ISOMURA of Japan, in describing the background against which decisions regarding the dispersal or concentration of population in Japan were taken. He went on to describe what he called the "new comprehensive national development program."

. . . The concentration of population in urban areas in postwar Japan has been motivated to a great extent by social changes. In the Pacific War, the Japanese people were compelled to a dispersal of the population to an extent that had never been experienced before. Under a forced evacuation program, one-third of the people then living in urban areas were forced to move to farm villages and live in the same way as the farmers. Furthermore, the system of rice rationing, the staple food of the Japanese, which has in effect been carried on for the past 25 years since the Pacific War, implies a socialist policy for a country belonging to the Western bloc. These factors have homogenized urban and agrarian types of living, and the reluctance that had existed to migration from agrarian to urban areas has disappeared. On the other hand, urban areas became all the more attractive with the spread of new industrial plants. The concentration of population in urban areas over the span of 10 years from the beginning of the war and including the defeat, might thus be described as a rare demographic phenomenon.

If this trend had been unhesitatingly accepted as part of urban policy, regional development in Japan might have followed a different pattern. The slow progress in housing and land policy served as the prime mover for the dispersal of the population that had concentrated in urban areas to their perimeters. This population has settled down in the suburbs so that the urban area has taken on quite a different pattern—divided into the suburban residential district and the CDB (Central Business District). Only a small, relatively insignificant section of the suburban population is returning to the city center with the appearance of apartment houses. In terms of ecological pattern, therefore, the regional environment will become heterogeneous on the basis of the differentials in the structure of living between the city and its environs. There are signs that Tokyo and Osaka would take on the pattern of an "all-night area"—something quite rare in the world.

The concept of broader area development designed specifically for Tokyo, Osaka, and Nagoya, and the concept of the development of new industrial cities, specifically in Sendai, Okayama, Oita, and other places, was the main trend throughout the 1960s. Local dispersal policy led to the concentration of population in big cities. The New Comprehensive National Development Program probably crystallized this trend into one concept and was designed to encourage further progress both in the economy and in industry.

This program, which is looked upon as a "large-scale project," incorporates ideas totally different from the so-called small-scale community projects, because its object is the development of super-speed railways, highways, airports, ports, and harbors. Its objectives reach out beyond the planning of prefectures, cities, towns, and villages and could be translated into action either by the state or by a very strong nongovernmental development organization.

The New Comprehensive National Development Program can be described as the total of development plans mapped out by autonomous local bodies, which plans are then subordinated to a new large-scale development program.

Regional development in Japan has hitherto been designed for power decentralization and dispersal so as to bring local autonomous bodies into the ideological context. There is, however, as in the past, a growing tendency toward power centralization and concentration in the big cities. Deficiencies in the regional living environment, notably that of big urban areas, have increased conspicuously. It might be asserted that the political and administrative posture in which no drastic measures have been taken for local dispersal has in a way deadlocked regional development in Japan.

Reviewing the issue of urbanization strategy as part of general development planning, ARIE SHACHAR summarized the present situation.

. . . Few countries have, with any degree of explicitness or comprehensiveness, formulated a national policy of urbanization. In many countries, national planning is mainly sectoral, lacking the spatial dimension of the development process. National development plans rarely specify a target distribution of urban and rural settlements or a desired structure of the urban system. The neglect of the spatial dimension in national development plans is due to insufficient knowledge

164

concerning spatial organization and socioeconomic development. Having a verified theory of urbanization, which provides explanation and understanding of the complex processes bringing about the spatial organization of society on a regional and national level, is a prime condition for formulating a viable national urbanization policy. Friedmann's "Theory of Polarized Development" provides a theoretical framework for establishing public policies of urbanization and regional development. Works on the evolution of the urban system by Berry, or the multifaceted problems of urban size by Alonso, or the role of the different processes in the spatial integration of society by Pedersen and the spatial organization of modernization processes by Soja and Gould are recent contributions to the field of the spatial organization of society. Urbanization policies should be formulated within a theoretical framework and in the light of the lessons of past experience with deeper insight and understanding. Existing policies should be examined within a theoretical framework and on the basis of the lessons of past experience. The accumulated experience gained through the formulation and implementation of urbanization policies in various countries might be useful in establishing and carrying out these policies in other countries in the future.

Most of the participants expressed the views—in their papers, in plenary sessions, and in various study groups—that a strategy of development in general and for the urbanization process in particular is essential in determining governmental policies. From the very beginning, one of the basic issues of that strategy was prominent in the debates and deliberations: concentration in larger cities versus dispersal in smaller ones.

CONCENTRATION VERSUS DISPERSAL

The problem of concentration versus dispersal of urban activities and the various factors linked up with it was taken up at length in LOWDON WINGO's paper.

The arguments for deconcentration can be reduced to contentions that specific national objectives or values could be better realized through a more spatially diffuse pattern than what tends to occur when development processes are left to themselves. Thus, it is contended, such a policy would result in the allocation of a nation's productive assets so much more efficiently that scarce factors, such as new plants, machinery, and human capital would yield a substantially higher product. Or it is put forward that a less concentrated development pattern might achieve a more equitable distribution of "real"

165

national income, where equity is valued either as a social and political value or as an antecedent of a more productive economy based on the development of a rapidly expanding demand for domestically produced goods and services. Thus, the degree of economic concentration may, some students of development contend, have an effect on the ease with which the social, political, and economic transformation necessary for development takes place. Finally, social or cultural values held by the people of a developing nation may be reinforced or weakened by the concentration of the nation's energies in its economic core region. Other objectives or values of the country may also be put forward in the debate about the virtues and vices of deconcentration, such as economic or political stability, popular participation in decision-making, or national pride.

Clearly these objectives can, and frequently do, conflict. They are graced with little consensus on their proper ordering in the formulation of public programs and policies. Indeed, much of the contention surrounding the issue of metropolitan concentration reflects disagreements among the contenders on the proper ordering of national objectives. In the light of the confusion that this multiplicity of goals and values introduces into the appraisal of national internal development strategies, this paper will attempt a brief analysis of the implications of concentration of development institutions and processes in the metropolitan core region for some of these objectives and values independently considered. Since the case is usually argued on efficiency and distributive grounds, we will concentrate on them specifically.

CRITERIA FOR STRATEGY DETERMINATION

Economic efficiency is perhaps the criterion most frequently invoked in the controversy over a concentrated versus a deconcentrated strategy. The advocates of concentration contend that the effects of scarcity in such key resources as entrepreneurship, highly skilled labor, and specialized public capital can be ameliorated by spatial concentration, which expedites the mobility of resources among productive opportunities. Their opponents of underutilized resources outside the main concentration of economic activity make productive gains possible by the simple expedient of redistributing of economic activities accordingly. In a circumstance in which the key characteristics of reasonably perfect competition in product and factor markets prevail, we could perhaps demonstrate the superiority of the actual outcome to any alternative with some ease. But this is not really the case in developing countries; indeed, there is good reason not to accept such analysis at face value: The departures from the competitive postulates of neoclassical economics are numerous and consequential.

In the first place, the modern sector tends to develop strong monopolistic features, which result from the confrontation of technologies exhibiting economies of scale with the limited consumption markets that characterize these countries. Locational investments, however, rationally calculated by investors, need not, hence, be optimal in any social welfare sense. The prevalence of strong unions in leading industrial sectors, which characterizes some developing countries, can also lead to a less than optimal distribution of economic activities over the national economic landscape: Employers may make locational investments to avoid or escape the economic constraints imposed by strong unions; at the same time, strong unions in industrial sectors concentrated in the core metropolitan region will resist otherwise socially rational deconcentration policies to protect the economic welfare of their memberships.

The rich mix of public and private services produced in core metropolitan regions generates an economic environment that is, in the technical sense, a unique pure public good, nonreproducible in urban settlements of substantially lesser scales. There is suggestive evidence that virtually all economic groups, from the unskilled migrant to the entrepreneurs, managers, and professionals, view this environment, in contrast to any other in the country, as a substantial real income addition to their private welfare, a circumstance that results in migration decisions not always consistent with the socially optimal distribution of human capital. Other kinds of externalities in these core regions have opposing tendencies: Congestion degradation of the quality of air, water, and landscape and rising costs of public services (which are frequently "paid for" by accepting lower service levels) are real social costs that do not proportionately affect the investment decisions of the firms and individuals generating them. Finally, it would be difficult to establish the existence of a locational equilibrium between the metropolitan core region and the rest of the country at any one point in time, since the rapid changes unleashed by development keep all economic relationships in a transient state, thus making objective evaluations of alternative situations very difficult.

Such qualifications of the competitive assumptions of economic analysis result in so wide a divergence between private utility and social welfare that one cannot accept at face value propositions that the existing configuration of economic activity is best for society because it seems to be best for key sectors of the economy. It is also true that these imperfections do not establish that a less concentrated alternative should be superior.

Is there any way, then, in which we can more realistically approach the question of the relative efficiency of concentrated versus deconcentrated development? I think so, but such an enterprise will involve more rigorous analysis than it has been given to date; for example, the most accessible measure of the changes in social welfare is gross product (GNP, GDP, GRP) a measure with serious defects. Gross National Product is the sum of nonhomogeneous productive events, which, for our purposes, needs to be disaggregated into distinguishable interregional economic relations that can be separately evaluated. Consider a simple model of a national economy consisting of two regions, $\underline{M}$ (for metropolitan core) and $\underline{H}$ (for resource hinterland), each of which trades with a set of customer countries $\underline{E}$.

Look for a moment at the country's external relations, which might be expressed in the statement that imports of capital depend on the export earnings of both regions less the imports of consumer goods to both. Characteristically the hinterland region exports abroad consist of primary resources such as copper, petroleum, or agricultural products and, at least in early stages of development, overshadow exports from the metropolitan core, which consist of processed goods. The sale of primary hinterland products abroad tends, then, to support imports of capital and consumption goods to region $\underline{M}$, since region $\underline{H}$ has a low propensity to import except for the capital needs of its export sector, and one should note that these export sectors are frequently enclaves in the hinterland region from which few economic benefits accrue to the hinterland region as more broadly construed.

What, then, would be the impact of inducing export industries to move from $\underline{M}$ to $\underline{H}$? In the first instance, production costs in such industries would be likely to rise. Specialized labor would be more costly because it would probably have to be induced financially to surrender the real income advantages of the metropolitan environment; new plants would have to be built and would have to operate in a less advantageous environment with the result that the country's comparative advantages in these productive sectors would be eroded. Where countries are experiencing deterioration of the market position of their primary products, such exports may become critical factors in the rate of capital accumulation and hence require special attention, even careful incubation. In short, the major metropolitan regions have provided special environments for the development and growth of export manufacturers. Where these are important in the country's development strategy, generalized approaches to deconcentration could put them at a disadvantage in the world market and require export subsidies to maintain their competitive position.

As for the domestic economy and its subnational dimensions, the $\underline{M}$ region begins with several advantages over the $\underline{H}$ region. In the first place, it enjoys a scale of local final demand that permits realization of substantial internal scale economies in the production of many directly productive goods and services. Second, enterprises in the $\underline{M}$ region have access to highly specialized input markets and market institutions; the labor market offers a concentration of skills

168

and industrial experience not approached in any other place in the country; the major financial institutions in the country are to be found there; and the stock of public infrastructure supports a highly differentiated array of public services. Finally producers located in the M region can exploit the dense network of linkages with other activities that characterizes modern sector activities. Hence, it can not only produce a much broader array of goods and services than the H region but also can produce those produced in common with the H region at a lower cost. As a corollary, where the differences in unit costs in the two regions exceed the transfer costs between them, the M region will tend to export such products to the H region.

Deconcentration policies would basically take the form of diverting capital investments to the H region in the form of public works, new factories, or migrations of highly trained labor. Many such policies have concentrated exclusively on public works, on the assumption that better public services in H will substantially eliminate the comparative advantages; almost everywhere they have been tried, they have dissipated large amounts of public capital. Attempts to improve H region's endowment of human capital have taken two forms: (1) special inducements to skilled, managerial, technical, and professional occupations to migrate from region M to region H and (2) establishment of educational and training establishments in region H to equip the local labor force with needed skills. The migration inducements can take the form of income supplements to compensate for the loss of the environmental public good of the metropolitan core. If these augmented incomes are borne by the producers, they must be reflected in the unit costs of the product and so augment the productivity differences between M and H regions. Where such costs are assumed by the government as a labor subsidy, they are ultimately borne at the cost of public services foregone by some groups somewhere. Net product is reduced, and capricious distributive effects are introduced.

The government might build and operate new factories in H region or might offer inducements to private entrepreneurs to invest in new factories in H region. In either event, the government will have to subsidize the new factories to compensate for the basic competitive advantages to the core region until the competitive gap closes. Because the opportunity cost of such funds is high, there is a limit to the total scale of the government's involvement in such reallocation of capital.

Another approach might be for the government to levy taxes on persons or enterprises in M region in accordance with the value of the external costs they impose on others. Congestion and effluent charges might radically redress the cost pictures of various classes of enterprise in the metropolitan region—indeed, perhaps so much as to close the competitive gap between the two regions. If this were combined with a carefully organized development of infrastructure and a human capital program, some metropolitan core industries might find hinterland locations increasingly attractive, especially industries now exporters from region M to region H who could become import substitutes in region H. The second-order consequences of such a policy would be some reduction in social costs in the metropolitan city, inducing some expansion (or even migration from H to M) of activities whose profitability is sensitive to these costs. It is not obvious how these effects would be reflected in relative M and H growth rates, but intuitively it suggests a relative deconcentration of "heavy" industry and an accelerated concentration of the so-called quaternary services.

In general, it seems that careless deconcentration policies could have a negative effect on the country's foreign trade position in those special cases in which core region export manufacturers play, actually or potentially, an important role in the country's foreign trade. In the case of domestic commerce, conventional regional development programs may result in large-scale and continuing claims on the public purse without effectively redressing the productive balance between regions M and H. A comprehensive program of compensatory taxation on congestion and pollution, working together with a strategic program of capital investment in H aimed at inducing metropolitan exporters to H to relocate in H, could result in a more effective interregional allocation of resources.

It should be kept in mind, of course, that, as economic development progresses, the competitive positions of M and H are subject to an orderly evolution of sorts, in the absence of policy intervention. The case for net diseconomies of urban scale seems to be very strong beyond a certain city size, which is only to say that the unique net advantages to firms of locations in metropolitan regions should decline with further growth and reach zero at some point further up the scale. The position of these points will vary from industry to industry, of course, but the principle would seem to apply aggregatively, also. The point is that, if M is large enough, continuing growth will reduce its inherent cost advantage over region H. At the same time, if H is small enough, its growth will reduce its cost disadvantage independently. Thus, it appears that growth in both regions will tend to close the gap, permitting an increasing diffusion of capital in all forms from M to H.

In general, then, deconcentration policies will not harm and may serve national welfare objectives where they involve the transfer from the metropolitan core region to the hinterland of enterprises whose direct requirements for highly differentiated public and human capital are limited and that would find it profitable to move, if they were to be not only taxed for the value of public services directly consumed but also assessed for the direct social costs created in the form of congestion and environmental degradation.

It is possible, of course, to shift an enterprise to the hinterland in such a way as directly to improve measures of hinterland income distribution without directly impairing those in the metropolitan region, if such an enterprise generates incomes that are relatively low in metropolitan terms but relatively high in hinterland terms. But note that this special case might have a neutral effect on national distribution measures or even a negative effect, and these conclusions omit consideration of induced or multiplier effects on the regional economies.

Hence, it is clear that no prima facie case can be made for the benevolent income distribution impacts of deconcentration policies. It is not beyond reason that such policies could exacerbate the maldistribution of income in a country measured in terms of the national frequency distribution of incomes while reducing interregional disparities in per capita income. Until we have better knowledge about income impacts on regional economies or interregional shifts in economic activity, each case will have to be separately evaluated. This evaluation might proceed by taking the regional frequency distributions of incomes as dependent variables that are functions of eight variables and then proceed by examining the impacts of the proposed shifts on each variable for each region. As a final step, changes in national income distribution would be appraised.

Clearly objections can be made to these procedures for appraising income distribution impacts of deconcentration, and we concede their difficulty. But the policy questions are vitally important for the development objectives of these countries, and conventional wisdom provides no unambiguous guidelines. Beyond the extravagances of trial and error, then, such an analytical approach would seem to be unavoidable.

In conclusion, the economic logic of subnational development does not by itself inform us very well about the extent to which the national objectives can be advanced by public policies addressed to altering the settlement patterns of developing countries. Great harm is clearly possible, but this does not preclude the prospects of a carefully defined program of deconcentration making a substantial contribution to the achievement of the development objectives, not only of the nation as a whole but also of the individual regions. Such a program can begin as a carefully formulated set of hypotheses to be tested as empirically as possible before becoming key elements in national plans and programs. Indeed, such a process of hypothesis-making, testing against reality, and embodiment in policy is the essence of planning. It is indispensable in the formulation of national internal development policies that seek feasible settlement patterns to advance national goals. The key hypothesis here, we believe, is that the growth of metropolitan regions and the economic development of hinterland regions can be made complementary aspects of national development.

A STRONG STAND FOR DECENTRALIZATION

RANAAN WEITZ took a different viewpoint, which he presented in his opening lecture on "Rural-Urban Relations in Developing Countries." His is a strong and unequivocal case for urban decentralization as the most suitable policy for most or even all of the developing countries.

. . . The rapid growth in the size of cities and the number of city dwellers began with the industrialization of Western Europe. The transfer of workers from agriculture to industry and services was accompanied by a movement of population from village to town. Occupational mobility, which was the outcome of more efficient methods of production in all three economic sectors, was directly linked to geographical mobility.

The connection between economic development and the growth of cities in the Western world was not accidental. The continued existence of an urban population is primarily dependent on a regular supply of food. As long as agriculture was based on subsistence farming, there were limits to the possibility of any growth in the urban population. Moreover, transport facilities were such that towns could rely only on their immediate surroundings as a source of agricultural produce. It was only when scientific and technological progress led to improvements in agricultural efficiency, the development of a supporting structure, and the extension of commerce and industry that the way was clear for the growth of urban centers. The acceleration of this process, which took place during the last three decades, led to the formation of giant cities stretching over increasingly large areas and encroaching upon rural districts. Such giant cities rely upon the largest hinterland possible, in fact, one can say that the whole world is their hinterland.

The fact that urbanization in the developed countries has culminated in the current development of giant cities has led many planners and policy-makers in the developing countries to the conclusion that such a trend is not only inevitable but desirable. Development policy should, therefore, aim from the start at the creation of large cities. This approach—which is sometimes declared openly and sometimes just assumed—has been supported by many scholarly arguments trying to prove that large cities have a number of special advantages that speed up the process of development.

Economically the advantages attributed to the large city include agglomeration and external economies, especially the existence of a well-developed supporting structure, an expensive labor market with a larger number of skilled workers, and a high concentration of consumers. All these factors afford enterprises in the large cities a measure of efficiency not to be found in smaller settlements. Underlying this assumption is the belief, conscious or unconscious, that agriculture cannot play any significant role in the process of development and that stress must be placed mainly on industrialization.

Socially, the city is seen as the catalyst in the process of modernization and social change. The assumption is that the larger the urban population, the greater the impact on the process of modernization, since more and more people will come within its sphere of influence. Among other arguments in favor of large cities is that, in a large concentration of population, it is possible to supply a better quality of services at a lower cost.

In addition to this consideration, there is, undoubtedly, a further motive behind the desire of the local leadership to encourage large cities—the desire to show that the country is on the road to progress and development. To the underdeveloped countries, the large urban complexes, which in the wealthy countries are the centers of industry and services on a high level, serve as a symbol of progress and efficiency. Therefore, relatively substantial means were and still are invested in the largest cities.

Is a policy designed to encourage such an approach desirable? Does it meet the needs to today's developing countries? This question has recently been asked in many countries. It seems indisputable that the tendency toward greater concentration of population creates problems as yet unsolved in the developed societies and much more so in the underdeveloped societies, while in no way providing an answer to the basic problems of development that face the developing countries at the moment or in the foreseeable future. Some of the harmful results of these trends are pretty well evident: congestion resulting from overloaded transportation, pollution of air and water, and increase in the average and marginal per capita cost of providing public services. The disastrous growth and spread of blight areas known as mushroom cities—barriadas, favelas, gecekondu, and so on—areas where the implications are not merely physical but also deeply cultural, economic, and political, leading to the phenomena of "primacy" and "dualism," and so on.

The various forms of malaise that have come to the fore in rich countries have an even deeper impact on traditional societies. Many assumptions that were accepted as gospel only a decade ago prove to be quite different in reality. Thus, rapid concentrated urbanization neither reduced the gap between town and country nor brought more

173

and more people within the sphere of influence of the town. The rate of population growth in most developing countries is so high that, in spite of the increased migration to the towns, the rural population is still growing, while a considerable percentage of the migrants who reach the towns do not improve their standards of living and merely exchange rural poverty for urban subsistence living.

However, the basic disadvantage of an unbalanced urban structure lies in the inability of a distant town to supply agricultural, rural districts with the services required to rescue them from stagnation and start them on the way to economic growth.

In addition, the deeply penetrating changes within the social structure and traditional system of values is breeding an upheaval that will not bring the desired progress and anticipated development in its wake.

THE NEED FOR RURAL TOWNS

The developing countries neither can nor should copy the territorial pattern of population distribution usual in the developed countries today. Such a pattern is not appropriate to their require-ments for economic development. Even in the developed countries, doubts have arisen about its suitability for the needs of society. A different approach is needed for urban-rural relationships that can lead to the creation of a spatial structure unlike the one developed in the advanced countries. The structure needed should be appropriate to the conditions prevailing in the developing countries today while, at the same time, being capable of accelerating the process of develop-ment, especially in its first critical stages.

There are three major aspects to the process of development that impinge directly on the individual: employment, services, and social relationships. For all three aspects, a model of spatial distribution based on large urban concentrations provides no answer to the fundamental problems of the developing countries. The question is whether or not it is possible to create a model of population distri-bution that can help speed up the progress of development in the conditions prevailing today in developing countries.

At the onset of urbanization in the developed countries, the increased concentration of population was essential for technological and organizational reasons. Occupation mobility was, therefore, linked to geographical mobility and led to mass migration from the rural areas to the big cities. The city was the focus of economic expansion and social change. Today, there are technological and organizational potentials that facilitate a division—at least to some extent—between occupational and physical mobility.

174

The possibility of transporting energy over large distances at relatively low costs, the existence of many kinds of industry that do not require locales with special conditions—that is, conditions that can be found only in big cities—and new methods of infrastructure-building that are relatively quick and cheap are essential. Therefore, as to technological and organization facilities, there is nothing today to prevent the concentration of urbanization process in comparatively small towns widely distributed throughout the country.

Urban decentralization is not merely possible. For the developing countries, it is essential. In order to speed up the process of development, a system of rural towns based on a hierarchy of functions is needed. Without such a system, it becomes almost impossible to set up the industrial structure necessary for the development of agriculture, which, in turn, can accelerate national development. The rural towns are necessary in order to fulfill three main functions of the development process in the developing countries.

First, they provide the basis for activating the supporting system. Creating a supporting system that can actually support the development process in the rural areas involves more than just creating something that never existed before. Its function is to provide active support in the transition from a farm with a closed economic structure to a farm beginning to produce increasingly large amounts of various kinds of produce for the market.

Before such a new framework can be activated and developed, there is a need for professional workers and entrepreneurs such as teachers, doctors, engineers, technologists, planners, agricultural instructors, and so on. Such people are not prepared to live in the village, and there is no need for them to do so, since normally they will serve the population of a number of villages. They require an urban center where they can live and find acceptable services and amenities.

Second, rural towns can serve as an appropriate location for the development of industries that must be dispersed in the rural regions. Agriculture cannot grow alone; concomitant development of industry is essential not only for the growth of the national economy but also for the advancement of agriculture itself. The nonagricultural sector must be able to absorb both surplus manpower no longer needed in agriculture and the increased output resulting from more efficient agricultural production. At the same time, it must be able to provide the agricultural sector with the goods and services vital to its development.

Because of size and character, less capital-intensive industries do not have to be located in the big cities. On the contrary, a considerable proportion of them can be dispersed throughout the rural areas and centered in rural towns. In this way, they can contribute to the development of the interrelations between agriculture and industry without necessitating large-scale investment in a ramified system of basic facilities between the large urban centers and the agricultural hinterlands. The establishment of industrial enterprises along with the introduction of improvements in agricultural production is likely, therefore, to close the economic cycle, which is vital for the process of development as a whole in the conditions prevailing in the developing countries.

The closing of the cycle that joins industry and agriculture in the early stages of the development process can, therefore, be made a practical possibility if appropriate industrial enterprises are dispersed throughout the rural areas. This involves locating relatively small factories with a suitable technological level in small urban centers scattered throughout the country. At the same time, it is clear that not every industry is suitable for the rural districts, and the feasibility of different types of industry must be carefully examined in the light of the special conditions of each separate region.

Rural towns, therefore, are essential for such linked development between industry and agriculture. Here agriculture and other ancillary industries can be concentrated; here surplus manpower can be absorbed as it is gradually released by improved agriculture.

Third, rural towns can bring urban culture to the countryside and hasten the process of modernization. The proximity of the town provides the farmer with both an incentive for change and a source of greater prospects. He can find there a market for his produce, better services, and an alternative source of nearby employment if he should wish to leave agricultural work. Those who leave their farms are able to maintain contact with their home villages since the distance between town and country is not great. If they wish, they can even continue to live in the village and work in the town.

So far, we have discussed rural towns without reference to size. For such a town to be viable and to fulfill the functions required of it, it must be large enough to maintain an effective level of services. It is difficult to determine an optimal size, for this changes from place to place and from time to time. We still lack adequate criteria for judgment. Some think that the ideal is around 100,000 inhabitants; others fix the minimum size at a much lower level. In his study of development towns in Israel, Berler concluded that the minimum size varies with the standard of living and the standard of expectations of the population. According to his estimate, the size was around 10,000 in 1950 and rose gradually to 25,000 by 1968. Notwithstanding all the studies carried out recently about the urbanization process and the relationship between size of towns and their functions, this question still remains open. The question can be formulated thus: What is, in fact, the take-off point of a town with regard to its size?

It may be assumed that the minimum size required for the effective functioning of the town is too large to guarantee that all the villages coming within its sphere of influence will have satisfactory services at a reasonable distance. There is a conflict between the requirements of a supporting system whose lowest echelons must be within a convenient distance from the villages and this requirement, which will determine the efficient functioning of the town itself, including provision for the satisfaction of those who keep the supporting system working. As a matter of fact, this is the point we have called above the "take-off point" of a rural town.

From the point of view of the supporting system, smaller towns serving smaller areas are preferable, whereas the economic and social considerations of an efficient operation tend to push toward larger and more widely spaced cities. Can this gap be bridged in a way that will satisfy all demands?

The gap can be bridged by means of the "quiet centers" that serve as intermediary foci of the activities between the village on the one hand and the medium-size town on the other.

THE CONCEPT OF THE "QUIET CENTER"

What is a "quiet center"? This is a physical unit containing only industrial and service installations without living quarters. The "quiet center" is the rural "business district." Workers are there only during working hours, and leave after work to lead their lives elsewhere.

The concept of the "quiet center" grew out of the patterns of regional cooperation in Israel. In the course of development, both the settlers themselves and the planners realized that the individual village could no longer operate various services and economic activities on its own. Groups of settlements pooled their resources and set up the joint enterprises and institutions on a much larger scale than they had managed by themselves. In this way, they reduced the running costs of the enterprises and facilitated the introduction of technological innovations and the mobilization of highly skilled labor. All the service facilities owned by one group of settlements are usually located at a single point in order to reduce the cost of maintenance and to facilitate their use by the surrounding communities. The people who operate those services, however, are mostly resident in the villages. This is so because most "quiet centers" in Israel are established at a later stage of development, when the villages already have surplus manpower released from agriculture and the cultural gap between farmer and professional is no longer significant.

In Israel, this trend resulted in the hierarchy of "quiet centers" ranging from a small center serving a few villages to a large regional enterprise supported by over 200 villages. All these centers have a common purpose. They all function as centers for services and industries for groups of rural communities, and they are all owned by these communities and managed by their representatives.

At first, only the small centers were established and were known as "rural service centers." They provided civic and economic services for a population of several hundred families. With the development of agriculture and the transition from mixed to specialized farming, these centers no longer met the needs of the settlements, and an interesting development occurred whereby the centers were functionally divided into the following classifications:

1. Village-Group Center: providing farming and social services to from four to eight settlements, mostly moshavim;

2. Regional Center: designed to serve 10 to 20 settlements, providing regional services and sometimes social and cultural institutions;

3. Interregional Center: includes enterprises designed to serve 25 to 50 settlements;

4. Area Center: in which are concentrated all the large enterprises that are owned jointly by regional bodies and their respective settlements. These enterprises are almost entirely of an industrial character.

This experience demonstrates that under suitable conditions it is possible to generate a continuous and dynamic territorial adjustment to technological and scientific changes and innovations in agricultural production and living standards. This development has been made possible thanks to a completely new creation in open space: the "quiet center." Thus, the "quiet center," or rather the hierarchy of "quiet centers," was used in Israel as a tool to divorce occupational mobility from geographical mobility completely.

The idea of the "quiet center" is fundamentally a simple one that can be used whenever it is necessary to bridge the gap between requirements for efficient urban functioning and the need for agricultural development. The supporting pillars of this bridge are the "quiet centers."

As the whole town grows in size in the course of development, it is the "quiet center" that bridges the gap between town and villages. On the one hand, it provides a place for those activities that can be located in rural areas, and, on the other, it helps check the exodus of people from rural areas. From the point of view of rural-urban relationships, the advantages of the "quiet centers" lie in their ability gradually to absorb certain enterprises that do not necessarily require the scale provided by the big cities.

In conclusion, it must be stressed that the prevailing strategy of development regarding the problems of rural/urban relations must take a new turn. Emphasis should be shifted from the big towns to a network of small towns or so-called rural towns. The rural towns must be given economic, organizational, and political support in order to become the focus for an over-all national development effort. By becoming so, they will serve as a basis and a lever for the creation of the much-needed supporting system on the one hand and for the dispersal of industrialization on the other. The rural town can, thus, become a viable entity, from the viewpoint of size, functions, and locations, because of the network of "quiet centers" that will link rural towns with the surrounding villages, and, so, a new set of relations can be established between the rural and urban spaces, which will provide practical solutions to the most pressing problems besetting the developing countries today.

AN UNDECIDED ISSUE

The issue of the strategy of urban development as reflected in the question of concentrated patterns or a centralized urbanization process was extensively and hotly debated at the Conference, both in the plenary session and in various study groups. The sum of all the debates is that this issue was left undecided. WILLIAM ALONSO referred to the problem in the following words:

. . . The main approach to the spread of development in most of the world seems to be to have growth centers or growth poles. The Israelis and some of the others have emphasized dispersion of industry in the countryside, and I think the scale of this nation has something to do with that. Most other discussions seem to indicate concentrated decentralization (to decentralize from the big place you have to centralize in smaller places), and, of these, in the modern industrial growth sector, there are two extreme models, which, with apologies to the two nations, I might characterize as the Indian model and the Italian model.

The Indian model tried to achieve decentralization by providing the means for small industries to go to small places. This was done through industrial estates, village development, and so forth, and it was not a success. In spite of electricity and the fact that people can pedal their bicycles from the villages to these industries, it has at best been a very qualified success for decentralization, and it appears to me that this is because small industries are very open systems. They need a lot of support, a lot of flexibility; they must be set in a rich matrix, and, when you pull them out of the big city, that matrix is lacking, and therefore, they are not as adaptable and not as capable of surviving.

The other extreme has been the Italian one, which led off with a big industry in a small place. They claimed that, because a big industry is very powerful, with its own accountants, lawyers, technicians, and so on, it does not need the supporting environment, so they put steel, petrochemicals, and so on in rural places.

This did not induce development either, for the opposite reasons. These big industries can go out precisely because they do not need the environment, with the result that they have very little influence on the new environment either. They do not need other people; therefore, they do not, or at any rate, they have not, induced development.

Professor Mills said that he found no great relation between primacy and development. Professor Brian Berry made a similar finding many years ago. Today, he points out that, in a dynamic sense, perhaps this is not so. There are all kinds of unusual countries: countries that have two capitals, countries that are partitioned, and so forth. I have myself been working with some Latin American data of a different sort, basically taking the average distance of the total population to the capital over the last 40 years. I find that in all South American countries the average distance of the population to the capital is decreasing. In other words, the population is still moving toward the center.

JOHN FRIEDMANN looked at this matter from a different angle:

. . . It might sound cynical if I were to say that a nation gets the cities it deserves, or a nation gets the regions it deserves, so I am not at all sure that these particular spatial forms are in fact exportable without a prior change in social and economic organization. The physical patterns themselves are not exportable. Professor Canaux's cellular city implies a cellular social structure. Dr. Weitz's quiet centers imply a cooperative social structure. If these can be brought into being, it is quite possible that the physical form that the society will be contained in will take this particular shape or some analogous shape.

I am reminded of the new British towns, or the new Israeli towns. There is now a great deal of discussion in the United States about new towns. But, in actual practice, what is called a new town in the United States turns out to be a suburban subdivision 9 times out of 10, and this is not because of some conniving scheme of the developers but simply because land in the United States is a commodity to be bought and sold on the market. It is not land held in communal or collective ownership. This is one of the reasons, perhaps the basic reason, why new towns take a different form and shape in the United States.

With reference to Dr. Weitz's paper, I think that, in addition to the structural argument, there is also a strategy argument that must be made explicit. I think, and I think this was pointed out by Dr. Mendez, that implicit in Dr. Weitz's paper is a strategy of agrarian development as the key strategy for national development. This may, in fact, be a sound strategy; I am not here either to defend or attack it, but it certainly is a clear-cut alternative to industrial strategy, which leads to quite different conclusions, such as an emphasis on road tolls for example.

Friedmann went on to discuss relations between city core and periphery:

. . . I would like to present the city size criterion: a colonial model of urbanization, or what some of my colleagues know as the corporatory model.

We begin with one, two, or three dominant cities, which are closely interconnected with each other in a functional way, and we call this the core area. Surrounding this is a peripheral area, which is dominated by the core. The periphery is dependent on the core because the intensive development at the core needs peripheral resources for its sustained growth. Core and periphery equal an economic system in its special dimensions. It is, therefore, the relevant unit for observation.

From this basic model, we can draw three consequences for development policy, all of which are based on the idea of specialization and trade between core and periphery. In the first case, we shall assume free movement of labor from periphery to core, in which case we get intensive development at the core, extensive development at the periphery, and relatively high levels of living in the periphery.

If labor does not move freely from periphery to core, though, as is true in the international situation across country boundaries (and to a certain extent even within a country where there is some slowness of population movement), then we still get extensive development in the periphery, intensive development in the core, but more people in the periphery and, therefore, a lower level of living.

The third possibility is to create centers of intensive development in the periphery itself—to take a portion of the core and move it out. These centers of development have to be capital, skill, and communications, intensive and innovative. In the course of time, these various cores will become interrelated with each other and form a larger economic system. I believe this is the real issue before us of regional and urban development.

181

Some voiced quite definite views about the issue under discussion and did not leave it open as did the former two participants
Thus, for instance, ATO BEKELE HAILE voiced his firm opinions
on the centralization of the urbanization process in the big cities
and on federating smaller cities with bigger cities for the benefit
of all.

. . . My idea is that the developing countries would benefit more
if they were to create a federation of towns, in order to coordinate
their energies and resources for the interregional development of
the space. It has been mentioned that we have mushrooming towns;
we would have to coordinate these and see that these towns also take
the environment into consideration. The only way to do this is to
control the intratown spaces by federating the small towns with the
major town of a region or province. This is one scheme. The other
scheme would be to see that the central government participates more
vigorously, and I think much is being done along these lines in Kenya.
This should take the form of expertise and regional planning, subsidie
control, and supervision. This is how we can develop realistically
and not play with the myth of democracy by leaving the community
of each town to decide its own fate by itself, because it is only part
of the whole nation and not an entity in itself.

Some were inclined to accept the general proposal for
decentralization but differed both from those who would like to
see it carried out simultaneously with the development of larger
cities and from those who would like to see the emphasis shifted
from the bigger to the smaller cities as a major turning point in
development policy in general and in urbanization policy in particular, for the developing countries. The following are examples
of such views.

Dr. BRUTZKUS formulated his opinion in the following words

. . . I believe that the crucial point in the whole question of a
more decentralized pattern of towns is the spread effect; the trickling
down never occurs automatically. Even if it is justified by economy,
there are always some social, psychological, or political factors that
prevent it. Countries like Uruguay or Argentina, for instance, are
no more developing than developed countries, with a population of
60,000 in one metropolitan area in Uruguay.
If the decentralization pattern is to be goal, then a very early,
very strict, and very consistent policy is necessary. I agree with
Dr. Weitz that that is not all, but it is the first and most important
prerequisite. This was to a certain degree the case in Israel,

implemented under very specific conditions, not always applicable; but there was a very early, very strict policy, based on a plan that was not well coordinated and not well implemented, but it was based on a very definite policy.

A comment written by EDMUNDO FLORES also dealt with this subject.

. . . Decentralization does not mean that industry is going to stop operating in the large towns and move to the periphery. Such an absurd move would increase unemployment and aggravate the remaining urban problems. Industrial decentralization means the process by which certain types of industry, which are noxious and produce contamination, are relocated far from urban concentrations and new labor-intensive activities are created in the city in order to absorb the natural increase of the work force and the unemployed. In other words, decentralization implies a selective relocation of activities as well as an increase in the rate of creating new sources of work. Changes in industry, services, housing, and population are the critical variables, on which the progress of a city, its development or decadence, depends, and eliminating industry in all the cities is out of the question.

JOSE BENJAMIN SOKOL voiced a stronger view in favor of centralization policy and strategical outlook as expressed by Dr. Weitz.

. . . I would like to make some brief comments on Dr. Weitz's paper. I found it stimulating, very pragmatic, and realistic in the framework of developing countries, especially in the area of Latin America. I think Dr. Weitz's regional development within an agro-industry base is quite sound within the context of Latin American development, and it could lead to halting migration from the rural to the urban areas.
As Dr. Weitz also said, I think each country should have its own special kind of aspirin to solve its own headaches, and not import solutions from countries with populations of 200 or 300 million.
Nevertheless, there are some points I would like to raise within the general framework of regional economic development. Regional economic development should be looked at from the context of the general economic policy of the country; in a country like Israel with an open type of economy and which trades with the rest of the world, it is possible to develop this agroindustry base within the quiet center, as Dr. Weitz has shown. But, in developing countries where some very protectionistic types of policy have been pursued in the

last two decades, a number of problems arise in developing this type of regional planning.

Because of the differences in cost conditions between countries and due to the size of markets, there is the problem of developing industries for exports. This imposes a considerable constraint in the development of this type of regional operation.

There is also an assumption that there is a homogenous type of population in each town, small town, or area in the market economy. In the developing countries there are rural populations largely out of the market economy, and an attempt is being made to incorporate them in large areas, in order to give them certain opportunities. This leads to a third point. In a developing country there are a lot of restraints, for budgets are very limited and insufficient resources are available for the services and infrastructure required for the development of these small towns.

A CASE STUDY

A case study being carried out on the problem discussed in this chapter was presented by ARIE SHACHAR; it concerned the policy of population dispersal in Israel and the effects of this policy on the urbanization trend and the development process. The following is the essence of the case study:

. . . In evaluating the goals of the national spatial policy, one phenomenon emerges that has far-reaching implications: the "dispersal-of-population" policy, which was formulated in order to achieve various national goals (occupation of empty areas, resources utilization, regional integration, and rank-size structure), had evolved over the years to become the prime national goal, in a spatial context. The pursuit of the dispersal-of-population policy was a persistent one and was firmly backed by all agencies concerned, even though it became evident that the achievements of some of the original goals were not proceeding satisfactorily. The transformation of the dispersal-of-population policy into a national goal in itself is the result of deep commitment of the central authorities to the idea of the development towns and their existing spatial distribution. Large-scale changes and modifications in the dispersal-of-population policy during its initial implementation stages would have meant disaster—a massive relocation for the inhabitants of the development towns. The outcome of this phenomenon is that, once a spatial configuration of national urbanization policy has been established, it is very difficult to change the basic dimensions of that spatial configuration.

The extent to which the objective of the dispersal of population has been achieved can be measured accurately by applying geo-statistical techniques for measuring point distributions. In order to evaluate the spatial results of the dispersal-of-population policy, the "standard distance" of the total population was computed for each year during the period 1948-67. The results show a continuous growth of the standard distance from year to year, beginning at 45.0 kilometers in 1948 and reaching 54.2 kilometers in 1967. The standard distance of the population of the development towns grew at a much larger rate, beginning at 35.8 kilometers in 1950 and reaching 82.4 kilometers in 1967. The standard distance measures prove, without any doubt, that the objective of the dispersal of population has been achieved, and it is remarkable how the empty areas in the northern and southern periphery of the country were gradually populated over the last 20 years. As most of the new towns are located in the southern and northern districts, it could be stated that they were mostly responsible for the success of the dispersal policy. Of the 470,000 people living in new towns at the end of 1967, 217,000 were located in the southern district, while 136,000 were located in the northern district, thus forming a more dispersed spatial pattern.

It is important to find out how the dispersal policy affected the demographic dominance of the Tel Aviv metropolitan area.

Percentage of Total Jewish Population

Year	Tel Aviv District	Northern District	Southern District
1948	42.1	7.4	0.8
1967	34.1	10.1	11.2

The table shows a considerable drop in the relative share of the Tel Aviv district as a result of the relative growth of the northern and southern districts. It seems that the dispersal policy succeeded in limiting and scaling down the relative demographic dominance of the primate city, while increasing the relative demographic share of the peripheral regions.

The dispersal of population was much more successful in the southern region than in the northern one. The new towns of the southern region were growing much faster than those of the north. The result of this growth pattern was a gradual spatial shift of the Israeli population toward the south. This southern shift is represented by the gradual southward movement of the mean center of the total population. The importance of the new towns in this southward movement is shown by the much larger displacement of the mean centers of the new towns, compared to the centers of the total population. Combining the results of the geostatistical analysis of the standard distances and mean centers, we come to the conclusion that the new towns were the main agent in carrying out the considerable changes in the spatial configuration of the population, which were the result of the national urbanization policy.

As the dispersal-of-population policy was formulated in order to accomplish the several national goals of a spatial nature, it is important to proceed in the evaluation, by analyzing the degree to which these goals have been achieved.

The goals that are of highest importance to the spatial integration of society are (1) the change from a primacy structure to a rank-size structure, and (2) the building of a complete urban hierarchy to enhance regional integration. Actually, these two goals might be achieved through the same type of urbanization policy, namely, establishing the missing levels of the urban hierarchy and limiting the growth of the primate city.

Plotting the city-size distribution on log-normal paper for various years along the urban development process enables one to evaluate the changes of the city-size structure. This figure depicts the changes of city-size distributions during the last 40 years. It is evident that the urban system has changed from a primacy situation (1931-44) through an intermediate (1953-59) to a full rank-size (1967). Following Berry's developmental model, we can trace the particular path through which the city-size distributions have changed. We come to the conclusion that the goal of changing the city-size structure of the urban system has been fully achieved. Assuming that reaching the rank-size distribution was an outcome of establishing a complete urban hierarchy and of the increasing complexity of the economy, it is open for further investigation as to whether the change in the city-size distribution should be regarded as a goal per se, in a normative way, or whether it might be regarded as a result of a primary urbanization process like the development of urban hierarchies.

A higher level of services would have had some effect in decreasing the very high rates of out-migration that were plaguing most of the new towns. Cities of larger size, with a wide and diversified economic base and a more stable population, would be instrumental in diminishing existing inequalities between the new towns and the core area in income, social access, employment opportunities, and the level of amenities and services. Very many of the arguments for a concentrated effort in a "growth centers" policy are applicable in this discussion of the desired parameters for the planned urban system and the future spatial organization of Israeli society.

The final argument for some modification in the present urbanization policy in favor of fewer new towns, each of a larger size, will be the following: The national urbanization policy did achieve most of the national goals. Through the development towns program, an extensive urban periphery was created, with most of the characteristics of peripheral areas, mainly the dependency relationships with the national core. Overcoming the inherent deficiencies of a dependency situation requires a concrete and sustained effort to develop the periphery in economic, social, and political terms. This enables us to define clearly the national goal for the new urbanization policy in the coming years: to incorporate the periphery within the core, thus achieving complete spatial integration of the country.

Although the official Israeli policy was for dispersal and undoubtedly gave great impetus to national development on the one hand and helped to cement goals and objectives on the other it also made way for many problems that still have to be solved.

CONCLUSIONS

The treatment and debates on the fundamental question of concentration versus deconcentration of the urbanization process were not concluded in any clear-cut way. When we sum up the papers and discussions at the Conference on this basic issue, two points emerge quite clearly. First, the matter is of vital importance to the developing countries and has a bearing on most issues dealing with the development process strategy and the development and formulation of policies of implementation; there was unanimity on this issue among the participants, both scholars and policy-makers. Second, our state of knowledge and proof of analysis is still insufficient for clear-cut decisions on the subject.

Doubts about the adequacy of the tools of analogy and criteria of success for dealing with this issue were expressed by EDWIN J. MILLS when analyzing the case study presented by Shachar.

. . . I want to offer a brief protest against Professor Shachar's criterion of success as regards the policy of population dispersal in Israel. What we have been told is that a policy of population dispersal adopted by the central government of 1948 has, in fact, been executed in the succeeding 20 or so years. That can hardly be surprising where the central government has complete control over land use and housing policy. If the central government decides it is going to disperse population, it may be assumed that it is going to disperse population, for it holds these two powerful instruments of control over where people live and work.

However, this is not the relevant criterion in the sense of policy. The economic success or failure of a policy of population dispersal has to do with the gain or loss of welfare of the people as the result of population dispersal. For example, we are told that some services were not as easily available to the people in the dispersed population as they were in the larger cities, say, Tel Aviv or possibly Jerusalem. That entails a loss to the population that can be measured.

There is a loss of consumer surplus because of the fact that no one could consume as much of the service as they would have, had they resided in the Tel Aviv area; or there is an increase in transportation cost because they must come to Tel Aviv in order to obtain the service.

Similar effects can also be measured in other aspects of decentralization policy: for example, whether plants that are located in dispersed areas incur higher or lower transportation costs with their inputs and outputs than they would have had they been located in the Tel Aviv area. We can also find out with a little imagination and calculation how much more or less infrastructure has had to be built in the dispersed areas than would have had to be built had the population been concentrated in the larger cities. I submit that it is only when we make these calculations that we know what the economic costs or benefits of such a dispersal policy are. It may well be that, even though the economic costs, as I suspect, are substantial, the policy was nevertheless a success.

It may be that military or other benefits of dispersal justify the economic cost, but I do not see how the people of Israel can make up their minds whether it was worthwhile unless they know what the economic costs or benefits were.

What Mills said about the case study of Israel is probably true for the case studies of most developing countries.

Thus, one of the major issues of the Conference has remained open, and the attention of scholars, professionals, and policy-makers should be drawn to this subject. Emphasis should be placed on further study of the strategy of urbanization with regard to the dispersal of population in space and the more specific issue of concentrated versus deconcentrated urban centers.

9

ELEMENTS OF
URBAN PLANNING

As the process of urbanization proceeds uncontrolled, planning for urbanization is a must, recognized by all concerned, and, as <u>DAVID AMIRAN</u> put it,

. . . We have to realize that urbanization is upon us, it is here to stay, and it will probably have even greater impact in the future on the way in which we live. Great advances in medical science have increased the numbers of people, and great advances in agricultural technology have greatly decreased the number of people required to produce the food for these increasing populations. Taking these two factors together, we have no other choice but to agree that there will be more and more people in towns and cities and more and more people in large cities.

This being so, I think the only course of action left to us as thinking human beings is to plan for this type of pattern of life, of increasingly deruralized populations, of an increasing percentage of humanity living in large towns.

The need for planning was further elaborated by <u>S. ECKSTEIN</u>.

. . . The moment we are not satisfied with the market mechanisms, we start planning and programing. I think we must agree that the two are in a sense contradictory because, if we could rely on the market mechanism, there would be no need for planning. Let the markets take care of themselves. The moment we have to plan, it means that we have to do something that the market mechanism by itself cannot do. We talk about all kinds of inducement, tax inducements, but we know that in the countries with which we are dealing, all these things are completely ineffective.

What we really need is to attain a radical change in the power structure, and, after we have changed the power structure, either we arrive at a completely centralized system, in which I do not believe, or, if we still want to work with the market mechanism, we have to do something about the motivational structure, with motivations that people will accept in order to adjust to what we social and political planners have in mind.

Another problem is that our theory is simply inadequate to deal with these issues in a market system. Not that the solution of technical problems is not enough; taking social aspects into account, the use of these technical tools is simply inadequate.

YEHUDA TAMIR stressed planning and implementation.

. . . Plans that are not executed do not spell development; plans that are executed are development. We sometimes use planning as an excuse not to do things. We say that the plans are not ready, that we need better plans, that it takes two years to prepare a five-year plan, and then we have three years to execute it; but, important as planning is, it is only as important as the extent to which it serves the purpose of development. Planning is not an end in itself.

DEVELOPMENT PLANNING AND URBAN PLANNING

Comprehensive Planning. The comprehensive approach to development discussed in Chapter 7 also applies to the planning process, as LLOYD RODWIN put it in his address to the Conference.

. . . We are presumably dealing with the issue of urbanization in developing countries, and it is a most striking, novel thing that in countries throughout the world—not just the poorer or less prosperous developing countries—for the first time in the history of the world, a national policy for urban and regional development is emerging. The great task that confronts us is how to make this policy part of national development strategy, how to incorporate it as part of national economic and social policy, and how to devise the appropriate institutions to do this.

The fact is that hardly anywhere in the world today is this policy being carried out satisfactorily or in a manner that we can point to as a kind of model. It is an interesting and belated kind of phenomenon and, if one stops to think of it, the kind of phenomenon that one would expect to occur belatedly. That is to say, it is easier in most countries to deal with sector problems, to deal with the problem of housing, of agriculture, of industry, of infrastructure, than to tackle the very difficult problem of seeing the relationships between components. It is much easier to come to grips with the more isolated sectors, yet the great issue of our time is to see that dealing with these isolated sectors alone is bound to result in serious inadequacies in patterns and approaches to development.

Plans into Action. ALBERT WATERSTON contended that after development strategy is formulated, it should be translated into plans, programs, and projects that should all be related to the finances and real resources. Waterston went on,

. . . When you examine this, you will see that this logically structured approach is defensible only if each step in the procedure is rational in itself and is then rationally interrelated to the other step. First, you have a conceptual framework model that is internally consistent; second, you see if the variables in the model incorporated in the plan are critical ones for the social unit concerned in the municipality, rural area, nation, or region; third, you determine if the data on which the plan is based are reasonably accurate and complete; fourth, you see if the implicit assumptions in the plan concerning the environment in which the plan is to be implemented are correct; and, fifth, you see if the plan's objectives reflect the social needs.

I think that an examination of these elements, if we had planned in detail, would show that there are serious flaws in this approach. Consider the matter of internal consistency. Much of the time planners spend in planning is based on trying to attain internal consistency. Quite correctly, the planner admonishes us to avoid ad hoc hunches. Arthur Lewis said, as between the hunch and bad statistics, take the hunch and bad statistics. We put a heavy premium on internal consistency, and there is a great deal to be said for the value of internal consistency; not only does this relate to inputs and outputs, but it also reveals the interrelationships of factors affecting development.

I have examined a great many national plans and many of the master plans of urban communities, and I would say that on the whole only 5 percent of those plans are internally consistent, and that is a very high estimate. However, even when a reasonable level of internal consistency is achieved, the results are frequently of little practical value because they give us only partial answers to planning problems.

For example, one of the objectives of the plan is to increase the rate of growth as rapidly as possible. This may be interpreted, say, at 7 percent per annum. We take a strategy and continue. The argument is that, if you increase the size of the pie, you permit a greater amount of it to filter down to the lower levels. Is this true in fact? In the United States of America, for example, where the rate of growth has been very good, the census department of the government has announced that, to this very day, there are more than 25 million people who are living at a level below the minimum subsistence standard.

If the United States of America has not been able to do it, is it reasonable to expect even with planning that you can have it in the underdeveloped world? The evidence is all negative. Pakistan blew up when the rate of growth achieved was a record 8 percent per annum. I found that the rate of growth of one of many countries of Latin America, Colombia, was 7 percent per annum, a highly respectable rate. Yet, as I traveled through the country, I was appalled to see the poverty in the rural areas.

This is basically what causes people to move into the urban areas, although there are many other factors as well. I have come to the conclusion that we must face the fact that these objectives of increasing the size of the pie do not by themselves, even in the course of decades, lead to meeting the social needs to any appreciable extent. What are the social needs in Colombia? The statistics of unemployment show 13 percent, but I feel that they are vastly higher than that, and there is no evidence that that need is really being met.

How can we ask planners to ignore the social, political meaning of this? I on occasion go into many countries to try and deal with problems that I meet. I have found this approach ineffective. More recently, I have attempted to apply a different technique in the field. I said this type of planning is technique oriented; we have a kit of tools, we come in, and we try to use them, and, of course, to adjust them, we fail very often, but we try again and argue that if we repeat it long enough we shall succeed.

Another possibility is to approach the problem not as a technique-oriented problem but as a problem-oriented problem. What is the problem of a country? In one country I found that the problem was that you had to look at it as a problem, so I started with the social need, whatever that social need might be, unemployment and so on. I found what that need was. Then I went on to find out what there was in the way of resources to meet that social need, both local and otherwise. The second thing I did was to ask myself what I would have to do in the way of projects and policies. This I added up into a strategy; and then I end up with a target, finally generalized into an objective. Here I find—if I had time I would be happy to give you examples—that I really meet social needs. I direct my attention to that from the beginning, and the rate of growth is only secondary. Naturally, I try to maximize it, but my prime problem is to meet the social needs in accordance with the situation of the country.

This is said to be a problem of implementation. It is not. There is no implementation! If in the process of formulating a plan you take into account the problems that you are going to meet in implementation, there can be no divorce between plan formulation and plan implementation. If you are really interested in planning you always remember implementation. You never, never deal with any formulation of a plan without taking implementation into account.

The need for urban planning to be incorporated into a comprehensive national and regional plan embracing economic, social, and physical aspects was stressed at the Conference by many other participants.

DAVID PINES, in his paper, analyzed the concept of planning.

. . . Planning is rational decision-making regarding a set of sequential actions through time.

Short-term planning refers to actions to be carried out in the near future only. Long-term planning refers to planning in which some actions will be carried out at some point in the distant future.

Planning is required when two conditions hold: (1) the present satisfaction of the decision-maker depends on events that may occur in the future; and (2) events in any given period that are relevant to the decision-maker are affected by action carried out in the preceding periods.

It can be observed that, in the above definition, orientation to the future of the decision-making is emphasized rather than the interference in the automatic mechanism of the free market. Moreover, the above definition does not restrict the concept of planning to the community or to public decision-making.

The product of the planning process is the plan. It is composed of two parts: the program and its anticipated outcomes. The program is the operative part of the plan. It specifies the sequence of actions to be taken. The second component of the plan is forecasts of the outcomes resulting from the execution of the plan, which are relevant to the decision-maker.

The planning process is assumed to be rational decision-making. This means that alternative courses of action exist, from which one is selected according to some rational rules. In selecting a plan, it is verified that the plan is a priori feasible and at least not inferior to any alternative feasible plan.

A plan is defined as a priori feasible if the following conditions are met: (1) the actions (policy variables) included in the program are within the direct control of the decision-maker who is responsible for the plan; and (2) given some independent forecasts and the interrelationships that hold between actions, independent forecasts, and outcomes, the plan is consistent. By independent forecasts, I mean those forecasts that are assumed to be independent of the actions embodied in the program.

A plan is defined as inefficient if there is an alternative feasible plan that is better than the one in question regarding all the relevant outcomes.

The ultimate purpose of planning is to select the best feasible plan that can be elaborated within the means available to the planner. In this sense an optimization problem is inherent in any planning problem. This definition of the planning problem does not mean, however, that it is necessarily a mathematical programing problem in the strict sense. Often, only a few discrete alternative programs are considered, rather than the whole feasible set. (The reason may be the high cost of formulating alternative programs.) But an application of "cost-benefit analysis" to a finite number of discrete alternatives is also represented in the above formulation of the planning problems. In other words, "cost-benefit analysis" of a finite number of alternative programs is not a substitute for the "optimization approach" but rather a special application of this approach.

William Alonso, Leslie B. Ginsburg, and others mentioned the need for urban planning and regional planning as part of general development plans. As Ginsburg put it, "No true regional planning is possible unless it operates within the framework of a national plan. So far as planning for growth is concerned—whether it be population growth or economic growth—how far can one carry out growth development in one region without some compensating factors elsewhere?"

SPECIFIC CONDITIONS FOR PLANNING IN DEVELOPING COUNTRIES

There was complete agreement among participants at the Conference that conditions in the developing countries necessitate a different approach from development planning and urban planning in developed countries. Planners cannot copy the approach or the techniques and tools used in urban planning in the developed world. All these should be adjusted to the specific conditions of each developing country separately.

Past Trends of Development. NATHANIEL LICHFIELD, in his paper, examined the difference in the path of development of Western countries in the past and developing countries at present. He came to the conclusion that developing countries should not follow in the path of the developed, though the profile of growth in the developing countries somewhat resembles past growth in Western urbanized countries.

. . . Historical study shows that, although the rate of advancement of the socioeconomic indicators was not uniform, the profile of their growth in currently developing countries corresponds with those of developed countries. Thus, it suggests that the future path of developing countries might be forecast with some confidence in general if not on particular indicators.

As literature shows, however, there are compelling reasons for thinking that the correlation between economic growth and urbanization for developing countries in the future will not necessarily be the same as for developed countries in the past. For one thing, the indicators just mentioned show that, while there are clearly common underlying tendencies, the urbanization of developing countries is proceeding more rapidly than did developed countries in the past (national population growth is faster and also the rate of rural migration from the land) compared with improvements in the socioeconomic indicators; this divergence might have all kinds of explanations, including the possibility that many developing countries are overurbanizing for their stage of economic development.

Another reason is in the differing political climates of developed and developing countries during their developing stage. While in Europe economic change was the catalyst for political change, in developing countries since World War II, it is political developments— in particular, independence from colonial rule—that are themselves forcing social and economic changes.

Yet another reason, which is not unrelated for the greater relative political maturity of the developing countries, is that economic growth in the contemporary world is not regarded as narrowly as it was in the last century. There is greater consciousness today of the aims of more equal distribution of wealth and economic efficiency and also of the indirect costs of economic growth that are not shown in national income accounts and to overcome which a slowing in the rate of economic growth as so shown is desirable. Finally, there is the influence of planning in contemporary developing countries at the three levels that are of significance here (national, regional, and local), which was absent in the corresponding stages of growth in the developed countries.

Perhaps it is this last reason for divergence between the history of the developed countries and the future of the developing countries that is the most important. It is now possible for countries to attempt to shape their future in the social, economic, physical, and locational spheres. While experiments in this direction since World War II have shown the difficulties as much as the solutions, they nonetheless demonstrate sufficient achievement to inspire some confidence that, in the not too distant future, comprehensive planning of the kind indicated will become a reality. The signs are hopeful; let an

economist rather than an urban planner testify in relation to towns:
"Urbanization is not the result of cosmic forces or organic growth
following immutable laws of nature which can be observed but not
influenced by human behavior. Within limits man can control his
environment—a need for problems solving where urbanization occurs
has produced increasingly successful efforts towards social control
through planning."

For the reasons just indicated, it is not thought profitable to
trace from historical analysis the contribution that urbanization has
made to past economic development and simply to apply the results
to the future of developing countries.

As has been pointed out, the search for a positive urbanization
policy needs more detached analysis of the dynamic relationship
between urbanization and industrial development, analyses that go
beyond statistical correlations. Since these do not exist, it is only
possible to speak in general terms. The same point could be put
another way. Common observation of the urbanization patterns and
problems of the developed countries spell caution in following historical paths, a caution reinforced in that the aim of contemporary
urban and regional planning in developed countries is to remedy the
consequences of past economic development and industrialization.
Indeed, so serious are the problems in developed countries that the
content of urban and regional planning itself is being extended to
cover the social crises in the cities and also the threat of pollution
in the urban and rural environment.

If, however, the experience and practice in economic growth and
urbanization of the developed countries are not to be taken as the
guide for developing countries, then perhaps economic theory can
help.

Should Developing Countries Copy the Western Approach? Sharp
criticism of the basic approach to planning and development,
which is due to a large extent to developing countries' copying
Western education concepts, was raised by LESLIE GINSBURG,
who stressed that a fundamental gap exists in concepts between
Western thinking and that of the developing world. This fact is,
in many cases, not recognized even by scholars from the developing countries.

. . . Those of us who have had the experience of working with
people from developing countries, who go to work in their own countries, have the very sad task of trying to get across to them. We had
to get over providing an education that did not necessarily equip you
in Latin, Greek, and Roman Law or confer an Oxford degree. This
is one of the great problems that the colonial powers, Britain, France,

the Netherlands, and Spain also, in Latin America, have left in these countries: that the standards of education both for professional people and for universities, are neither high, nor low—they are wrong.

The standards are based on those of nineteenth-century Spain, nineteenth-century England, nineteenth-century France, and the native pedagogue, the Kenyan or Ugandan professor wishes to remain in this kind of false glory of a European professorial outfit because he is unique in his country. He does not really like the idea that other people become professors with a Ungandan or some other degree, which has nothing whatever to do with Oxford but is now really an African degree, because he will no longer be unique.

This is a hard thing to say, but I believe that it is absolutely true. Though perhaps I do not know enough about this, I think we could learn enough from Hong Kong and Singapore as to whether a Chinese attitude to education has in fact given a slightly different slant to the teaching in those universities from the kind of teaching all over French and English Africa and Spanish Latin America.

The man from Nepal, trained in England, tries to take English planning to Nepal. And this is where it goes wrong. He likes to be supported by importing another expert from England because this will make him seem "an OK man," whereas what he should do is to go back to Nepal and say, "What a lot of rubbish I learned in England. Now I can take the methods that were suitable and use them; and forget all the other things that are useless."

I wonder how far the developed countries are right in continuing with U.N. and AID, with every Western foundation that is spending money because it does not want to pay income taxes. How wrong are the Western countries, and how right, in putting on international courses in their own countries, whereas these should be held in Dakar, Nairobi, and in Colombo. We are told that, if the courses are held in Dakar, only the French-speaking Africans will come; if they are held in Nairobi only the English African will come; but, if they are held at the Sorbonne or in London then a whole group will come, and you get a better mixture of people being educated.

I do not think this is right. I do not think nearly enough international effort has been made by Americans, English, and French to educate Indians, Ugandans, and Ghanaians in Africa. The fact that it is thought "nice" to get a post-graduate degree from a non-African, non-Latin American, or non-Indian university is the basis of what is wrong in so much of our professional education. If we cannot put it right at that level, what chance have we at the primary level where it is even more important to learn things about one's own country. You get the children in mission schools in West Africa learning from their English-type teachers, painting water colors of the kind you will find hanging in the vicarage of an English village.

It is high time that the emerging countries grappled with their own educational problems in their own way.

It does not matter if they go wrong. They will be going in their own direction, not copying the Western way of teaching, which has been too deep and too narrow for too long and needs to expand in other ways.

A similar opinion was expressed by RAANAN WEITZ, who stressed the fact that copying the Western approach might be especially harmful to the rural population drifting to big cities.

. . . An approach to planning, and planning methods that were developed for a certain society, cannot be applied to another society, and the result is that actually we do not have a proper tested approach for development planning as a whole and therefore, not for urbanization planning in the developing countries.

We cannot copy the developed countries, and more than that we cannot follow in historical footsteps. We need a new, quite a different concept, approach, and technique of planning for those societies that are in an entirely different situation from the societies that today constitute the developed countries.

If the rural areas are denuded, the more talented and skilled will be pulled to the big city, which will not be able to answer their needs. If that continues for another 10 years, it will lead to a blind alley, a suffocating dead end.

DENIS JOHN DWYER also criticized the application of Western models and tools to the planning process in countries of the Third World.

. . . One of my children once asked me, "How do I capture an elephant, armed only with a telescope, a matchbox, and a pair of tweezers?" As I obviously didn't know, he said, "I'll creep up to the elephant and look at it through the wrong end of the telescope. It will be so reduced in size that I will pick it up with the tweezers and put it in the matchbox."

I use this as an illustration of my fundamental attitude. I equate the elephant with the problem of urbanization in the developing countries, and I equate the telescope with indiscriminately applied Western experience. I do not regard urbanization as a single, unitary, universally singular process. To me, it is used in different forms and meanings, depending upon the prevailing historical, economic, social, and cultural conditions, and that is why I am worried. Eighty percent of what has been said at the Conference could have been said at a Conference on cities in Western Europe or the United States, or other highly developed economies and societies.

I come from Hong Kong, where I have lived a number of years, and everything in my experience in Asia so far has reinforced this kind of doubt in my mind. Looking across the spectrum of the social sciences, I have noticed the great debates that have taken place in recent years about the Western and the colonial interpretation of the social sciences and certain of the arts such as history when applied to the Third World countries.

Very little of this self-doubt that has struck very many of the social sciences has seeped over into urbanization studies in the Third World. Even today, with honorable exceptions such as the world-known work of people like Lloyd Rodwin and John Turner, much of the work in the developing countries is pretty much paper planning mainly based on Western lines.

Today, more than half the urban populations of the world live in developing countries. These people are overwhelmingly poor, apart from a certain very restricted elite, confined, often too closely, to the capital cities. They are poor in a greatly differing degree from the poor in the highly industrialized countries, and this is the fundamental fact that should condition most of our urban planning for the Third World.

All too often both the visiting experts or the local planners, usually trained in a Western planning school, consider the situation in terms of "them" and "us." "We" are the small elite of the West, or the local elite; "they" are the vast mass of the urban population in the Third World. The objective always seems to be to try somehow and make "them" somewhat closer to the model of "us." I think that, in the prevailing demographic social and economic situation of the Third World, this is never likely to be a realistic project within the foreseeable or even long-range future.

Take the work of John Turner on housing, for example. It is quite clear from this work that there is no conceivable solution for housing problems in the Third World on accepted Western lines. Let us look at industrial development. Is it at all realistic to conceive that the vast number of people in Third World cities, either through natural increase or migration, can be employed in regular factory or tertiary occupations? Is that level of development, the expectation of that kind of economic development in the Third World generally, a realistic one?

What about urban land-use theory? Much of it depends upon the value of land. Yet we have a situation in the Third World where perhaps between 20 percent to 50 percent of the urban population pays no attention at all to the value of land, because they are in fact squatters. These are the kinds of situations that raise very serious doubts as to general applicability of statements derived from the Western experience.

What we need is a very much greater body of investigation and knowledge in the disciplines of social geography, sociology, cultural anthropology, and psychological study. Only when this kind of research is carried out, can we expect our planning to become much more applicable to the needs of developing countries, which now form the majority of world urban populations.

Similarly, ALBERT WATERSTON mentioned the erroneous use of Western tools in developing countries. However, as Waterston put it,

. . . There are many tools available to us that we are not applying because we are in outer space looking for something, some gimmick, some new way of dealing with a problem, that is, after all, one that is a changing human problem, and we are not using the tools we have. This is not to say we need not do research; it is merely that we are not using what we know. We either apply everything in our kit of tools or nothing, and the answer lies in between.

Delegates from the developing countries stressed that planning and development in the developing countries should embrace large portions of the population, so that the population should and would participate in the development effort with realistic plans stemming from local conditions.

TAN CHOK KIAN added the following comments:

. . . The best plans in the world on physical planning or urbanization may be useless. The plans must be flexible; they must be realistic. By flexible, I mean that these plans have to have more than one option; they must be adaptable to several ways of implementation. But they must also be realistic, by which I mean that the people who plan must know and take local conditions into account. This is a very important point to be remembered when inviting experts to our country to assist us in our plans. The experts are there to give of their wide experience, of the breadth of their knowledge on a particular subject, but eventually the work has to be done by ourselves, for we know our country best. When they first arrive in the country, the experts admit that they need some time to learn what the conditions of the country are and then apply their knowledge.

Thus, it is important that we in the developing countries know that in the end we must find the solutions to our problems ourselves; and, even if we are given all the resources in the world, all the expertise in the world, the final ingredient in the successful completion of any plans is the will of the people, the will of the workers to carry these plans out. In the last resort, the plans must have the participation of the citizen.

However, I would like to caution that this point should not be overdone; because citizenship participation is somewhat like democracy; it can be overdone. You cannot get everybody in the country to say what he wants and to make decisions; because you will have many decisions and you will have many different people wanting to do things in their own way. Finally, somebody has to make the decision; so, within the context of participation, the decision-making process has to rest on a final authority. One of the ways we in our country have found to get these things done effectively is by setting up corporate bodies' statutory boards, which have definite terms of reference and a definite system to attain certain objectives.

Some Specific Points for Planning in Developing Countries. RAM C. MALHOTRA called for planning and development that coincide with the expectations of the masses and have an impact on large parts of the population rather than a concentration of limited projects.

. . . We have two alternatives of development, two approaches. Most of the donor countries who came forward suggest having concentrated development in certain areas. They call it regional development. Instead of dispersing sectoral programs all over the country, for example, instead of having a school in district "A," health facilities in district "B," and water facilities in district "C," why not put them all together in one district, so that we can have at least one region developed, then we can continue region by region. But, if you work it out, you will find that it will be centuries before all the regions or all the villages are developed, and people are not prepared to wait so long. Moreover, what are the criteria to be applied in selecting the areas? Is it to be the planners, or the politicians selecting their own constituency? This charge has already been made.

We may begin making the kind of mistake Dr. Ginsburg talked about: the failure of the planners trying to force on people the things they think they should have instead of trying to develop the things that they really need.

I would say that the other approach is not to try to plan what we think the people need by ourselves but to develop a set of objective criteria that can be applied in an equitable manner and let the people see for themselves that the government or the planning authority or the agency is there to help them to help themselves. In other words, they will have to do certain things on their own, and whoever comes forward will win the first reward, will be given the assistance. If this is done on an equitable basis, then, of course, it will be accepted and people will come forward; but, if the approach is to concentrate on one area because the government thinks that this area should be developed, this is not going to be acceptable.

Giving every region an equitable share of grants-in-aid means nothing because the resources are so limited and each share is so small that it does not make any sense at all. Then there is the theory that we should try to concentrate development in a certain area, but concentrating or selecting a region for a concentrated effort should not be left to the bureaucrats or politicians. Certain objective criteria should be developed to determine allocation of resources for development on a regional basis.

A description of the specific conditions in the developing countries and the conclusions that should be drawn as to planning and development policy was given by some of the participants who have been engaged in development planning in those countries.

WILLIAM ALONSO, in his paper, described the conditions in developing countries regarding availability of basic data, the administrative setup, and their implications on the approach to planning:

. . . Conditions in the developing countries argue for planning that relies on policies based on an understanding of the ongoing social processes and on flexible responses rather than on detailed forecasts and master plans. This is because their weak data introduce a great deal of error into forecasting, because their bureaucratic departments are heavy and unresponsive, with a thin and overextended cadre of able technicians and administrators, and because their situations are unstable in the short run and undergoing profound structural changes in the longer run.

Planners in developing countries often bewail the lack of some data and the poor quality of what data are available. It is often thought that, if only the data were available, the elaborate mathematical planning models developed in the economically advanced countries might be applied. Foreign experts in these techniques are often consulted, and young national planners aspire to master what they regard as scientific sophistication. This is a fundamental error because the poverty of the data is an intrinsic condition of underdevelopment, not a happenstance. Rich and frequent data are the by-product of the organization of an advanced economy. When weak data are put through the mathematical machinery of a complex model, they deteriorate through the compounding of error, and the output becomes worse than the input. It is as if one tried to build skyscrapers out of wood and reeds; the structure would collapse.

This is not to say, of course, that the available information should not be used. Quite the contrary, its very scarcity makes it especially valuable. But it cannot be used in terms of fully articulated quantitative models. The important thing is the understanding of the processes of the urban system, and within this context the planner must put together and use his incomplete information as a detective puts together his fragmentary clues, using to the utmost his judgment and ingenuity to join formal data with any other information to produce indicators of the condition and performance of the system. When information is poor, one cannot have confidence in the prediction of specific events, including the actions of the government itself or its consequences. Rather, one must rely on general strategies based on the best possible understanding of the ongoing processes, while retaining the flexibility to respond to the unfolding of events and to new information.

The approach of strategic intervention is also dictated by the usual conditions of the planning and administrative bureaucracies in these countries. These bureaucracies are typically fat at the bottom and thin on top. At the bottom they are commonly overstaffed, undertrained, and inefficient to the point of immobility. Routine matters lose their way in that labyrinth, orders from above are not carried out or are distorted from their purpose, and new or unusual needs meet with no responsiveness. Indeed, in many cases the system is so rigidified that corruption, whatever its faults, is the only lubricant that keeps the machine working.

The situation at the top is different. There, a small number of able and energetic technicians and managers typically find themselves overextended and lacking in staff support. There are extremely limited resources for planning, for ensuring the correct implementation of decisions, and for following up to see how previous decisions have worked out in reality. Thus, there is a limited capacity for action, since effectiveness will depend more on the personal attention of the leadership than of the routine carrying out of programs by the bureaucracy. Since action itself becomes a scarce resource, it is most important that the actions taken be important rather than trivial ones, and it is by reference to an understanding of the processes of the system that an issue or an action may be recognized as important.

Detailed long-range urban plans that are an inventory of specific future investments and programs are further inappropriate in nations undergoing profound and often sudden changes. In many countries the national leadership is often changed by coup or revolution, and diverse crises are frequent, such as sudden deterioration of the terms of trade, fiscal crises, or even war. Since the national government is de facto the metropolitan government is most of these countries, in part because of the disproportionate importance of the capital in national economies, these sudden changes belie the picture implicit in long-range comprehensive plans of a smooth and steady development. Underneath these short-range crises, there are the

deeper tides of social transformation, affecting customs and life-
styles, redistributing power and privilege among social groups.
Since few can lay claim to a clear vision of the future structure of
the society, not too much stock can be put on detailed plans for the
physical city that will be the container for that society. Where the
society is in the process of change, urban plans must themselves be
processes, not static pictures.

Comments on the views expressed by Professor Alonso
were made at the Conference by EDWIN S. MILLS, who came to
the conclusion that the specific conditions in the developing countries described by Alonso call for less effort on comprehensive
planning and more effort on the provision of minimal services,
infrastructure, and housing.

. . . The implication is not just the one outlined in Alonso's
paper, namely that comprehensive mathematical programing or
planning is inappropriate in developing countries, but rather the
more general one that they tend to plan too much, whether it is done
by mathematical programing, intuition, or any other means. In other
words, all the criticisms of mathematical planning apply equally to
nonmathematical planning of the same kind, at the local level. The
moral that I draw from the paper is that too often in urban areas in
lesser developed countries, people who are trying to do things find
not only that they have the barriers imposed by their terrible
poverty but that they also have to fight the bureaucracy in order to
be allowed to do things for themselves. I have overstated the case
to some extent, and what we are talking about is a tendency and not
a universal fact, even if what I say is true. If there is any merit
to this view, the implication is that much less effort should be devoted
to comprehensive or total planning with much more effort in the
public sector, to the provision of minimal services on a very broad
base for the poor people that come to big cities in less developed
countries in such large numbers.

I refer to such things as facilitating the construction of housing,
rather than large-scale projects of building middle-class housing,
which inevitably, in a poor country, cannot be built for very many
people. Instead, I think the suggestion made in Professor Alonso's
paper is that it would be much better if efforts on the part of the
public sector were devoted to making it easy for low-income people
to find the materials for housing, or to acquire appropriate tenure
(whatever that might be in particular countries) to the results of
their efforts, so that they can benefit from any later sale of whatever
capital investment they have undertaken. This would give them an
incentive to make a greater investment either of their own time and
materials or conceivably of hired labor in the construction of housing.

It is also obviously necessary for the public sector to provide
the appropriate kind of infrastructure—levels of sanitation and minimum levels of education and transportation have to be provided. I
do not know how much reorientation is involved as the result of the
actual planning process in large cities in South America, Africa,
Asia, or elsewhere. If I interpret the implications of Professor
Alonso's paper correctly, it is a very sensible redirection: simply
that planners ought to continue to do what they are in fact doing.

The specific conditions in the developing countries calling
for different planning methods and different targets in urban planning in developing countries were discussed at length by experts
who have spent some time in these countries.
MARSHALL B. CLINARD stressed the importance of urban
community development in emerging new urban units within the
existing urban centers.

. . . I have in mind a population of some 2,000 to 5,000, like a
village. This kind of work is being done in the cities in Venezuela,
and in Colombia. It is being done on quite a large scale in the cities
of India, creating what we call "urban community developments,"
something like community development in the villages, only we have
to build a unit in which they elect their leaders, in which they have a
small council that is responsible for sanitation and health, physical
improvements, education, etc. This work has been done on an increasing scale in Manila. It has a long history of self-help groups in the
cities, and in some of the worst of the slums of Hong Kong.
The development of the civic responsibility in self-help and
building is not only needed by squatters; it is needed in the high-
rise buildings in Singapore, Hong Kong, and other cities. I suggest
here some of the things that can be done from a study of self-help
within the cities of developing countries, if they form themselves
into units of around 2,000 and set out with their meager resources
to try to make changes for themselves and for the community.
Urban community development, self-help, decentralization,
is really the problem of the cities, establishing new methods of
social control, overcoming the diversity, indifference, bridging the
gap between coming from a large joint family and belonging to a
nuclear family within the city, of dealing with young people who come
in alone.
I do not think it is basically a matter of housing. I do not think
it is a matter of economics. It is a problem of the developing way
of life. In my study of an African city, one slum area had a large
number of problems and another slum area did not. The interesting
thing was that they looked almost the same physically; in fact, the

one with most problems had, if anything, better housing. The one
with the most problems was better off economically than the other.

While Professor Clinard stated that the problem in urban planning is not that of housing, JORGE E. HARDOY argued that the
problem of housing and building technology as well as the provision of services should be given special attention.

. . . Human agglomerations of the size we foresee cannot be
built with the low-level technology we now employ. We now have
more advanced technology and have learned to use more resources
than a generation ago, but the techniques we use in building cities
are still very primitive in comparison with other activities where
the safety and comfort of human beings are also involved. Most
cities in developing countries still employ building techniques that
are not very different from those used two or three generations ago,
and in some cases even centuries ago. To make things worse, when
a government decides to modernize its process of planning and
building cities, it generally favors techniques and a technology that
are alien to the cultural background, the resources, and the local
conditions of the country or the regions.
There are no basic standards or basic norms for investment
in the urban areas, though many governments have tried or are
trying to set them for education, health, security, recreation, housing,
and even the construction of cemeteries. Uneven standards in social
services, community equipment, and basic amenities between cities
widen gaps of opportunity and salary that already exist. A minimum
standard for urban services, community equipment, and basic amenities should be established for all cities and towns according to the
size of population. Such standards could be based on what we could
consider the essential services needed by each community according
to regional criteria.

Professor KARMON spoke on the difference between urbanization in developed countries and the process that is taking place
in developing countries. He stressed the need for finding a common language between planners on the one hand and national leaders
on the other, and he dealt broadly with the conception of the town
in the eyes of those responsible for its planning and development.

. . . I would like to discuss this common language. Professor
Mabogunje said that the decision on the development of a town is
bound by ideology, by the picture in the mind of a political leadership. In translating this into geographical language, I would say it
is a question of conception. What is the conception of a town and its

208

task not only in the eyes of the political leader, not only in the eyes of a planner, but also in the eyes of those people who live in it and go to live in towns. What makes towns in Africa especially significant is the fact that about 70 percent or 80 percent of the population have been living in any particular town for not more than some 10 to 15 years. The rapid growth of towns in Africa has created municipal bodies without any tradition of town living. People coming to live in a town do not know that they are going to live in a big town with all its problems. The only thing they know is that they are going to a place where they hope to find employment, and this tremendous growth of African towns is in my opinion the main problem of the town.

If we compare urban development in developed countries, we all become aware of the problems of pollution, of conservation of environment, and so on, but these towns do not have one problem— the prospect of further rapid growth—because, when in some countries today's rural population has been reduced to 8 percent or 12 percent of the total population and the urban population has reached almost 90 percent, there is no reserve there for growth, except by immigration. However, the urban population in most of the African countries is still probably only 12 percent or 14 percent, with 85 percent still living in rural environments. This is a reserve for growth of towns in dimensions that none of us can imagine because most of these people, and especially the youngsters going to school, put pressure on a town unequaled in a developed country, though it may be equaled in Asia.

The town of Tema, for example, which is the modern port of Accra, the capital of Ghana, was planned by one of the best planners in the world, Constantinas Apostolos Doxiadis of Athens, on the best planning principles imaginable. The buildings were constructed according to climatic conditions. The town was divided into neighborhood units, not only according to income groups but also according to a certain mixture of income groups in order not to divide the town into separate sectors. Rules were laid for maximum densities in each sector of the town, and when the town began to be settled in 1962 everything went according to plan. It was a modern town of African planning. Then they developed the port of Tema, which attracted industries. The Volta Dam at Akosambo was constructed and attracted laborers.

In the conditions of underemployment or concealed unemployment in rural areas of Africa, there are at least five to six applicants for every job offered, and all those applicants came to Tema. According to the rules of planning, they were not allowed to live in town, so they set up shantytowns in villages all around the town of Tema, which were not subjected to the planning controls.

There were some lucky people who had kinsmen living in Tema—
a brother, a cousin, a member of the clan. How can someone with
a home refuse hospitality to a cousin? In African thinking this is
completely impossible. The cousin comes, looks for work, is lucky,
and finds work, so why not bring his family? His family moves in
with his cousin, then the two wives quarrel and one of them sets up
a kitchen outside in the garden. The best planning has not been able
to prevent this kind of development, which produces densities much
higher than any planner ever envisaged. Anyone who knows anything
about towns in development countries knows that this process is
repeated over and over again, in all countries in Africa, and I assume
in most of Asia.

Therefore, the progress and process of urbanization takes on a
completely different character from that of the developed countries.
It is commonly acknowledged that since antiquity the town has been
the form of human organization that always claimed progress, culture,
civilization.

Today, the measure of development of a country is taken on the
percentage of its urban population; the higher the urban population,
the greater, statistically, the development of the country. Thus, in
the judgment of politicians and planners alike, progress means
urbanization. But, while this conception has been accepted generally,
the town has changed its character. In the last decade, we suddenly
talk no more about urban progress, only about urban problems, urban
pollution, urban explosion. This means that, while the developing
countries have taken over the idea of a town as being the main instrument of progress, the developed countries are suddenly regarding
the town as their main problem. Actually, the planners of the developed
countries have imposed a tool on the developing countries that has
been proved to be a danger; they have advised developing countries
to use a tool they themselves can no longer handle. I think that this
is the real problem of the town in the developing countries. I think
we should rethink the subject of whether the town, the big town, and
the metropolis are really the tool for development, for it may be that
all of us who are engaged in technical aid, in advice and planning
for developing countries, impose our conception of the town on a
society when we should probably be thinking in other directions.

Professor Karmon's approach is thus in line with that of
the other participants who referred to the specific condition of
urban planning in developing countries and believe that a different
approach is needed. One cannot and should not apply the methods
or tools used in developed countries. Urban planning in developing
countries should be adapted to the social order prevailing there.

PATTERNS AND MODELS OF THE URBAN SYSTEM

After the above examination of the specific conditions for
urban planning in the developing countries, the next issue that
arises is which urban patterns should be encouraged and which
are the most appropriate models of the urban system for the
developing countries.

Urban Patterns for the Developing Countries. In his paper, LLOYD
RODWIN analyzed the different urban patterns. The issues dealt
with were scale, density, grain, and physical organization of
development. Rodwin did not always suggest the pattern to be
followed, as this depends on local conditions in each country, and
only studies and research can lead to conclusions as to the desired
appropriate pattern.

. . . An important set of issues concerns the form of growth that
would best serve the needs of developing countries, both in metropolitan areas and in other growth centers. The main urbanization
options in terms of form involve issues of scale, density, grain,
and physical organization of development. Unfortunately, as might
be suspected, all too little is known about the costs and benefits of
growth options that do exist. Nonetheless, we do know enough to
give us a sense of some of the problems that ought to be skirted and
some of those that might be successfully explored.

For example, research on optimum scale and density is complicated by so many value-laden issues, frustrating data-gathering,
and analytical problems that it would be prudent to avoid these questions. If research on scale and density were encouraged, it is unlikely that the results would be decisive enough to guide action.
Other approaches, however, such as examining the economies of
scale of public utilities and of likely economic activities, as well as
the minimum scale and thresholds of development necessary to
serve certain urban functions or to achieve certain effects on growth,
attitudes, and migration, might prove very helpful. It should prove
quite feasible to evaluate the economic, administrative, and even
social functions served by cities of varying size and type in different
developing countries and the effects of the mix of different industries,
service activities, and infrastructure facilities on growth investment
patterns, development effects on the hinterland, etc. We have enough
research prototypes, such as the work of Colin Clar, Hautreux and
Rochefort, and B. Malisz and the studies of economic character and
functions of cities by the Civil Aeronautics Administration—to cite
only a few examples—to make a reasonable assumption that such
studies can provide useful guiding decisions on suitable scales of
development for satellite cities and new towns.

A related question is whether to emphasize the building of new communities or the expansion of existing cities. In Great Britain, the current tendency is to favor large new cities over town expansion on the grounds of efficiency, and the likelihood is of greater development effects as well as more innovative and management capacity. However, the emphasis in France and elsewhere has been on the expansion of existing large cities (although the French are now building some new cities mainly around Paris). Expansion is emphasized on the grounds that existing cities often have important advantages of location and inertia and that expansion generally involves less conflict and less "robbing of Peter to help Paul." Despite the recent initiation of a New Towns program for the Paris region, this point of view still predominates in France. Because of contrasting perspectives and experiences, it would be desirable to encourage a comprehensive, comparative study of the economic problems and opportunities and the development effects involved in the current New Towns approach followed in Great Britain compared with the policy of developing regional metropolitan centers (metropoles d' equilibre) now being pursued actively in France. To undertake such comparative studies would require the assistance of the appropriate government agencies, i.e., the Ministry of Housing and Local Government in Britain and the Delegation for Territorial Planning and Regional Action in France. It may also be possible to involve other groups such as Political and Economic Planning (which is now involved in a major study of urbanization in Great Britain) or comparable French organizations such as the Institute of Applied Economic Research, Regional Section (ISEA). It is worth emphasizing that this kind of comparative research is likely to be more valuable if the aim is to determine circumstances under which one set of policies would be more appropriate than another for different types of nations to follow rather than which set of policies is correct or superior in all cases.

Physical development patterns may vary from dispersed to concentrated and from linear to multiple nuclei. Indeed, it is possible, as seems now to be happening in Great Britain and elsewhere, for growth to be like "beads on a string"—in short, to show both linear and multiple nuclei characteristics. More needs to be known about the development effects of these patterns. We have evidence that suggests that innovations in ideas and in the diffusion of the economic effects of new development occur more effectively in hinterlands with hierarchical urban patterns. If so, this suggests that, when urban growth centers are promoted, emphasis should be placed on the ties created between the growth center and the other urban settlements in the hinterland. Studies could be made in developing countries to see how ideas, income, and other economic effects are diffused to their surrounding hinterlands. In particular, one could study how the influences differ with variations in settlement and mobility patterns for different city sizes and types.

There is increasing evidence that the growth of urban centers has significant effects in transforming the markets for agriculture and even the practice of agriculture. This is true for the new patterns of agriculture being developed at the mouth of the Orinoco in Venezuela, and the transformation of agriculture in the area surrounding Adana and Ankara in Turkey, to cite only a few examples. We need to learn more about how these effects vary with the size and patterns of cities. We also sought to export the changes in information, education, health, and transportation programs that might complement programs promoting urban growth centers, in order to reinforce the spread effects and to extend these urbanization influences and opportunities to the population of the hinterland.

LESLIE GINSBURG seemed to favor the urban pattern that helps to control or at least guide the growth of the big cities. In his paper on the "Strategies for Regional Growth," Ginsburg deals at length with urban planning aimed at achieving such a pattern.

. . . Controlling growth—how far is this really possible? I am referring here to urban growth resulting from in-migration and from local population growth. With it goes industrial and commercial growth with a good traditional location, plus a large labor force, plus a large local market, plus good transport facilities, which together must always add up to rapid urbanization. Nowhere in the world have policies succeeded that actually controlled this type of urban growth except where the society was rich and technically advanced, as well as law-abiding and with an administration able to implement land-use control policies. At all levels of development, this capacity to understand land-use controls, and to be able to implement policies in relation to them, is absolutely fundamental.

Britain, the Netherlands, and Scandinavia are probably the only countries where such controls are fully effective, and, even so, the pressures for housing and office space and industrial land are so great that only by carefully balancing political demands with actual allocations—resulting in revision of town plans—can the appearance of land control be maintained.

Plans that guide growth rather than attempt to control it are likely to prove the more successful and are, therefore, more realistic. Should strategies, however, set out guidelines for development—employment policies based on likely investment programs lead back to population needs—these, in turn, through demographic studies, lead to sizes of population. Here again, the variations within even the most controlled plans can be considerable. Mothers and babies may be statistics at some point, but they operate within a set of rules not always understood by the best demographers!

Population parameters can be attempted and housing policies put forward to establish land allocations for maximum and minimum growth. While even minimums may not always be reached in European situations, it is unlikely that even the maximums will suffice in rapidly developing areas where open-ended plans must be the order of the day.

A framework for communications and for land allocations is essential, but with this must go the budgeting program and a training program to enable self-build housing to go ahead in a reasonable manner.

Provided land can be obtained by development agencies at the right price, the provision of basic services on the ground—and they need to be very basic—plus offers of building components, such as roof beams at special prices or long-term payment, could be more effective as an attraction to develop there than any disincentives elsewhere. Another problem is the difficulty of providing sites for low-income families sufficiently close to industry or commerce, which, having already become established, wishes to expand on those sites. The journeys to work and the fantastic cross-city congestion that result are so tedious that one despairs at any planning being able to provide better living conditions for any except the protected rich.

Industrial and commercial locations are very difficult matters to lay down in a regional strategy except in the most general sense. Yet, in the final form that urbanization is likely to take, it is these locations that affect so much else—especially the transportation network and its capacity for expansion in the future. Foreign investment is so eagerly sought after that national governments override regional planning organizations if the foreign investors push hard or even pretend they are not interested unless they can operate from certain sites. Here, one may ask if a whole country were covered with a series of regional strategies, and in all these there were consistent policies governing location, could such strategies be adhered to more easily? This is a subject where a large number of individual case histories would be needed to establish any norm of behavior. It is a matter, though, that should find a clearly defined place in every regional strategy.

If one is concerned with spatial allocations, then the actual shape the region is to take must be considered seriously. All too often a regional plan is prepared as a policy document without the physical implications being fully understood or explored. After people, land is a nation's most precious commodity. Once built over or developed, it cannot be "undone" except at great cost. Why are humans such dirty animals as to despoil so much of their heritage so soon in its development?

For many years, the concept of the "contained town" with new growth in the form of "satellites" dominated planning thinking. With it went the rural center equivalent, ringed by key villages—a typical urban-rural planning concept basic to so much country planning in the United Kingdom, the Netherlands, and Israel. Flexibility of transport—especially the country bus and the lorry—has nearly killed this concept, for the rural dweller takes the bus not to the key village or the rural center but right through to the large city. The large city is dominating all, for the thresholds of growth have themselves expanded so that the best range of facilities may be available to the greatest number in the biggest places.

The planner has made a virtue of necessity. The containment of the big city is virtually impossible, so back to the untried linear forms, first suggested by various reformers in the nineteenth century. Now linear expansion is considered the most feasible way of letting the urban areas grow within some sort of controlled framework, but, with this, we must take care not simply to allocate housing and more housing in endless geometrically precise belts along unmade wide and dusty highways, while all the employment and social facilities somehow integrate themselves elsewhere.

Transport policies for low-cost mass transit are also integral to any regional growth plan for urbanization. Can the plans ensure that the budget for this type of enterprise is incorporated in the scheme from the beginning? How far are the ad hoc free-enterprise bus services, mammy wagons, and shared taxis likely to be able to cope? How many so-called experts and planners ever actually use the services the poor urban workers have to use? Using the services for a week, and at various seasons, can teach a great deal more than mere statistics or service. If some form of mass transit system cannot be built into the policy, then should linear forms of expansion be planned for at all? The motorcar is a costly item in developing countries, and in many cases fuel is costly as well. Why plan to build in freedom for the motorcar everywhere, when one knows that eventually it will clog itself up as it has been doing everywhere in the world where given free rein?

Many planning policies are based on outdated concepts of zoning. How far should regional plans consider these? Early urban developments, outside the government quarters or early colonial central areas, were so often a mess that planners, native and expatriate alike, tended to introduce European and American zoning ordinances in an effort to regulate land uses, yet in so doing they separated functions too much, created further long journeys, and seriously affected land values by creating central area plateaux incapable of easy expansion.

Some of the participants at the Rehovot Conference presented urban models they had designed. Some of these models may be regarded as suggestions that have not yet had a great deal of experience, like the model suggested by Jean Canaux, and some were models used in the relevant countries, like those presented by Felipe Herrera for Latin America and David Tanne for Israel.

The "Flexible" Urban Model. JEAN CANAUX of France has designed a flexible model of urban structure, which he suggested for adapting to different locations and different circumstances. This model makes it possible to combine considerations of space, time, economics, and law, according to any foreseen future. Canaux argues that, despite variations in urban populations, in spite of the fact that every city is a particular case, there are still some common features that can be isolated. He went on to describe his ideas:

. . . Certain physiological and psychological characteristics are common to all men, even though all men are different. These differences are the basis for division of labor and subsequently lead to cohabitation, for, outside working hours, they prefer to spend their time among people whose tastes conform most closely to their own. Places of work and business quarters will, therefore, not have the same social structure and will consequently also differ from residential quarters in the physical sense (building, access, etc.), because these regroup people according to criteria that are partly contradictory.

Some people prefer quiet, some like excitement, but the acceleration or slow-down that man is capable of enduring without physiological side effects in a common vehicle of public transportation is the same: approximately 1.5 m./s./s. Therefore, all methods of transportation will try to reach this speed limit but will be unable to exceed it. It is enough to know this speed limit in order to calculate the duration of travel by public transportation, whatever means of transportation is used in the future, because the frequent stops exclude the possibility of traveling faster than 90 km./h., and even that is possible only if the road system is "independent," i.e., with no crossings or other complications.

In such conditions, if one wishes to restrict the distance between public transportation stops, on one hand, and residences or working places, on the other, to a 10-minute walk, or to 500 m., one arrives at neighborhoods of 1 km. in diameter, with public transportation stops in the center. The distance between public transportation stops only slightly affects the average time needed for commuting, as the intervening distance can be covered at maximum speeds. The distances between stops can thus exceed 1 km., leaving continuous interstitial spaces between stations.

A town ceases to be a shapeless agglomeration; it resembles an archipelago of built-up islands, each approximately 1 km. in private cars, as well as public and open space. The neighborhoods that can already be reached by public transportation at stops in their centers now become accessible to private vehicles along their outside boundaries, thus reducing the risk of accidents. The interstitial space, which creates complete communities out of neighborhoods, also serves to connect them economically through better communications and socially through meetings of people using common facilities. In such a system, any residence can be located at less than a 10-minute walk from leisure areas. Culture and even leisure can thus be reintroduced into the system of human habitation, from which it is now so often excluded in favor of production.

A trait shared by all men is the wish to choose their own way of life. As the town planner cannot offer man the choice of his standard of living, it is even more imperative that he provide him with the widest possible choice of housing.

In a residential quarter, the most restrictive factor affecting the way of life is population density. Therefore, the town must offer a whole gamut of residential quarters with various population density rates. Moreover, neighborhoods of equal densities must have distinct characters of their own, arrived at by the interplay of built-up areas, land use, and open space. Whatever the temperament or character of potential residents, each must find surroundings conforming to his individual taste. We have thus made use of both differences and similarities.

In order to complete this sketch, we must recall the distribution of certain social phenomena within the entire archipelago, that is, population density, number of employment opportunities, consumption of water and power, the value of land and business premises, and the need for collective facilities.

The average intensity of such social phenomena is known to decrease as one moves away from the center (population density is the best-known example). Research carried out recently has shown that the simple exponential model $D(r) = Ae^{-br}$ can be applied, with a high degree of precision, to almost any situation observed and at any period of time—provided that the two sole parameters A and b are properly chosen. Moreover, this model is remarkably well suited to methods of mathematical analysis; it can be most easily used. It can be considered a preferable formula of the "law" regarding decreasing population densities, as this law seems to arise from statistics based on multiple causes, making action practically impossible. Elementary caution dictates respect for this law even in a new town, as projects that defy it are bound to produce unbearable tensions. The use of average figures does not prevent the planner from giving each neighborhood a character of its own, or even from assigning highly different population densities to neighborhoods situated at equal distances from the center.

A model like this has been found to produce rather remarkable results; in one instance where it was applied, the average duration of a trip from door to door was 18 minutes and the maximum duration was 45 minutes, at the level of 1 million inhabitants using public transportation. This is undoubtedly an achievement of which no existing city is capable. And yet, in this plan, a quarter of its area is totally assigned to open space and one-eighth is held back as reserve land.

The urban structure thus described

(1) offers the greatest variety of different environments;

(2) facilitates the distribution and collection of all fluids and solids;

(3) suggests correspondingly suitable administrative, political, and social structure;

(4) describes the city in easily understandable terms, giving each person, even visually, a sense of belonging to several coexisting social groups that nonetheless form one whole;

(5) makes growth and renewal feasible by entire neighborhoods;

(6) creates harmony in the mineral and vegetable worlds;

(7) creates a structure applicable even to existing cities where a network can be determined along which the age of the existing buildings and the low value of land and business premises will gradually make it possible to create a continuous interstitial space.

The main advantage of this model lies in its versatility. The use of this structure makes it possible not only to prepare one plan, that is, to forecast one single future for each town but also to put at the disposal of the planner a cluster of possible alternative figures to choose from, taking into account the unforeseeable elements inherent in the present.

In order to clarify these ideas further, let us assume an example expressed in figures: a town of 40,000 inhabitants, for which a five-year town plan has to be devised. Land allocation and financial resources have to be decided upon within the framework of the plan, because, if these decisions are made separately, they become fortuitous, placing the entire project in jeopardy. When this town reaches a population of 60,000, we assume that it will become necessary to double its area and, therefore, to create two new neighborhoods. This growth is close at hand both in time and space; therefore, it is possible to outline, at least, the first of these future quarters and to begin procedures for the acquisition of land and, consequently, the granting of necessary funds.

However, for the next increase of 20,000 people (from a population of 60,000 to 80,000) it will be sufficient, within a fairly large circumference, to initiate preparatory measures for the construction of one or several neighborhoods, as well as roads and facilities within the interstitial space. Within this area, only provisional concessions will be granted for indispensable construction works. Financially, a few indemnities over a period of 10 or 15 years will undoubtedly suffice.

Finally, for ultimate growth (this town may some day reach a population of 500,000) it is enough to adopt the principle of spatial organization of the archipelago type, i.e., to decide in advance, that, whenever a neighborhood reaches 1,000 square meters in size, an empty space of approximately 500 meters has to be left between this and the nearest future neighborhood. It is not necessary to decide at this juncture either on future location nor on land acquisition. Nevertheless, if this principle is adopted, it is possible to make sure that the town will still be capable of functioning when such a large population is reached.

In this manner, forecasts can be put into a certain perspective, where that which is near both in time and space is defined in legal as well as financial terms, while land policies and funds can be less precisely formulated regarding operations more removed in time and space. Thus, the collective discipline required in a town becomes progressively less restrictive and in fact less necessary as the size predicted for it becomes larger. Such a harmonious interaction of space, time, economics, and law makes the adjustment of a town to circumstances feasible only through the application of such a polyvalent model as I have described.

The "structure" thus obtained is multidimensional, containing the germs of its own development, somewhat similar to a genetic program. Through such a structure, a town becomes a system within systems, thus achieving a higher level of organization than before. The town can, then, be considered the result of a shrinking of a regional space containing townships and villages. Organization attains another level, and, as always happens in evolutionary processes, this level is reached by multiplication, specialization, and differentiation of component cells. In order to achieve this, functional discontinuities must be introduced into the probability range of development in order to avoid a malignant growth.

Urbanization in itself is not evil, but the rules and means governing good urban processes must be discovered. This is one of the most urgent tasks of our times.

The Israeli Urban Model. DAVID TANNE brought before the Conference the Israeli experience in urban planning based on the principle of population dispersal. As a result of this policy, the pattern existing before 1949 and based on extreme primacy gave way to a new pattern on Rank City Distribution.

. . . In 1949, the Population Dispersal Plan came into being stressing the following principles as its aims:

(1) reducing the relative degree of urbanization in the coastal plain;

(2) redistributing the population by means of dispersing it throughout the country;

(3) developing balanced regions through an integrated hierarchical structure of interdependent urban and rural settlements;

(4) absorption and assimilation of large numbers of immigrants.

The obvious and seemingly only solution to these tasks (in the light of the previously enumerated constraints) appeared to be a balanced, predetermined, and well-planned network of new towns to be built and designed to absorb the new immigrants.

The physical Master Plan that followed the Dispersal Plan set down the first directions for such a solution. It identified the different regions, made a first attempt at determining their desired population, and also set the pattern for the new towns.

This pattern involves a hierarchical structure of five levels, the first two largely rural, and the other three urban:

(1) Village: about 500 inhabitants;

(2) Rural service center: about 200 inhabitants designed to serve up to 8 villages;

(3) Small town: 6,000-10,000 residents to give administrative, cultural, educational, and medical services to about 30 surrounding villages;

(4) Medium town: 40,000-60,000 residents, affording services on a regional level and room for various industries;

(5) Cities: with a population of more than 100,000.

This pattern was constructed along the classic European model, notably that of Christaller. It called for 26-30 new towns (depending on the definition of a new town). Its emphasis, as Table 8 shows, is on small and medium-sized towns, and its locational policy in accordance with the plan itself put these new towns mainly in the less inhabited North and South.

These, then, were the guidelines along which the new towns in Israel were conceptualized and according to which the system was broadly built.

Tanne then described the criticism that was directed at this pattern.

TABLE 8

Population Targets for New Towns, According to Plans, 1951, 1957, and 1963

Population of Town	Number of Towns in Plan		
	1951	1957	1963
Up to 9,999	4	5	1
10,000-19,999	3	7	11
20,000-29,999	3	3	4
30,000-39,999	3	3	7
40,000-49,999	3	3	1
50,000+	1	3	4
Total	17	24	28

. . . In recent years much criticism has been directed at the new towns. This criticism ranges from a categorical denial of the whole concept to finding faults in the policy and in the practices of its execution.

The critics are quick to note several points of conflict and crisis that the new towns have undergone and their frequent failure to achieve regional significance and social and economic integration. They also cite the large sums that had to be invested to correct these shortcomings, and the few cases in which, in spite of all attempts, the town has not yet managed to take off on an unaided course of development.

When viewed restrospectively in the light of present knowledge, it is undeniable that there is much truth in these criticisms. It is the contention of the author of these lines, however, to take issue with these critics, maintaining that, although undesirable, the pragmatic development of new towns in the manner employed was historically unavoidable for various reasons:

(1) The needs of the state were of such magnitude and so pressing that immediate measures were the only solution. An embarkation on academic researches, although desirable, was out of the question because of the time this would necessarily take.

(2) The problems that faced the state in the first few years were unique, as was the experiment in new-town-building. Even the best of critics could not at that time suggest anything but a tentative unproven theory, as good or as bad as the one adopted.

(3) Even if an alternative policy had existed at the time, the severely restricted funds of the new state may not have been enough to make its enforcement possible.

(4) The opinion sometimes voiced among critics that no policy at all was needed and that people should have been left to settle freely in the existing cities is of mere theoretical interest. It is impossible either to affirm or to refute the notion that the predicted calamities may not have taken place.

(5) Finally, much of the experience and evidence on which current criticism is based did not accumulate until many years after the process of town-building was started, and largely because of it. It is quite probable that it would not have become available at all had not the policy been implemented.

Thus, criticism of the policy is itself an integral part of the implementation process—a necessary result of a dynamic system and one that cannot exist without it.

It is freely admitted that the true nature and dimensions of the problems to be encountered were not realized at the time and that much of the work during the first few years was done, as it were, in the dark by a tedious process of trial and error. Only by repeated retracing of the measures taken and continuous evaluation could the experience be gained and the data collected. This eventually led to a better and deeper understanding of the problems at hand and facilitated both the rehabilitation of existing towns and the comprehensive planning of more new and better towns.

The constant follow-up method employed led to several revisions of the original population-dispersal plan. All in all, the plan has been revised seven times, each revision reflecting current thoughts about the desirable population distribution. Needless to say, none of these projections ever quite materialized, and the final result is more of a compromise between the natural population tendencies and the planners' efforts.

To complete the picture, it should be added that, by 1971, 30 new towns were established. Even though the urbanization of the coastal plain has not stopped, it has been significantly reduced. The concentration of population there declined from 80 percent in 1949 to some 69 percent in 1971; at the same time the population of the peripheral regions had risen from 8.5 percent to 21 percent. The difficulties and failures, according to Tanne, were mainly of social origin. Furthermore, there was failure to achieve regional integration and a lack of a comprehensive policy for the planning process.

ARIE SHACHAR also dealt, in his paper, with the pattern of urbanization developed in Israel after 1949, namely the dispersal of population through the establishment of new towns known as Development Towns.

. . . The planning of the development towns was concerned, primarily, with their physical aspects. The planning authorities were responsible for determining the location, size, and urban design of the towns. Economic planning during the initial stages of the program was not applied on a local scale and was applied quite rarely even on a regional scale. Social planning dealt mainly with anticipated demand for public services in education, health, and welfare, but not in the broader aspects of cultural adaption and social integration.

The planning considerations concerning the location and the size of the development towns deserve special attention, as they represent one of the very few cases in which physical planning of an urban system was on a geographical theory of spatial organization, the central place theory. The central place theory provides a description and explanation of the hierarchical structure of an urban system, interrelating in quantitative terms the size of an urban settlement, the size of its zone of services, and the average distance to the nearest urban settlement of the same hierarchical level. As most of the development towns were planned as service centers for the rural districts around them, it was relevant to apply central place theory in planning their location and size. The planning department has defined small regional units on a nodal base, allocating each of them to an existing urban center or an anticipated development town. The location of a development town was planned to achieve regional centrality; as far as the urban center is dependent on its rural hinterland, it must dominate its district, and, therefore, the site of the town must be at the crossroads of the regional traffic and at the very focus of its economic activities.

In order to fill the wide gap in the urban system between the rural settlement (level A in the hierarchy) and the large metropolitan areas (level E in the hierarchy), the planning authorities intended to insert three intermediate levels of settlements: B Center, defined as a "Rural Service Center," of the size of a few hundred inhabitants, catering to the needs of 4-6 rural settlements; C Center was planned to be a small town, with a population of between 6,000 and 12,000 inhabitants, and service areas within a radius of 6-10 km.; and D Center, which was planned to be a middle-sized town with a population of 15,000 to 60,000 inhabitants, including central regional institutions and services. The development towns were planned to be C and D Centers, and their locations and sizes were to be determined within the spatial organization of a planned hierarchical urban system. A few urban settlements, those on the "Resource Frontier," were to be located according to the distribution of natural resources, and their future size was determined according to estimates of the potential utilization of the resources.

We can summarize the three major factors affecting the size and the location of the development towns: (1) the spatial organization of the urban system and regional integration as expressed by central place theory; (2) the spatial distribution of resources; and (3) the spatial pattern of a few small urban settlements existing before 1948, which were used as nuclei for building development towns.

The result of the national planning, on a macro-scale, was a general scheme for ultimate geographical distribution for an assumed target population to be reached about 20 years hence. These schemes were not forecasts with great chances of fulfillment, but rather working hypotheses, proposing the most desirable spatial distribution of population, yet with a reasonable chance of being realized.

Spatial organization and the model developed for the rural areas in Israel were presented by Raanan Weitz (see previous chapter). This model, based on four types of Rural Centers including what Weitz called a "quiet center," is unique to Israel. However, as Dr. Weitz stressed, the idea might be suitable and also provide solutions to developing countries.

Latin America: Past and Future Models. The traditional urban model and the future urbanization model for Latin America were presented by FELIPE HERRERA in his paper "Nationalism and Urbanization in Latin America."

. . . The underdeveloped city has at the same time been the center of a national space limited by historical factors and the periphery of a metropolitan economic space whose commercial interests usually determined the parameters within which the national economies were developed. Within this scheme, the driving impulses of economic growth were determined basically by exogenous factors; the local benefits of development were, in fact, by-products of the commerce between an overseas center that purchased and financed production and the countries producing raw materials.

In these circumstances, the capital cities of independent countries or of colonies or protectorates were virtually the only places equipped with basic infrastructure roughly adequate for the requirements of trade and for the needs of the population directly associated with the country's economic and administrative activities. The rest of the population remained in rural areas, where raw materials were produced or mineral deposits were worked for export, and where the reinvestment of the benefits of trade was limited to what was strictly necessary to maintain the levels of production that external markets could absorb.

When the national states of Latin America were consolidated in the second half of the nineteenth century, the new political functions of the urban areas and the diversification and interchange of foreign markets also made for further domination by the capital cities. These practically monopolized the functions of foreign trade and became the only places to concentrate the reinvestment of national savings generated by exports. A large share of these savings was absorbed through urban and suburban expenditure benefiting a thin stratum of landowners, exporters, and public officials.

Beginning in the 1930s, signs appeared of a growing deterioration of foreign trade, which led to stagnation of production and subsequently to a reduction in the capacity of rural areas to absorb manpower. Concurrently, a genuine revolution occurred in the field of health, owing to the progress of medical science and the development of communications. Acting together, these two phenomena resulted in an explosive increase in the pressure of population in the countryside. The expansion of transportation served once again to initiate sweeping migratory movements, which even now are bringing about a rapid and massive displacement of the population and thus a radical change in the traditional pattern of population distribution.

Moreover, the process of import substitution that began in the 1940s was largely in manufacturing industries. It is well known that these activities tend to be located near consumer markets. This could not but provide further impetus for the growth of the largest urban centers. Indeed, population statistics show sharp increases in the largest cities during this period. Many Latin American cities thus have entered the category of the most populous in the world. Buenos Aires is fifth in population; Sao Paulo, seventh; Mexico City, ninth; and Rio de Janeiro, eleventh. Sao Paulo has the highest growth rate of all these, and, if its growth continues at past levels, this metropolitan area could possibly become the largest in the world by the end of this century, with over 40 million inhabitants.

Other "emerging" cities also have grown rapidly, in the short span of two decades increasing the number of large cities of Latin America. At the same time, the total population residing in this category of cities has risen. In 1960, Latin America had 9 cities of over 1 million inhabitants; in 1970, there were 15 in this category; and, in 1980, there will be 26. Latin America is rapidly becoming a subcontinent of cities and markedly of large cities.

In the most recent decades, Latin America has entered a process of fast-moving political changes. Steps toward regional integration and the new nationalistic orientation of many of its governments indicate that the region is searching for a more distinctive identity. If achieved, this goal will require an increase in its share of world trade, as well as an expansion of national markets. In terms of urbanization, this approach implies a change in the traditional model, which will require (1) that the larger cities become less dependent on external pressures and more effective centers of their national economies and (2) the completion of national networks of urban centers that will permit better use of a still largely unexploited interior space.

The new urbanization model, as summarized by Mr. Herrera, should have the following characteristics:

(1) The still more intensive growth of national centers until they reach a scale sufficient to produce the conditions required for the creation of secondary centers (possibly 5-6 million inhabitants). Since the smaller countries do not enjoy the conditions required to reach this scale, they will have to associate in subregional compacts or accept the domination of another regional center.

(2) The decentralization of growth poles (new activities) toward regions with greater potential. This will require mechanisms for the transfer of economic and technological resources from the larger national centers.

(3) The creation of supporting systems (infrastructure and urban services, especially technical and financial) in new development centers

(4) Greater participation by the population in production and consumption through policies for the redistribution of product and social investments.

The few case studies of urban patterns given here, and the theoretical models suggested, all point to the fact that, with changing economic, social, and political conditions, the urbanization pattern must change. Developing countries should not copy the urban pattern of Western developed countries. New models suited to their local conditions should be developed.

CONCLUSIONS

The debates and papers on the subject of urbanization planning stressed the urgent need for planning in the light of the rapid process of urbanization.

It was also agreed that urban planning be part of a comprehensive development plan covering all disciplines. Planning alone, however, will not lead to the desired goals, it should also include programs and specific projects for implementation.

The fundamental gap between Western thinking and that of the developing countries and the completely different conditions in the developing countries call for a different approach to planning there. Many of the planners, both those from Western countries and those who just studied there, have failed because they used tools that could not be applied to developing countries.

In order to be able to plan for developing countries, one should study the social, cultural, economic, and political processes taking place there.

It was agreed by all that, despite inferior conditions for planning in the developing countries (lack of data, lack of means, social difficulties, etc.), urban planning there is essential, and it should embrace large parts of the population and meet the expectations of the masses.

However, some of the participants pointed out that such efforts in all fields of urban development have little chance, as means are limited. Therefore, some advocated limiting urban development to the most pressing issues like housing or the provision of minimal services. In the mind of others, the most pressing issue was community development and not housing.

Regarding the desired urban pattern, it was suggested by many of the participants that urban growth should be controlled or at least guided to avoid overurbanization. To achieve this, various urban models were suggested. These models differ from one country to another, but most of them contain the basic idea of controlling growth through the establishment of new urban centers, thus reducing the extreme primacy of certain urban centers. Such patterns were suggested in Great Britain, Israel, a group of Latin American countries, and some African states.

In some cases, on the other hand, as in France, for example, the policy has been for the further expansion of existing large cities.

The majority of participants, however, were of the opinion that the desired pattern should be for more decentralization. It was pointed out that urban models should be flexible so that they can more easily be adapted to conditions.

Regional planning is an essential stage in the implementation of urbanization policy. One group of the participants in the Conference addressed itself almost exclusively to this issue, but the subject came up in discussions of other groups as well.

This chapter is devoted to the notion of planning, to conceptual planning methods, and to their application to the spatial organization of socioeconomic systems. This elaboration is confined, however, mostly to planning in general and to regional planning in particular as processes of decision-making, rather than to urbanization analysis and policy. The latter is discussed and elaborated in other chapters of this book.

This chapter is based mainly on the paper "Application of Activity Analysis to Comprehensive Regional Planning," which David Pines submitted at the Conference, and also draws heavily on ideas and views expressed within all the groups in discussions that refer to the main subject. However, this chapter is not a summary, and it does not profess to reflect the whole spectrum of views related to the subject that were expressed and discussed. It comprises three main parts. In the first, the concept of planning as a constrained optimization procedure is discussed. In the second, the concept of comprehensive regional planning is defined, and the merits and demerits of comprehensive planning are elaborated. In the third, two basic approaches to spatial planning are discussed: The first is activity analysis; the second is cost-benefit analysis of predetermined alternatives. An evaluation of the two approaches is suggested in the final subsection.

———————
———————

Written by Dr. David Pines.

PLANNING AS A RATIONAL STAGE IN THE
PROCESS OF DECISION-MAKING

The Concept of Planning: Some Definitions. There are numerous
definitions for the concept of planning. In general, two elements are
emphasized in most of them: (1) intervention of the community in the
course of development; and (2) orientation to the future.

Physical planners, on the one hand, emphasize orientation toward
the future; economists, on the other hand, tend to emphasize the aspect
of public intervention in the free market allocation process. This
approach can easily be traced in the discussion between Nathaniel
Lichfield and Dr. S. Maital, regarding the need for planning. The
"proplanning" argument expressed by the former referred to the
shortcomings of the market mechanism in allocating resources. The
"antiplanning" argument expressed by the latter referred to the advantage of the perfect market mechanism.

We prefer here to adopt a very broad definition: Planning is
rational decision-making regarding a set of sequential actions through
time.

Short-term planning refers to planning in which all actions are
to be carried out in the near future. Long-term planning refers to
planning in which some actions are to be carried out in the distant
future. Planning is required when two conditions hold:

(1) The present satisfaction of the decision-maker depends on
events that may occur in the future.

(2) Events in any given period that are relevant to the decision-
maker are affected by actions carried out in the preceding periods.

It may be observed that in the above definition the orientation
to the future of the decision-making process is emphasized rather
than the interference in the automatic mechanism of the free market.
Moreover, the above definition does not restrict the concept of planning to the community or to public decision-making. Decision-making
of a household regarding future expenditures and composition of asset
holdings would be defined as planning. But I would hardly define central decision-making about current intervention in the allocation of
resources as planning. In other words, public control of allocation
of resources per se is not necessarily planning according to the above
definitions.

The product of the planning process is the plan. It is composed
of two parts: the program and its anticipated outcomes. The program
is the operative part of the plan. It specifies the sequence of actions
to be taken. The second component of the plan is forecasts of the
outcomes resulting from the execution of the program that are relevant
to the decision-maker. Accordingly, a plan is described by a vector
(A_j), (Z_k) where:

(A_i) = vector describing the program. The component X_i
is the level of action i (i = 1, . . . , α)
(Z_k) = vector of outcomes. The component Z_k is the level
of outcome k (k = 1, . . . , β).

The planning process is assumed to be rational decision-making.
This means that there are alternative courses of action, one of which
is selected according to some rational rules. In selecting a plan, it
is verified that it is feasible and at least not inferior to any alternative
feasible plan. These concepts are further elaborated in the following
two sections.

The Concept of a Feasible Plan. A plan is defined to be a priori
feasible if the following conditions are met:
(1) The actions included in the program are within the direct
control of the decision-maker who is responsible for the plan; or,
using John Friedmann's formulation, "First, planning must be joined
to effective power for implementation."
(2) Given some independent forecasts and uncontrolled interrelationships that hold between actions and outcomes in the real world,
the plan is consistent. By independent forecasts, I mean those forecasts
that are assumed to be independent of the decision-making embodied
in the program.
Using formal presentation, a plan is said to be a priori feasible
if the following condition is met:

$$f_e \left[(X_i),\ (Y_j),\ (Z_k) \right] = 0$$
$$(e = 1, \ldots \gamma;\ j = 1, \ldots, \delta)$$

where

(X_i) = vector of describing a program that is composed of
actions chosen within the jurisdiction of the
decision-maker, i.e., actions with regard to which
the decision-maker has direct control (control
variables, policy variables, or instruments).
(Y_j) = vector of independent forecasts. Each component,
Y_j, refers to the forecast of variable j.
(Z_k) = as above.
f_e [   ] = interrelationship e.
To substantiate this concept further, consider a simple economic
system of three sectors and two primary factors of production.
Suppose that the input-output coefficients are fixed and reflected in
the following table:

| | Buying Sector | | |
Selling Sector	A	B	C
A	.1	.1	.1
B	.1	.1	.6
C	.3	.1	.0
Labor	.2	.5	.3
Foreign Exchange	.3	.2	.0

Assume that the government controls the level of investment, and its investment budget is R. Let the set of actions be composed of

X_1 investment in sector A
X_2 investment in sector B
X_3 investment in sector C

Suppose that the set of relevant outcomes is composed of

Z_1 = level of induced employment
Z_2 = demand for foreign exchange

If input-output relation is according to the above table, then the functional relation between (X) and (Z) can easily be computed:

Sector (1)	Direct Effect (2)	Indirect Effect (3) = (4) - (2)	Total Effect (4)*
Induced Employment by Investing $1			
A	.20	.36	.56
B	.50	.20	.70
C	.30	.48	.78
Induced Demand for Foreign Exchange by Investing $1			
A	0.30	0.14	0.44
B	0.20	0.10	0.30
C	0.00	0.23	0.23

$$* (4) = F (I - A)^{-1}$$

Where

    F = row vector of the direct labor coefficient in the case of employment and direct foreign exchange coefficient in the case of demand for foreign exchange.
    I = unit matrix.
    A = matrix of input-output coefficients.

231

Using the figures in this table, the set of feasible plans is defined by

$f_1 [\ ] = 0 \equiv$

$(Z_1, Z_2) - (0.56X_1 + 0.70X_2 + 0.78X_3, \ 0.44X_1 + 0.30X_2 + 0.23X_3) = 0$

$f_2 [\ ] \equiv 0 \equiv X_1 + X_2 + X_3 - R = 0$

The set of $f_e [\ ]$ is often defined as a set of constraints. The composition of this set is illustrated by Prof. M. Hill as follows:
"Constraints Arising from Political and Institutional Factors, including international agreements and relations between national and local governments which are generally set by law, institutional structures, and tradition . . ." and . . .

"Constraints of a Technological and Engineering Nature. These relate to what is physically or technologically feasible; these constraints can be thought of as production functions or input-output relationships. For instance, the metropolitan water resources planners must decide how much water is available in a watershed and its likely distribution in terms of the assimilation characteristics of streams in the area, operating characteristics of reservoirs, and the technology of treatment plants. This will then indicate the range of feasible alternative plans. If these constraints change over time, forecast of change in technology over time will be required."

The anticipated outcomes of a plan (Z_k), may not be realized even though the plan is a priori feasible. First, a plan that is a prior feasible may be a posteriori infeasible. The reason is a deviation between the independent forecasts, (Y_j), and their realization. Such a deviation is generally inevitable, since most of the independent forecasts refer to stochastic variables. The deviation must be attributed to bad luck.

Second, the anticipated outcomes may not be realized because the plan is a priori infeasible. Infeasibility can result from inappropriate definition of the feasible set. This is the case if some of the significant interdependences that exist in the real world either are not accounted for in the set $f_e [\ ]$ or are accounted for but with an inaccurate set of parameters. Inaccuracy of the parameters can be illustrated by using the above example of fixed input-output coefficients. Suppose the planner considers only the direct effects of the investment program on employment and foreign exchange: In that case he incorrectly defines the feasible region by $(Z_1, Z_2) - (0.2X_1 + 0.5X_2 + 0.3X_3, \ 0.3X_1 + 0.2X_2) = 0$ and $X_1 + X_2 + X_3 - R = 0$, rather than by the set of constraints described above, which accounts for the indirect effects as well.

Failure to account for these interdependences appropriately is sometimes to be charged to the planners but mainly to the

232

shortcomings of the existing state of the art. This last point is emphasized by the comments of J. Bergsman, who claimed that, in the present state of the art, "we do not have the knowledge of how the system works" and of D. Sheffer, who asserts that "our tools of controlling development are not sufficiently developed."

Feasibility also means that the program specifies instruments that are under the control of the decision-maker. If the decision-maker cannot carry out the actions recommended by the program, the plan is infeasible. An extreme case of infeasibility occurs when there is no decision-maker who can adopt the plan and enforce its program, so that the preparation of a plan becomes an exercise rather than a formulation of effective policy-making. Unfortunately, this extreme situation is not exceptional but rather common. Professor Friedmann, for instance, asserts that, "In most countries, the role of national planners is to advise on policy. Yet, being divorced from the instrument of action, national planners have no means of getting their advice accepted." This refers mainly to experiences in comprehensive planning and will be further elaborated in the subsequent sections of this chapter.

COMPARING ALTERNATIVE PLANS AND COST-BENEFIT ANALYSIS

The term "cost-benefit analysis" is used here in the broad sense rather than the narrower meaning that Professors Hill and Lichfield adopt. Thus, cost-effectiveness analysis, planning balance sheet, and goal-achievement analysis are all considered to be specific techniques of cost-benefit analysis in broad terms.

Inherent in any planning process as a stage of rational decision-making are the basic objectives. The key role of the basic objectives in the planning process was emphasized by Hill. Referring to metropolitan planning, he gave examples of objectives such as "national economic growth, economic stability, regional economic growth, distributional equity, environmental quality, health, and safety, etc." Some other objectives were mentioned by J. R. Boudeville: "internal and external integration, a lessening of inequalities, an increase of interdependencies, a strengthening of consensus."

Whatever the specified objectives, they become operative only after a corresponding set of criteria is selected. A criterion is defined here as a direct or indirect measure that can be applied for ordering plans with respect to a given objective to which the criterion corresponds. To substantiate this, consider the following set of objectives and the corresponding criteria:

	Objective	Criterion

<table>
<tr><td>(1)</td><td>Increasing the rate of growth.</td><td>Rate of increase in GNP.</td></tr>
<tr><td>(2)</td><td>Reducing inequality in the distribution of income.</td><td>Lorentz coefficient of per capita disposable income inequality.</td></tr>
<tr><td>(3)</td><td>Preserving wildlife.</td><td>Number of species that survive.</td></tr>
<tr><td>(4)</td><td>Providing for the aesthetic quality of the area.</td><td>Ordering alternative plans by the city architect.</td></tr>
</table>

The level of performance of a given plan can be expressed by a vector of the level of each criterion, (C_g) where C_g is the level of criterion that corresponds to objective $g(g = 1, \ldots, \Sigma)$. This level of performance depends on outcomes and/or actions (otherwise the actions are irrelevant to the objectives). Formally, this relation can be expressed by

$$c[(C_g), (X_i), (Z_k)] = 0$$

Once the set of criteria that corresponds to each plan is determined, plans can be ordered with respect to every operational objective (i.e., an objective with respect to which a criterion can be defined). Let this ordering result in a vector (O_g^m) where O_g^m is the rank of plan m with regard to objective g.

Comparing the level of performance in terms of ranking of any pair of feasible plans, m and n, may result in one of the following two relations:

(1) One plan, m, in the pair is superior to the other, n, regarding some outcomes, and is inferior to the other in respect to none, i.e.,

$$(O_g^m) (O_g^m) (O_{g''}^m) = (O_{g''}^m)$$

where g is a nonempty subset of the integers $(1, 2, \ldots, \Sigma)$ and g'' is a set of the integers $(1, 2, \ldots, \Sigma)$ not included in g.

$(V_g^m \text{———} V_g^n$. In this case plan n is defined as inefficient.

(2) Neither of the two plans compared is inefficient. If we carry out the comparison for every pair of feasible plans, two sets can be distinguished. The first comprises those plans that are not inefficient in any comparison. This set is defined as the "set of efficient feasible plans." The second set comprises the rest of the feasible plans.

When we eliminate inefficient plans, the number of plans to be further evaluated is reduced. It may even happen that only one plan is included in the efficient set. In this special case, the cost-benefit analysis is complete. Suppose, for example, that the set of objectives and the corresponding criteria are the four in the above illustration; then, if there is a plan that is ranked as the best with respect to each of the four criteria, it can be defined as "the best," whatever the importance of each objective, in relation to the others.

However, once the set of efficient feasible plans is ascertained and there still remain more than one efficient plan, it is impossible to select the best plan without adopting some sort of objective function. The objective function uses the set of values of criteria of each plan, (C_g), in order to determine the rank of each in terms of preference. This ranking may be ordinal or cardinal according to the specific model adopted. Conceptually this stage of selecting the best plan out of the list of efficient ones can be formalized by computing $\phi[(C_g)]$, which corresponds to each alternative plan, and selecting the one that renders the highest value.

The planning process can thus be formalized in terms of solving a problem of constrained maximum:

$$\text{Maximize} \qquad \phi[(C_g)]$$
Subject to
$$f_e\left[(X_i), (Y_j), (Z_k)\right] = 0$$
$$c\left[(C_g), (X_i), (Z_k)\right] = 0$$

This does not mean, however, that the planning process is a solution of a mathematical programing problem in the strict sense. On the one hand, neither must $f_e[\ ]$ be formulated in analytical terms nor are X_i, Y_j, Z_k necessarily continuous variables. Often, a few discrete alternative programs are considered, rather than all the feasible set. Such an approach is, for example, suggested in the paper by Professor Lichfield. On the other hand, a mathematical programing approach to resource allocation does not necessarily represent a meaningful planning model. This is the case when there is no specification of the policy variables (X_i). This can be illustrated by the stimulating paper presented by Walter Isard.

The paper submitted by Professor Lichfield refers to the evaluation of four different patterns of urban growth in Israel:

(1) Official Plan: This was prepared by the Ministry of Interior in 1967 for the period 1985. The plan was conceived to establish a continuum from the small rural settlements to the large cities based upon a Christaller-type concept of a hierarchy of towns.

(2) Urban Clusters: Structuring of groups of small towns in such a way that they can compete or compare with large urban centers for variety, choice and quality of services, employment opportunities, social life, etc.

(3) <u>Growth Centers</u>: Development of major urban centers away from the coastal plan would provide development poles and regional urban nodes counteracting the attraction of the major urban concentrations.

(4) <u>Linear Development</u>: Emphasis on transportation lines as the main skeleton for development. The spatial distribution of population follows development along transportation lines ending at major poles of development. The development axis will, in time, take the form of strings of urban concentrations, smaller or larger according to local conditions.

These four alternatives do not reflect all the spectrum of possibilities and, as Professor Lichfield admitted, "may not even include the optimal solution." However, once these discrete four alternatives are defined, their feasibility is examined and cost-benefit analysis is applied.

Though this procedure is not identical to solving a mathematical programing problem, it is still a procedure that identifies a feasible subset and can be used for identifying efficient plans within this subset. Of course, if this "efficient" set includes more than one plan, an objective function is indispensable for determining the ranking of the alternatives and selecting that most preferred. This can be illustrated by the statement of Lichfield: "because of the data limitation, the analysis will not give a clear-cut answer, but a tentative conclusion at the time of writing is that 'urban clusters' is the best of the three new alternatives, and it has certain merits and demerits in relation to the official plan."

Unfortunately this conclusion is not further elaborated in Lichfield's paper, but it nevertheless implies that the merits and demerits of the preferred strategy, i.e., the "urban clusters," were weighted by some sort of objective function.

There is a serious problem involved in this procedure, which is discussed later in this chapter. The point to be emphasized at this stage is that this procedure of cost-benefit analysis is not inconsistent in principle with the solution of constrained maximum problems inherent in any planning procedure.

The model discussed by Isard is formulated in terms of an analytical constrained maximum problem. Yet it is not, and is not designed to be, a planning model, since the instruments are not explicitly specified.

The model presented by Isard is designed to determine optimal resource allocation through time. Its specific problem is to ascertain the locational pattern of growth of a new industrial district that serves an existing city. The model determines the level of production in the new district, the level of activities in the existing city, and the allocation of product among consumption, investment in productive activities, and investment in pollution abatement.

The objectives of this hypothetical resource allocation problem are to increase consumption, to decrease the amount of labor, and to reduce pollution in the existing city. The criteria of these objectives, i.e., (C_g) in the above notation, are the quantities of two consumption commodities (the first is produced in the existing city, the second is produced in the industrial district), the amount of labor input in production and the level of pollution.

These criteria are assumed to be a well-defined function, i.e., c[ ] in the above notation of the anticipated outcomes. Since some of the outcomes are defined directly in terms of the criterion (the consumption pattern and labor), these outcomes appear as components of (C_g). The level of pollution is defined as a function of the level of activities in the existing center, the level of production in the new industrial district, and the distance of the new industrial district from the existing center.

It is assumed that a well-defined social welfare function exists, i.e., ϕ [ ] in the above notation, which specifies the weight of each criterion. This function is the integral of the welfare level at each time period through the planning horizon.

The social welfare function is maximized over a feasible set defined by a set of constraints, i.e., f_e [ ] in the above notation.

(1) production function relates output to input (labor and stock of capital as a proxy to the flow of capital services);

(2) supply of any factor of production (labor, capital) equals its demand;

(3) supply of any product (product of the center, product of the new industrial district) equals its final demand (consumption, productive investment, and investment in pollution control); and

(4) net increase in the stock of capital within a given interval of time equals investment during the same interval of time.

Thus, the model presented by Isard seems to correspond exactly to the formulation of the planning problem suggested above. But there is no specification of the control devices, i.e., the actions required for the implementation of the solution. In terms of the above formulation, there is no distinction between (X_i) and (Z_k).

It can be deduced a priori that the model is designed to determine exactly the specific allocation pattern of each factor and the distribution of product between consumption and investment as well as the distribution of the product and labor quota among individuals. But, then, the question of feasibility may arise, i.e., whether the decision-maker has such control.

Of course, if we use some assumptions to be discussed later on, the model can be assigned a less comprehensive role. It can conceptionally be used to determine zoning regulations, on the one hand, and a compulsory norm of maximum pollution tolerable, which will vary according to location, on the other hand, while leaving the decisions regarding the specific allocation of resources to market forces. Alternatively, the model can be used to determine the level of tax that should be levied on pollution in order to guarantee the required locational separation between the existing city and polluting activities as well as the use of suitable abatement devices.

The conceptional model presented by Isard illustrates a particular allocation problem that maximizes a certain social welfare function, subject to the availability of resources. In order to represent a planning model even on a conceptional level, the control variables (X_i) are to be specified and the outcomes (Z_k) should be shown to result from the control variables.

In the above formulation of the planning procedure, objectives are represented by criteria, (C_g) as arguments in the goal function, i.e., $\phi\,[(C_g)]$. Very often, however, objectives are also represented in the set of constraints: A minimum level of performance regarding some objectives is required. Accordingly, a plan that provides for less than this minimum level is defined as inadmissible.

Formally, an additional set of constraints is added to the ones discussed so far. The set discussed so far includes two groups: The first specifies the interrelationships between instruments or actions (X_i), independent forecasts (Y_j) and outcomes (Z_k), i.e., $f_e\,[(X_i), (Y_j), (Z_k)] = 0$. The second refers to the dependence of the level of performance of the plan in terms of each criterion (C_g) on the outcomes of the plan, Z_k, i.e., $c[(C_g), (Z_k)] = 0$. The third subset now added is

$$(C_g) \geq (\overline{C}_g)$$

where $(\overline{C}_g)$ represents the minimum level of performance of each criterion. Some of the $\overline{C}_g$ may be zero, signifying that no minimum level is a prerequisite of the plan. Some are positive, representing prerequisites in terms of the level of performance. Hill discussed the role of this set of constraints, which reflects standards flowing directly from the fundamental objectives, e.g., health and safety (public health standards, safety standards on highways, etc.).

The distinction between this set of constraints and the two proper ones is very important. The proper ones are binding from the standpoint of the decision-maker. The third one discussed is not binding and is formulated tentatively to be reconsidered again. They are used to overcome the difficulty involved in formulating an explicit objective function.

Consider, for instance, pollution control standards used as constraints (e.g. by zoning regulations and investment in infrastructure) in determining a locational pattern of land uses. These standards reflect the basic objective of reducing pollution. In principle, this objective, once represented by proper criteria, should be incorporated into the objective function. But, very often, the decision-maker cannot adopt any clear value judgment regarding the trade-off between, for example, GNP and pollution, i.e., the amount of GNP that is worth sacrificing in order to reduce pollution by one unit. Rather, he has perhaps a rough idea about the range of prices (in terms of sacrifice of GNP) of pollution that is not acceptable and the range of prices that is.

The technique is to find solutions for alternative standards and to examine the transformation function between pollution level and GNP. From the marginal rate of transformation, the decision-maker can obtain some impression on the justification of the standards. Of course, this procedure is very difficult and ambiguous in cases when more than one objective is to be treated in this sensitivity analysis.

To this category of constraints, one can perhaps add what can be referred to as "absolute targets." These are objectives of high priority so that a very high price (in terms of alternative objectives) is attributed to them. Such is perhaps one objective of preserving national shrines.

PLANNING AS A CONTINUOUS PROCESS

The most important decision-making in the planning process is that which refers to immediate actions. The rest of the decisions, which refer to actions in the future, can be reconsidered when the time of their implementation falls due. As a matter of fact, it is not only possible but also necessary to reconsider previous decisions, for, when the time comes, new information may have become available. This does not mean, however, that the modified decision is independent of the original planning. On the contrary, some actions have already been carried out and affect the new decision-making. This point deserves more elaboration.

Consider, for instance, an investment project that is planned to be carried out during a two-year period. Initially, the project is considered to be profitable when taking into consideration all relevant costs and benefits. When the project is still in execution, it may be worth reconsidering its profitability in view of new information that has become available. However, the fixed investment, which has already been made, is irrelevant to this reconsideration. This obviously reduces the relevant costs of the project and, therefore, increases the probability that the soundness of carrying on with the project will be confirmed. However, if the new information differs substantially from what was available before, the project should, perhaps, be stopped even at the cost of abandoning the capital already sunk in it.

Modification and updating of plans does not prove that the original decisions were bad. These decisions might have been good relatively, for the information that was available when they were made. Their updating may result from new information not available before. Furthermore, plans that are not reviewed at short intervals are likely to become a posteriori infeasible. The fact that old plans are discarded every 5 years although they refer to 20-25 years does not signify that the plan was useless. The operative part of the plan refers to the short term only.

All this boils down to the argument that even long-term planning is not a one-time process of decision-making regarding actions to be carried out in the long run. Rather it is a continuous process of decision-making regarding actions to be carried out in the short run in view of considerations that refer to the long run.

COMPREHENSIVE REGIONAL PLANNING

Regional Planning. Planning is defined here as "regional" if the decision-making is specified in terms of locations that are not all included within one city. In other words, the actions, (X_j), determined in the regional planning process are spatially specified and, using the terms of John Friedmann, refer to "supra-urban space—that is, any area that is larger than a single city." In this definition, no distinction is made between interregional and intraregional planning. This distinction is only a matter of the aggregation in the definition of location. For instance, suppose that, by whatever principle, the "supraurban space" is divided into some "supraurban subspaces." Suppose each action, X_i, is then locationally specified in terms of one of these supraurban subspaces to which it refers, then the planning can be defined as interregional. But, if the subspaces according to which locations are specified are not "supraurban spaces," then this is intraregional planning.

This definition is very broad and is not necessarily confined to public decision-making. Private firms may elaborate on a regional plan for maximizing profits through time. Moreover, regional plans may be confined to small-range actions. Thus, there may be regional plans for transportation, regional plans for industry, and regional plans for the educational system. If the set of actions determined by the regional planning is broad, then it will be referred to here as comprehensive. This will be further discussed in the subsequent sections.

Comprehensive Regional Planning. "Comprehensive" is an adjective often used in conjunction with regional planning, yet it is much less frequently clearly defined. Comprehensive regional planning is defined here in terms of the conceptional structure of the planning process elaborated above.

The planning functions of the public are most often distributed among different agencies according to their responsibility. Most often there is a "division of labor" between "economic planning," "industrial planning," "land use" or "city planning," "transportation planning," etc. Each of these differs by (1) the agencies responsible for its performance; (2) the set of policy variables, with regard to which a decision is made, i.e., the vector (X_i); (3) the range of outcomes that affect the objective function via the definition of the criteria; and (4) the scope of the objectives embodied in the definition of the objective function.

For instance, "economic planning" is generally designed to determine resource allocation in such a way as to maximize some well-defined objective function. However, the spatial aspect of this allocation and nonquantifiable outcomes are entirely disregarded.

The policy variables determined in land-use planning are zoning regulations and perhaps investment projects of infrastructure. Most often, however, the economic outcomes of the plan are partially or entirely disregarded.

Transportation planning is designed to determine investment plans in transportation facilities. Most often only the direct effects in terms of the level of service of the transportation system are considered, while the indirect effects on land-use pattern and on economic performance are wholly or partially disregarded.

Planning is defined here to be more comprehensive if the ranges of policy variables, the outcomes evaluated, and the feasible plan considered are wider. Accordingly, the planning that simultaneously determines zoning regulations and the investment in the transportation system, while considering the level of service as well as the impact on land-use pattern, is more comprehensive than when carried out separately for land use and transportation. It is clear that comprehensiveness in this sense is a relative concept. There is no "comprehensive planning" but rather "more comprehensive" or "less comprehensive."

The advantages of more comprehensive planning are manifold. If there is one ultimate decision-maker, then more comprehensive planning is required to increase the probability of the internal consistency of the plans. Moreover, even though consistency is guaranteed by appropriate coordination, less comprehensive planning is likely to be associated with a lower level of over-all achievement from the viewpoint of the decision-maker.

Pooling jurisdictions and adopting common criteria are advantageous to different decision-makers who have distinct criteria for evaluating the same set of outcomes. Again, such pooling guarantees consistency and can improve the level of welfare of all the decision-makers participating in the pooling. Such improvement is possible when the policy adopted by one decision-maker affects the welfare of other decision-makers, i.e., when external effects influence the decision-making.

The Advantages of Comprehensive Planning: The Case of the One Ultimate Decision-Maker. Coordination between agencies that represent the same ultimate decision-maker is indispensable for rational decision-making. Without such coordination, some or all the plans of the agencies are a priori infeasible. Yet, coordination alone is not sufficient. It will be demonstrated that it is advantageous to pool jurisdictions and to adopt a system of comprehensive planning. First, the need for coordination is discussed. Then the advantages of pooling jurisdictions is demonstrated.

Very often the decision-making of one agency affects the outcomes resulting from decisions made by other agencies. More formally, the policy variables of agency a, (X_j^a), are exogenous variables of the agency b, (Z_j^b). Hence, the outcomes, (Y_k^b), of a program of agency b, depend, among other things, on the program, (X_j^a), of agency a. Similarly, the outcomes, (Y_k^a), of a program of agency a, (X_j^a), may depend on the program of agency b, (X^b). Internal consistency implies that, if the above interrelationships exist, then $(X_i^a) = (Z_i^b)$ and $(X_i^b) = (Z_i^a)$. Without such consistency, either one plan or both are a priori infeasible.

Such interdependence exists when land use and transportation are planned separately. It is known that the demand for transportation depends on land-use pattern. The level of service of a transportation system depends on the capacity of the system and the demand for it. Hence, the level of service resulting from a transportation plan depends, among other things, on the land-use pattern that is affected by land-use planning.

On the other hand, land-use pattern is considerably affected by the level of service in the various links of the transportation system. Hence, the outcomes of land-use planning depend on decision-making regarding the transportation system.

The above interrelationships imply that variables decided on by those responsible for transportation are independent forecasts for those responsible for land-use planning. Absence of coordination implies that either one of the plans or both of them are <u>a posteriori</u> infeasible in the sense that the independent forecasts of one agency do not coincide with the decision-making of the other.

Coordination is also indispensable in another sense. Suppose that both of the agencies belong to the same decision-maker, for instance, two departments of the same government. Then, internal consistency implies that both must use the same set of criteria, i.e., ϕ [ ] function, and that the same interrelationship must be assumed by both to exist among the variables, i.e., f_e [ ]/.

So far it has been demonstrated that coordination is required in order to ensure the feasibility of plans. Now we are going to show that coordination, as such, cannot always guarantee the best results and that pooling jurisdiction is indispensable.

Assume that, instead of a simultaneous process of decision-making, the coordination is carried out by small numbers of iterations. One agency determines its plan according to the same initial assumptions of the program of the other. The other takes the policy variables of the first as forecasts and optimizes its decision-making. The first modifies its forecasts accordingly and modifies its initial program. Suppose that ultimately the process converges in two consistent programs (program of each agency is identical to forecasts of the other agency). Is the solution necessarily optimal? It is clear that this is not necessarily so. It can be illustrated by the following example:

> Let the policy variable of the first agency be x and of the second y. Let the same criteria be applied by both: "maximize (x,y)." Then, the process of iteration ends when

$$\partial \phi / \partial x = 0$$
$$\partial \phi / \partial y = 0$$

But these conditions are not sufficient for maximizing ϕ (x,y). Suppose ϕ (x,y) is described by the following hill:

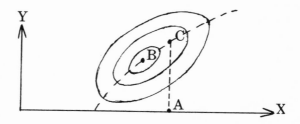

and the initial program of the first agency is A. Then the second agency, which is authorized to move vertically, will choose C. The first agency, which is authorized to move horizontally, will have no incentive to move away from C. Therefore, the peak of the hill, B, will not be reached in this iterative process.

Indeed, if the process of iterations is more sophisticated so that each agency is allowed to make only a small change at a time, it is possible that a higher point in the hill will be reached. But, again, this process does not necessarily end at the peak represented by point B. This is evident if at the same stage C is reached. There is no motive for either agency to move from it. But, if one decision-maker is authorized to move both in the east-west direction and in the north-south direction, he will certainly choose to move toward B.

In this illustration, it has been demonstrated that consistency in criteria and weights of both agencies and consistency between forecasts of one agency and programs of the other do not guarantee the best decision-making. Rather, coordination is necessary that is equivalent to performance of the planning process by one decision-maker. It suggests that institutionally it is preferable that jurisdictions be pooled in the hands of one planner so that all the main control variables are simultaneously determined in view of all the relevant outcomes. This is the meaning used here for the concept of comprehensive planning. This pooling of jurisdiction is advantageous as long as the interdependencies imply that the outcomes resulting from decision-making regarding one set of control variables are affected by decision-making about another set of control variables.

An example for the sake of comprehensiveness, in the above sense, is illustrated in the case of transportation and land use, which are closely interrelated. Given the zoning regulations, the transportation system affects the land-use pattern and the level of service of the transportation system. Given the transportation system, the zoning regulations affect, again, the land-use pattern and indirectly, the level of service of the transportation system. Hence, these two groups of outcomes are relevant both to the determination of zoning regulations and the improvement of the transportation system. Optimal decision-making implies one set of criteria and weights and simultaneous decision-making with regard to both systems. This requirement has recently been recognized. But, since most often the functions are located in different agencies, comprehensive planning is not implemented.

The Advantage of Comprehensive Planning: The Case of More Than One Decision-Maker. In the preceding section, it was assumed that there is one ultimate decision-maker who delegates his powers to different agencies. However, the set of criteria, i.e., the ϕ [ ] function, was assumed to be the same for all agencies. The need for comprehensive planning, i.e., pooling jurisdictions regarding control variables, may also prove to be advantageous to different decision-makers who have distinct criteria for evaluating the same set of outcomes, i.e., who have a different scoring function, ϕ [ ].

Consider two neighboring communities with independent agencies, each of which is responsible for the land-use and the transportation programs of its community. Each agency is supposed to take into consideration the effects of its decision-making on the welfare of its community only. The effects of its decisions on the welfare of the other community are disregarded. In this case, either the set of relevant outcomes of each decision-maker is entirely different or at least the criteria and weighing system of the two agencies differ. For instance, one agency may try to push noxious industries to the boundary between the two, thus reducing the nuisance to its constitutents, because the nuisance to the members of the other community is irrelevant. The outcome of this policy from the standpoint of the other community is different: It increases the nuisance.

Consider another example of external effect. Let the level of service of the transportation system in one of the two communities depend on the level of service in the other. This may be the case if the transportation system in one community accommodates trips to the center of activities of the other community. Again, when the decision-making of the two communities is independent, the benefit to the neighboring community resulting from the improvement is disregarded.

In both the above cases it is sometimes advantageous to both communities to coordinate their actions by pooling their jurisdiction, i.e., by adopting comprehensive planning. Let the nuisance effect on each community be defined as two distinct outcomes; similarly, let the level of service to each community of the transportation system and the costs imposed on each community for implementing the transportation project be defined as distinct outcomes. Then, a consensus may be arrived at for scoring alternative outcomes (i.e., objectives):

(1) Reducing nuisance in community A.

(2) Reducing nuisance in community B.

(3) Increasing the level of service of the transportation system for community A.

(4) Increasing the level of service of the transportation system for community B.

(5) Reducing costs of implementing the plan covered by community A.

(6) Reducing costs of implementing the plan covered by community B.

Using the above set of criteria, efficient plans can be determined that are advantageous to both communities, relative to plans that would otherwise have been decided. For example, suppose each community determines in advance the maximum costs it is ready to bear for the improved level of service (the price it is ready to pay per unit of time saved in trips). Suppose also that the transportation project to be carried out in the area of community A cannot break even when the benefit to community A alone is considered, but more than breaks even if the benefits to the two communities are taken into consideration; then coordination is clearly advantageous. Actually, the problems of distributing the net benefit of the common project still remain; but at least the set of efficient plans can be agreed on (each plan in the efficient set may differ, for instance, in the portion of cost imposed on each community).

Disadvantages of Comprehensive Regional Planning. The more comprehensive the planning, the less manageable it becomes. First, it is very difficult, simultaneously, to take into account resource allocation among sectors specified in terms of both location and time as well as spatial interactions of activities, If the variables are dis-aggregated considerably, most of the existing techniques become un-manageable. This point will be further elaborated later in the chapter.

Second, the current regional planning has no proven hypothesis to provide the planner with adequate knowledge about the way such complicated systems work. While econometric models yield satisfactory explanations for macroeconomic systems, this is not true so far for regional econometric models. Interregional econometric models were developed and tested only recently, and further experience is indispensable for their implementation in practical problems. This point was emphasized in the comments of Mr. Bergsman, which were quoted above.

Third, resource allocation models disaggregated in terms of both sector and location require much more data. Thus expensive surveys become indispensable. For instance, interregional planning of resource allocation requires regional input-output coefficients. These coefficients may differ substantially from one region to another in the production of primary commodities and services. Therefore, the average national coefficients and incomplete regional data are not sufficient to estimate the regional coefficient. This means that expensi regional input-output surveys are required.

Fourth, comprehensive planning is possible if a wide range of instruments are controlled by one decision-maker. (Such a case exists for instance, if budgets and other control devices are implemented according to programs arrived at in the process of comprehensive planning.) In general, though, comprehensive planning is not coupled with comprehensive instruments of power. This, according to Fried-mann, is the difference between comprehensive planning, which is removed from the management of effective power, and planning for specific sectors.

On this point Friedmann contended that,

"In most countries, planning for specific sectors of the public economy such as transport, housing, education, electric power, or agriculture is considerably more successful than either coordinated intersectoral or spatial planning at the national level. The reason is that sectoral planning is carried out by the very agencies that are in charge of making the programed investments. For instance, a Depart-ment of Transportation plans for the use of its own resources, including its legal regulatory powers, to achieve intended, if usually quite limited, effects. A Rural Electrification Agency does likewise; the allocator of its investments is not the unseen hand' of a competitive market but an explicit decision process in which technical factors are weighed alongside other considerations. Planning in these cases is used to guide the daily work of the agency. It provides the necessary in-formation and analysis, produces future projections, furnishes evaluations of costs and benefits, and in a multiplicity of other ways is tied into the formulation of policies, program development, and project design.

"Planning in this sense is effective because it is intimately joined to the exercise of power, that is, to control over the legal and monetary resources to carry out intended actions. Where planning is so integrated with action, it must operate under a set of realistic constraints that make its contributions immediately relevant to the managers of power. Plans are usually formulated in terms of the available instruments for implementing programs; questions posed by the potential use of these instruments are the problems to which planning will generally respond. Sectoral planning has, therefore, a close fit with the available instruments of power."

Thus, implementation of programs prepared within the frame-work of comprehensive planning requires a change in all the structures of decision-making, i.e., comprehensive planning implies compre-hensiveness in decision-making. In some sense this inevitably implies its centralization of decision-making.

PLANNING METHODS: TWO ILLUSTRATIONS

The subject of this section is not a survey of planning techniques. Rather, two basically different approaches are discussed. The evaluation of these two methods illuminates the limitations to which comprehensive regional planning is subject.

The first technique is activity analysis, which is widely used in planning in general. Its main disadvantage is the cost of solving big problems like those implied by comprehensive regional planning. The second technique is cost-benefit analysis, which is applied to a finite number of discrete alternatives. Its main drawback is the fact that only a small subset of the feasible set is considered and evaluated. In general, this method does not provide for a systematic technique that guarantees that the best or at least an efficient plan is really chosen.

APPLICATION OF ACTIVITY ANALYSIS TO COMPREHENSIVE REGIONAL PLANNING

<u>A Linear Programing Model and Its Basic Properties</u>. Suppose that there is a set of predetermined quantities of commodities, a_i ($i = 1, \ldots, m$). Assume that a set of activities (j) ($j = 1, \ldots n$) is defined so that a unit level of activity j is associated with direct revenue p_j and excess demand a_{ij} for commodity i. Thus, a unit level of activity j can be represented by a column vector

$$\begin{bmatrix} p_j \\ (a_{ij}) \end{bmatrix},$$

(a_{ij}) itself is a column vector of which the a_{ij} element is the excess demand of a unit of activity j for commodity i. The general activity analysis problem is to determine the level of each activity j, X_j, such that the vector (X_j) solves the following problem:

$$\text{Maximize} \sum_{j}^{n} P_j X_j$$

$$\text{Subject to} \quad A_{ij} (X_j) \leq (a_i)$$
$$(i = i, \ldots, m)$$
$$(X_j) \geq (0)$$
$$(j = 1, \ldots, n)$$

where A_{ij} is a matrix with columns (a_{ij}) $j = 1, \ldots, n$.

A vector (X_j) that satisfies the two systems of constraints is said to be feasible. A solution to the above problem is, therefore, a feasible vector that maximizes the objective function $\sum_{j}^{n} P_j X_j$.

One important property of such a problem is that, if a solution exists, then a vector (λ_i) exists defined as shadow-prices vector so that the following conditions must hold:

$$(1) \quad [\sum_{j}^{n} a_{ij}X_j - a_i]\lambda_i = 0$$

$$(i = 1, \ldots, m)$$

$$(2) \quad P_j - \sum_{i}^{m} a_{ij}\lambda_i \leq 0$$

$$(j = i, \ldots, n)$$

$$(3))P_j - \sum_{i}^{m} a_{ij}\lambda_j = 0$$

$$(j = 1, \ldots, n)$$

This vector can be determined simultaneously with the solution of the above problem by what is referred to as the dual problem. Assume that λ_i is the price of commodity i. Then 2 above states that the value of activity j minus the sum of values of the excess demands created by it, is not positive. 3 states that, if the value of a unit of activity j is smaller than the sum of values of the excess demands created by it, then activity j does not appear at a positive level in the solution.

These basic relations imply that, if decision-making regarding activities can be delegated to profit maximizers, rather than being withheld by the central planner, the resulting level of activities will be the optimal one, as long as the price system (P_j, λ_i) is operative. In other words, instead of centrally determining the detail of the program (X_j), the central planner can impose a price system (P_j, λ_i). This system can be used to calculate the net gain or loss of each activity as in the left hand side of 2; then, if the decision-makers are profit-maximizing entrepreneurs, the resulting outcome of their decision-making corresponds to the optimal solution of (X_j). To be more rigorous, the above assertion must be more carefully formulated; if the price system (P_j, λ_i) prevails, there is no incentive for a profit-maximizer to carry out activity that is excluded from the solution.

Linear programing is a special case of a general mathematical programing problem. Its specific characteristic is the linearity of the objective function and the system of constraints. In a general mathematical programing problem neither the objective function nor the system of constraints is necessarily linear. However, if the objective function is concave and the feasible region is convex, a set of λ_i prices can be established in such a way that the above delegation of decision-making, i.e., decentralization, is possible.

249

<u>Application of Activity Analysis to Planning of the Allocation of</u> <u>Resources and to Comprehensive Regional Planning</u>. It was argued above that the planning problem can be represented by a general optimization problem:

Maximize $\phi\,[(C_g)]$

Subject to
$$f_e[(X_i),\,(Y_j),\,(Z_k)] = 0$$
$$c[(C_g),\,(X_i),\,(Z_k)] = 0$$

Thus, if the functions $\phi(\ )$, $c[\ ]$, and $f_e[\ ]$ are formulated in linear terms, then the planning process is reduced to a solution of a standard linear programing problem.

Moreover, resource allocation models can be extended to include spatial aspects by introducing three modifications: (1) dividing the space into planning subspaces so that the land in each subspace is a distinct resource; (2) specifying the activities in terms of the subspace in which they take place; and (3) introducing transportation activities that allow for transferring some resources and commodities between any pair of zones. These basic ideas underly the various applications of the activity analysis model to regional planning.

Suppose now that, in a general resource allocation model, activities are specified according to location and transportation activities are defined in terms of shipments of commodities between locations. Then the model is comprehensive in that it simultaneously handles economic activities, land allocation, and transportation, taking into account the direct and indirect interrelationships between these three systems of variables.

Obviously, this comprehensive model is operative only if the decision-maker can implement its solution either directly or indirectly. He can implement it directly if he has direct control over the variables determined by the model. He can implement it indirectly if he controls the price system while participants in the market simultaneously tend to maximize profits.

<u>Comprehensive Evaluation of a Set of Discrete Alternatives</u>. Inherent in the definition of activity analysis is an evaluation of an infinite number of alternatives defined by a set of linear constraints. An alternative approach defines a small number of alternative plans and evaluates each one more thoroughly, taking objectives into consideration that cannot be accounted for otherwise. These approaches are illustrated in the papers of Professors Hill and Lichfield.

According to Prof. Hill, "For projects or programs that can be expressed in very specific terms and whose effects are predictable, evaluation techniques are available. These include cost-benefit analysis, cost-effectiveness analysis, the planning balance sheet, and goals-achievement analysis. Cost-benefit analysis measures the national economic benefits of alternative plans. Cost-effectiveness analysis compares the cost of alternative plans in terms of their comparative performance levels. The planning balance sheet records the advantages (benefits) and disadvantages (costs) of plans with respect to groups affected by them. Goals-achievement analysis compares the level of achievement of plans with respect to the preferred objectives of the community as a whole, as well as groups within it."

This basic approach can be illustrated by the Boston Regional Planning Project (which changed its name to Eastern Massachusetts Regional Planning Project). Four growth alternatives were defined, in terms of the metropolitan areas. The instruments, in terms of transportation, water, and sewer systems, were determined for each alternative. A predictive model, EMPIRIC, was used to generate forecasts of the relevant outcomes. These outcomes were evaluated, and two of them were selected for further evaluation.

Differing perhaps substantially in its degree of technical sophistication, the conceptual procedure presented by Professor Lichfield is nevertheless very similar to the above one. As mentioned above, four alternative spatial patterns of urban development in Israel are elaborated and evaluated. One of them, the "Urban Clusters," was tentatively selected as the most preferred urban development pattern.

In determining the feasible set of alternative plans, various models can be applied that vary in their degree of sophistication. Input-output technique, linear programing, econometric models, gravity models, etc., can be used as submodels in forecasting the outcomes of a given set of instruments. This enables the planner to account for linear as well as nonlinear interrelationships among the variables.

Linear programing is mentioned in the present context as one of the submodels used to simulate the feasible set of alternative plans. In this sense it is used in quite a different role than the one referred to before. (In the preceding section, linear programing was discussed as a complete planning procedure, which includes the definition of the feasible space, evaluation, and the selection of the best plan.)

Given the prices of commodities and assuming that the production functions are concave, competitive equilibrium can be shown to correspond to a solution of certain mathematical programing problems. Models of these types are extensively used to describe spatial equilibrium in the allocation of economic resources.

Provided that actual economic behavior corresponds to competitive equilibrium, such models can be used in a predictive capacity. For instance, suppose that the government considers the effect of an improvement in an intercities transportation network. Assume that the growth rate of the population and economic activities are predetermined so that the consumption and production of each city according to commodity is given. Then, if the competitive equilibrium prevails, the pattern of intercity shipments of commodities will correspond to the pattern determined by the well-known model of "The Transportation Problem." Hence, the linear programing model of the transportation problem can be used as a predictive tool for making forecasts of the effects of the improvement. It is thus used in the capacity of one of the relations f_e [ ] discussed above.

Note, however, that in this capacity the model is used as one element in the planning process. It is still necessary to determine alternative courses of action and to evaluate the predicted outcomes of each. In this limited capacity, activity analysis has nothing to do with these two later stages.

EVALUATION

The alleged shortcomings of applying the activity analysis approach to regional planning may be grouped in five distinct categories:

(1) Estimates of the required parameters are not available.

(2) The model cannot take into consideration intangible and nonquantifiable considerations.

(3) The model requires a priori specification of the economic structure of the region, i.e., the consumption pattern, production structure, and trade.

(4) Linearity does not characterize all the relevant interrelationships to be considered. Being confined to linear form, the model overlooks some crucial issues.

(5) Implementation of the model requires either a priori specification of prices or a social welfare function, while it is practically impossible to define such a function.

Considering these arguments carefully, one realizes that some of them are not relevant to the application of activity analysis to regional planning per se, but rather to regional planning in general. Some of these arguments are relevant to certain specifications of activity analysis models and not to others. Moreover, some difficulties are of operational character, and their importance declines with the development of computer techniques.

These points then deserve further elaboration. First, the absence of reliable data is in fact not specific to activity analysis but rather to any conceivable technique designed to determine efficient allocation of resources. For instance, if it is empirically difficult to estimate economies of scale, training effects, external economies, etc., then it is impossible to take these elements into consideration by any alternative technique. Similarly, without information about input coefficients and perhaps alternative vectors of input coefficients, one cannot determine the most efficient allocation of resources. In this sense the unelaborated argument of Meyer in his survey of regional economics is not relevant specifically to activity analysis but rather to any planning method designed to determine efficient allocation of resources.

Second, the model cannot really tackle all the intangible and nonquantifiable considerations. It is confined to components that can be quantified. But the model can still efficiently be used in cost-benefit analysis of activities that cannot a priori be assigned a weight. The technique is the tentative targets or standards already mentioned.

Suppose, for example, that this set of instruments includes zoning regulation and that one of the objectives is to increase the amount of open space, but that no specific value can a priori be assigned to a unit of open space. The planner can, in this case, tentatively introduce a certain amount of open space as a constraint. Then, using the shadow price, he can measure the marginal alternative costs of this amount of open space in terms of the measurable criteria included in the objective function. Moreover, applying sensitivity analysis on this tentative constraint, he examines how these marginal costs vary with the amount of land allocated to open space. This information can be used for modifying the initial targets that reflect objectives, the importance of which cannot be a priori assessed. The same technique can be applied to such objectives as the preservation of areas of historical and aesthetic importance and the like.

Third, a priori specification of the consumption pattern, production structure, and trade are not indispensable elements of this planning technique but rather depend on some formulations of the model. These a priori specifications are embodied in an input-output model, but not necessarily in an activity-analysis approach. (Alternative activities of production, trade, and consumption can be defined so that the model itself determines which combination of these activities is included in the solution, thus determining consumption, production, and trade patterns without an a priori specification.)

Fourth, linear relations do not really characterize all the relations, but as long as the objective function is concave and the feasible region is convex, linear approximations to these relationships can be formulated that are as close as desired to the nonlinear relations. The real difficulty that still remains is the increase in the size of the model resulting from such approximation. Thus a declining demand can be described by a stepwise function, resulting in as many new activities and constraints as there are steps. Once demands are identified and approximated by stepwise functions and appropriate constraints, there is no danger that too small a number of activities will appear in the solution, in contrast to the real world.

Even more serious difficulty is indeed involved if either objective function is not concave or if some of the constraints are not convex. In this case it is impossible to maintain the standard linear form of the programing. Convexity of the objective function is implied when decreasing costs and increasing returns characterize production. Thus, some characteristics of agglomeration cannot be accounted for by linear objective functions.

Concavity of a feasible region is implied by characteristics of many spatial interrelationships. Spatial interrelations, for instance, are often simulated by gravity or similar models that imply non-convexity. The same difficulty is implied by externalities and indivisibilities.

These difficulties can to some extent be tackled by using integer programing techniques. But, the application of integer programing is still confined to a relatively small problem and cannot yet be applied effectively to such big models as are required in comprehensive regional planning.

Fifth, the argument that the application of activity analysis to regional planning implies either an a priori specification of prices or the definition of a social welfare function requires special consideration. As was argued above, some scoring function is indispensable in any planning technique and is not confined to activity analysis. It is dispensable in a special case when the set of efficient plans includes one plan. If the scoring function is linear, then "predetermined price system" is used. If the function is nonlinear, then a "welfare function" is implied. (Note, however, that the adjective "social" was omitted from "welfare function," since the "welfare function" refers to the valuation of the planner, whoever he is.) Hence, as long as the analytical scoring function is defined, the problem is again reduced to the one of the linearity. The only additional reservation that still remains is that the scoring function is not analytical and, therefore, cannot be applied in mathematical programing at all.

Indeed, if either the region is small in relation to the national economy or if foreign trade prices are important, then it is necessary to make independent predictions of demand and supply for the tradeable commodities in any case. But, again, these estimates are indispensable in any planning method as long as these demands are important.

Most of the arguments against activity analysis are relevant to the planning process as such rather than to the activity analysis. But the activity analysis should be properly specified to take care of all the problems mentioned above. This specification raises some operational difficulties that cannot be overcome by the present computer programs and techniques.

The main drawback of the second method, i.e., evaluation of a subset of feasible plans, is the fact that it is at best suboptimization. This is especially apparent when the instruments can be defined in terms of continuous variables. For instance, public space, density, a public investment, etc., are in general continuous. Lichfield admits in his paper that "the method of selection of the alternatives is certainly not comprehensive in the sense of including all possibilities and may not even include the optimal solution." In other words, his method provides perhaps for comprehensive evaluation of alternatives that are not comprehensively selected.

CONCLUSIONS

To sum up, there are, on the one hand, regional planning problems that can be tackled efficiently by activity analysis techniques. A classic problem that can be solved by such a technique is the location of agricultural production in the surroundings of an export market, which are the areas where prices are determined by supply and demand outside the region.

There are, on the other hand, planning problems in which it is too difficult either to define the whole set of feasible plans or to formulate an analytical welfare function. This is especially relevant to cases in which increasing return to scale, externalities, and other now convex interrelationships are important.

There are, however, also other problems in which some synthesis of the two methods can be productive. Consider a case in which agglomerative advantages of industrial complexes can be defined. The rest of the activities that do not contribute to the agglomerative advantages can be determined by using an activity analysis model that minimizes, for example, total costs of interrelations. Each alternative is thus suboptimized over an infinite subset of feasible solutions. Thus, the total number of alternatives evaluated is substantially extended. Some of the advantages of both of the methods can then be realized.

11

**TRANSFORMATION
OF SLUM AREAS**

Since the advent of the Industrial Revolution, immigration of peasants into the towns in search of work, fortune, and a new way of life has been one of the major forces of progress and modernization. It has been the major force in creating the worst and most disastrous of all modes of human habitation—the slum.

All too often the dreams of a brave new world are shattered within days by the indifference of the city to the newcomer and by the lack of employment, facilities, and accommodations. All too often the city literally sends its new residents into the gutter, for lack of other lodgings, and the faster the rate of growth, the more people are likely to land there.

That progress and decay march hand in hand is one of the most frequently recorded of all social paradoxes, particularly in Western Europe, where men of letters have attacked it, from Defoe through Dickens to Shaw. The scope of the problem in the developing countries, however, owing both to the rate of migration as well as to its scope, is of quite unprecedented magnitude and has staggering implications. It is no wonder that it was one of the most hotly debated issues of the Rehovot Conference, where speakers from all over the world presented a chilling picture of the situation and made urgent pleas for plans that would solve the problem.

DIMENSIONS OF THE SLUM PROBLEM

ROBERT J. CROOKS introduced a new dimension into the discussions by terming the slums "transitional settlements." According to him, the growth of transitional urban settlement is

256

. . . very probably the most dramatic phenomenon accompanying urbanization in developing countries today. The most severe and dangerous conditions of the urban environment are to be found in transitional urban settlement areas, which are by far the fastest growing part of urban areas in developing countries.

The term "transitional urban settlement" is used here to embrace the many forms of slums, squatter settlements, and other uncontrolled settlements in developing countries. These settlements exist throughout the world under various names, such as shantytowns, marginal areas, favelas in Brazil, barriadas in Peru, ranchos in Venezuela, gecekondu in Turkey, bidonvilles in French-speaking Africa, or gourbivilles in Tunis. The use of the term "transitional urban settlements" reflects the desire of the United Nations to move toward a terminology that will eliminate the pejorative and legalistic connotation of the terms "slum" and "squatter" and that will be consistent with more than a decade of international experience, which indicates that the low-income sector of the population living in these areas, is potentially a dynamic and positive element of society.

These areas are "transitional" in the sense that their inhabitants are undergoing a social and economic change, often from a rural to an urban way of life, with the goal of full participation in the urban economy. An important distinction is that the effective land use of these areas is commonly of a long-term or permanent residential character. These are areas within which a transitional process is taking place.

Crooks went on to explain the need for tackling the problem, its characteristics, and its scope.

. . . The argument for devoting specific consideration to transitional urban settlements within the process of urbanization and developing countries may be outlined briefly as follows:

(1) a significant proportion of the urban population of the developing world now lives in these areas;

(2) this population is growing extremely rapidly both absolutely and in the proportion it constitutes of the urban population;

(3) the environmental conditions of these areas are man-made, shameful in their degradation, and commonly beyond the limited reach of conventional public housing programs;

(4) the people of these areas lack the economic mobility to escape from their microenvironment, which, therefore, constitutes the total physical environment affecting their lives;

(5) the environment of the urban areas as a whole and the degree to which the potential benefits of development can be realized are increasingly determined by the physical environment and social problems of transitional settlement areas.

The apparent homogeneity of transitional settlements—the low quality of housing and community facilities—conceals a wide range of deficiencies and an even wider range of outlook. In addition, conditions in these settlements are usually undergoing a process either of gradual improvement or of deterioration and are seldom stable.

Most often, however, the degree of environmental deprivation is severe. Families establishing themselves in these areas will commonly begin their existence there at the meanest of subsistence levels. Access to water will be difficult, irregular, and expensive, with the water itself in all probability being contaminated.

Inadequate or, more likely, nonexistent sewage and garbage disposal services will have provided fertile conditions for the breeding of vermin and pestilence. Living accommodations will be overcrowded, lack privacy, and be very hot in summer and cold and wet in winter. The surrounding areas will suffer from a high density of population and lack open space and ready access to transportation to other parts of the urban area. Fire will be a constant and devastating hazard. Access to normal community facilities such as health, education, and recreation facilities will be difficult or impossible. Sickness and infant mortality rates will be high and life expectancy short.

Whatever the story of the individual transitional settlement, be it newly formed or many generations old, it is probable that the majority of its population will now be young newcomers to the urban area, motivated by the opportunities that seemed to exist in the city. The incomes of these people as a whole are so low and unstable that they are beyond the reach of conventional institutional assistance mechanisms such as publicly assisted low-cost or low-rental housing and financial and credit mechanisms that would allow participation in the officially recognized housing market.

The nature of the environmental conditions of any area is to influence the behavior and social attitude of the inhabitants. In the case of transitional settlements, their inhabitants lack the economic mobility to escape for any significant period from their microenvironment, which exerts a correspondingly strong influence on them, in some cases creating frustration and dissatisfaction with their inability to participate more fully in urban life. It is apparent that the continued growth of these areas in their present form could lead to deep social problems and unrest of a magnitude that may act substantially to counteract the potential benefits of the development process.

Considering the present magnitude and rate of growth of transitional urban settlements in developing countries, the environment of these areas increasingly determines the environmental quality of the cities of which they are a part. It appears that about one-third of most urban populations in developing countries now suffer environmental degradation in transitional settlements.

Crooks was supported in his arguments by <u>DENIS JOHN DWYER</u>, who, also, outlined the dimensions of the problem.

. . . Today's Third World cities, in terms of their built environment and especially in housing provisions, can be said not simply to
be bursting but more accurately to have burst already at the seams.
Substantial and growing numbers of people live within or on the edge
of what perhaps may best be called spontaneous settlements. These,
at least initially, usually consist of dwellings of extremely flimsy
construction, lacking in basic urban services such as safe water
supply and sewers and without the benefit of legal land tenure. Such
settlements are often referred to in English as squatter settlements,
a term that, it is worth noting, automatically carries with it prejudicial
legal connotations. While, in general, it is erroneous to think of
spontaneous settlements as consisting wholly of recent in-migrants—
a survey carried out in Hong Kong of the occupants of inner-city
tenement premises scheduled for redevelopment between October
1963 and June 1965 showed, for example, that 16 percent intended to
move into squatter units and a further 6 percent into stone cottages or
village houses, many of which technically would also be squatter structures—such in-migrants are undoubtedly a highly important element
in the formation of spontaneous settlements throughout the Third World.
Spontaneous settlement has become a major element in the urban
form of cities of the developing world in the last 30 years. About one-
quarter of the population of Manila and Djakarta lives in spontaneous
settlements; in Hong Kong, despite the fact that the formation of such
settlements has been brought under effective control, the current
figure is 11 percent of the urban population. Comparable figures
elsewhere are 20 percent for Caracas, 33 percent for Mexico City,
and almost 50 percent for Ankara, and this situation will undoubtedly
soon become much worse. Turner has estimated, for example, that
by 1990, 4.5 million out of Lima's anticipated population of 6 million
will be living in <u>barriadas</u>. He has also pointed out that growth rates
of such settlements are now reaching 12 percent annually in several
countries, such as Mexico, Turkey, the Philippines, and Peru, or in
many cases double those of city growth rates as a whole.

While it is certainly correct to state, as Crooks does above,
that the "nature of environmental conditions is to influence the
behavior and social attitudes of the inhabitants," the behavior of
man on the other hand may also have considerable influence on
his environment—a point forcefully made by <u>M. B. CLINARD</u>:

. . . Too often, the slum has been considered in physical terms:
overcrowding, congested housing, and deficient physical amenities.

These factors alone, however, have not produced slum problems, and poor housing in itself does not cause crime and other forms of deviant behavior. . . .

One cannot conclude, moreover, that the poverty of the slum alone produces the problems of the slum such as crime. Economically deprived persons do not necessarily steal; rather, the norms permitting and sanctioning such behavior must be found in the immediate environment and incorporated into the individual's life organization. . . .

I, and I think our sociological studies, do not find that slums, and the products of slum life, both in the developed and the developing countries, are due to housing nor are they due to economics. They are due to a human way of life that develops in certain kinds of areas. This way of life that develops does not develop in all slums. I merely point out to you that the Jew lived in some of the most horrible slums the world has ever seen, both physically and economically, in Europe, and never did the bad sanitation, the crime, and delinquency develop that there is in New York City or in Europe and that has characterized other groups.

The Japanese-American has lived in the slums of my country and never was a part of it, either in crime, alcoholism, drugs, sanitation, or otherwise. I wrote an article on the slums of Tokyo that was printed a few years ago, called, "Slums That Are Not Slums." Some of you have seen some of the slums of Japan: The housing is very poor—wooden shacks, but they are clean and neat. They do not have much crime, or much of other kinds of sanitation and health shortcomings.

I merely wish to point out that a slum is a sociological phenomenon, and it is not the shacks that make the filth. Filth is made by people not using sanitary facilities that might well be erected by themselves. It is made by poor sanitation. I have worked in India for three years with the Ford Foundation in the slums. The dirt of Indian slums is dirt like that of New York City, or any other city. It is put there, dropped there, whether it be food, excreta, or any other article.

Slums, then, are not products of a physical situation. They are products of social ways of life. A sociologist does not regard a slum as a physical or as an economic phenomenon, but as a way of life.

The scope of the problem in the foreseeable future was also discussed by ROBERT SADOVE, whose outlook was far from optimistic.

. . . What appears to be the outlook for this trend toward continued rapid urbanization? What are the conditions under which it is taking place? Despite average per capita income and productivity differentials between urban and rural areas, unemployment in developing urban centers is high and getting higher due to increased rural-urban migration. It appears an almost universal phenomenon in developing countries that the investment required to employ the potential labor force productively has plainly outstripped the means available.

The Organization of American States estimates that for Latin America the average officially registered unemployment rate doubled between 1950 and 1965 to well over 10 percent and the rise has continued since. For some individual countries and cities, the situation is much worse.

Projections for the years ahead, unfortunately, give no basis for optimism of any early or automatic relief of these problems. Past demographic trends preclude any early reduction in over-all population growth or the growth of the labor force. Total population appears likely to grow in the next decade at much the same rate as in the 1960s. The rate of increase in the labor force may be somewhat below that for the over-all population due to lower participation in the labor force by people in the working age group. There are few grounds, however, for expecting the work force rate of increase to be significantly less, if at all, than in the 1960s.

It is difficult to avoid concluding that the deterioration of urban conditions under way in the 1960s will be further accentuated in the 1970s and 1980s unless determined action is taken along new lines to counter or accommodate current trends. To cope with the existing deficiencies of major urban centers in the context of the natural population growth rates—often exceeding 3 percent and at times reaching as high as 3.5 percent—would be difficult enough. In the context of continuing heavy migration from the countryside, the urban problem threatens to become explosive.

Attention should be drawn to the existing ratios between rural and urban population. In many parts of Africa and Asia, over 80 percent of the population is rural. In such cases, migration to the towns or even a small proportion of the natural increase in rural population will produce a large increase in urban population.

The implications are serious. The poorer developing countries where the rural percentage is at present very high will have to deal with the more rapid rates of urban growth, yet these are the countries that have fewer resources with which to cope with the urbanization problem.

The resource picture is no less discouraging. The capital requirements of the industrialization/urbanization process are in all countries particularly related to higher aspirations and standards than in the past. Most larger urban centers are closely connected with the more industrialized countries abroad, which they often resemble more closely than they do minor towns in their own country. This resemblance, or aspiration to resemblance, is to the disadvantage of much of the urban developing world; the costs involved in providing similar conditions of living are generally far beyond the means available in developing countries. Provision of modern transport, social services, education, and urban amenities on the pattern of the more developed world requires extremely high capital and operating costs.

The necessity of relating real infrastructure costs to the incomes of the people can be illustrated readily in the field of housing. The demand for housing in developing countries is largely "noneffective" because the intensity of need for housing bears little relation to the ability to pay for it. Housing is basically not the same problem in the cities of the developed countries as it is in the developing world. In the developed countries, the basic problems derive from social and institutional rigidities; in the developing countries, the problem is simply a basic lack of national resources.

It is not surprising to find that public housing intended for low-income groups is frequently occupied by middle-income families. In fact, perhaps three-quarters of the population in the major cities of the poorer developing countries cannot afford the economic rent of the conventional type "low-cost" housing. Even assuming substantial transfers by way of subsidies, total national savings are quite inadequate for the effort required. The problem is compounded by high land costs, limited mortgage facilities, and poorly organized construction industries. Therefore, for at least the poorer countries of the developing world, public provision of conventional low-cost housing for the urban poor directly or indirectly is simply not a practical proposition.

CONCEPTUAL PLANNING
FOR SLUM IMPROVEMENT

Many of the speakers at the Conference attacked the prevailing fallacies of high standards that often prevent the improvement of slum areas and the practical solving of the problem. On this subject, SADOVE wrote,

. . . The attention currently being given to slum settlements perhaps incorporates the only possible approach, i.e., one directed toward devising low-cost methods of providing settlements with minimal facilities for water supply, sanitation services, transport, and educational and health services to permit some satisfactory conditions for living, combined with a community development program based on a "self-help" principle.

A program of this kind will require a considerable shift in urban infrastructure standards if the large populations are to be accommodated. Such a shift may have a significant effect on the standards employed by the various aid-givers.

The "substandard" and the "inadequate" may have to be accepted in the short run because otherwise half or nearly half of the population will continue to be excluded from the benefits of economic development.

JOHN F. C. TURNER discussed the same subject and went to the more conceptual roots of the matter.

. . . We have an evident contradiction between what a central body considers the desirable minimum and what the users, each according to his own situation, consider desirable. The one is static; the other dynamic. The one perceives housing as a noun; the other as a verb.

The obvious solution to this dichotomy is to reduce the minimum standard to a level that the mass of people, through their own efforts, can meet. But there is an enormous resistance to this approach on the part of middle-class standard-fixers.

In situations of massive poverty, the minimum standard must be so low that it loses any meaning, so that there might as well be no standard at all. We must be more seriously concerned with situations in which central planners have established minimum standards of some significance and, in enforcing them, have actually contributed to the reduction of the housing stock.

Very often this means that areas of low-income housing are freed for upper-income development at the expense of development for lower-income groups. Unless the government of a nation with a transitional economy, which is between the preindustrial and industrial situation, has a large budget for subsidized housing (which indicates a gross maldistribution of wealth), it will be likely that a minority of the privileged poor, or the not-so-poor, will be housed at the expense of the unlucky majority.

In cities that have recently been small and that have lately been swollen by huge influxes of rural or small-town migrants, there is little filtering down of older housing stock. Furthermore, government housing programs are notorious for increasing new housing costs, and, with very high per-unit expenditure, such programs further reduce services that might potentially be available to those capable of creating their own homes.

Ingenuous planners have frequently exacerbated low-income housing problems through their often well-intentioned but generally counterproductive schemes for slum clearance and urban renewal. More often than not, the demolition of older housing, which brings low rentals and is inhabited at high densities, <u>achieves the opposite results on the pretext of improving low-income housing conditions</u>. Cases from all parts of the world are notorious; the West End in Boston, Nonoalco Tlaltelolco in Mexico City, and the Lagos Slum Clearance Scheme, for instance. In many and, perhaps, in most cases, the houses built (or the land vacated) were far too costly for the low-income families displaced and even for the middle- or upper-income users. In all three of the above-mentioned cases, the new properties were still only partially occupied years after construction—thus depriving both the poor and the public at large.

I think it is evident, then, that a quantitive, or "minimum standard" definition of housing actually leads to the minimizing, at best, of what the public sector can do toward the housing of the poor, and, at the worst, it may produce the absurd situation in which houses are torn down in a time of grave shortage and in which the people displaced are prevented from building their own homes.

In the view presented here, the housing problems created or exacerbated by conventional standards cannot be understood or solved, therefore, unless the issues of what we are dealing with are identified and resolved. These issues are conceptual and linguistic on the one hand and strategic and political on the other. Language defines desirability, while politics define feasibility, and, in any existentially significant activity, we must be concerned with both.

By "existentially significant activities," I mean those that can act as vehicles for personal fulfillment—assuming that fulfillment or maturity in turn depends on personal responsibility for making decisions about one's own life. Housing is one such activity, as are all those on which the "immediate ends" of life depend: the cultivation and preparation of food, clothing ourselves, the care of our bodies, and the procreation and nurture of children. Other activities, essential as they may be, are less amenable to personal direction or direct participation: the installation and operation of major communications systems, for example, or dealing with any mass-produced and mass-marketed item, whether one is a factory operative, a distributor, or a consumer.

If this distinction is not recognized, then what I consider to be the basic issues will seem irrelevant or meaningless. That is, the linguistic difference between housing as a noun and housing as a verb and the political difference between legislating standard rule and executing standardized games.

These alternatives, naturally, have profound implications in all spheres. On the one hand, we will—as we so commonly do—have supralocal agencies that plan for and provide for people's housing needs, with the result that the people so planned for and provided for turn into consumers or passive beneficiaries. On the other hand, if housing is treated as a verbal entity, as a means to human ends, as an activity rather than as a manufactured and packaged product, decision-making power must, of necessity, remain in the hands of the users themselves. I will go beyond that to suggest that the ideal we should strive for is a model that conceives housing as an activity in which the users—as a matter of economic, social, and psychological common sense—are the principal actors.

That is not to say that every family should build its own house, as the urban squatters do, but rather that households should be free to choose their own housing, to build it or direct its construction if they wish, and to use and manage it in their own way. In fact, these are traditional characteristics of local housing systems and are still open to use for those with high incomes.

Obviously, the agility and flexibility of a housing market depends on the openness of the system at all levels of production, so that the number and variety of producers and compatible and interchangeable products is maximized. In both material and human terms, the more open the system, the greater the potential benefits. The best results are obtained by the user who is in full control of the design, construction, and management of his own home. Whether or not he builds it with his own hands, it should be noted, is of secondary importance—unless he is very poor.

The relatively high-income owner-builder in the United States achieves a first cost savings of 50 percent or more, and these savings are proportionally matched by many very low-income squatter-builders in countries such as Peru. A squatter with a suitable building plot and secure tenure can and often does build a house that would cost twice as much were it built by a government agency.

Savings in first construction costs are considerably greater, of course, if operating expenses are taken into account—interest, insurance, and utility costs over a 20- to 30-year period are generally three times as large as the initial construction cost. Mortgage carrying charges constitute the largest part of operating costs, and these are greatly reduced when the principal is halved (or, as in the case of squatter "progressive development," mortgage financing is eliminated altogether).

The human side of the account is very much more difficult to assess. Most, if not all, observers agree, however, that user-controlled housing (when it is also materially economic) is far superior as a vehicle of personal, family, and social growth or development than housing that is merely supplied.

In an economy of scarcity, the mass of the common people, though poor, possess the bulk of the nation's human and material resources for housing. Their collective entrepreneurial and manual skills (and spare time) far surpass the financial and administrative capacity of even the most highly planned and centralized institutional system—whether dominated by the state or by private capitalist corporations.

The commercial market for new housing in low-income countries such as Peru is inevitably limited to the minority who can afford the costs of imposed standards and, of course, the profits demanded by capitalist enterprise in inflationary or high-risk economies. The publicly subsidized housing supply is also limited by the generally very small budgets available for housing and related facilities.

If neither the "organized" private sector nor the public sector of the economy can provide new housing for a huge and rapidly growing population (which cannot possibly crowd into the initially small and diminishing supply of old housing in zones of transition), then the effective demand must come from the people themselves, the "popular sector." This third sector is, in fact, the major producer of low-income housing in most low-income and rapidly growing cities. Norms practiced or legally required by the organized public and private sectors but impractical for the mass of the people are simply ignored. For example, if building land is restricted by private and commercial speculation, it will be taken out of the commercial market through organized invasion if no other land is available or if poor people cannot pressure the political authorities into expropriation on their behalf.

A "popular sector" capable of organized action on a scale the formally institutionalized sectors cannot control and composed of households whose housing priorities are relatively inelastic is, therefore, the dominant factor in the processes governing the production and maintenance of new housing in economies of scarcity.

If governments in countries with low per-capita incomes wish to avoid the disorder and diseconomies of unplanned direct action by squatters and clandestine developers (who are the major suppliers of low-income urban housing in these contexts), then their housing strategies must change. The only way of reversing the present deterioration of housing and the collapse of viable urban development is for governments to redirect their relatively scarce resources away from the conventional and now discredited closed housing projects and into the development of open housing service systems.

In reply to Professor Turner, DENIS JOHN DWYER said,

. . . There are certain significant difficulties in such possible programs, some of which Professor Turner himself acknowledges. One of the largest lies in the poor design and layout both of individual settlements and of communities when constructed almost wholly by unskilled and often ignorant workers who, if not direct migrants, may be only a very few years removed from rural hinterlands. At the

266

level of the individual dwelling unit, there is usually a marked tendency to reproduce known forms, either those of houses of the poor in the countryside or those of the urban slum near the city center. While there are instances, at the community level, some of which Professor Turner himself notes, or spontaneous settlements that have either begun or quickly assumed regular layouts and where the settlers themselves have voluntarily left space free for the later installation of community facilities, there are also many, especially in Eastern Asia, in which densities characteristic of such settlements are far too high and building patterns too chaotic to permit of their easy rationalization. Official programs based on the creation of new areas for spontaneous settlements in these circumstances might face formidable control problems.

Perhaps of most crucial importance, however, is the over-all view Professor Turner holds of the form of the city. This is never clear. The fostering of spontaneous settlement will, in a majority of cases it seems, inevitably imply a widely spread city of relatively low density with such settlements on the periphery, and, while this may have merit as a possible solution to the housing problem in certain circumstances, inherent difficulties of transport services, of the extension of roads, water supply, lighting, and sewerage, of industrial location, and of journey to work must also be recognized. Professor Turner himself quotes the case of Arequipa, Peru, which in 1960 had a regularly built-up area of 900 hectares and an additional built-up area of barriadas covering 1,100 hectares, with the average gross density in the barriadas being only 22 per hectare.

Lastly, Professor Turner's strongest argument, the self-improving nature of spontaneous settlement, also requires considerable qualification. Though this is a marked feature of certain Latin American situations and has rightly attracted attention as one of the most forceful examples of the creative forces latent among the urban poor of the Third World, it must be recognized that self-improvement is not characteristic of a large number of squatter cases. It is, for example, possible to set against the self-improving experience of the several parts of the Lima barriadas quoted, the generally static experience of the bustees of Calcutta, and most East Asian squatter areas seem to conform more to the Calcutta pattern in this respect than to that of the "improving" parts of the Lima barriadas. Professor Turner tends to relate improving activities to the level of family income, but in reality the situation is much more complex than this. Selective in-migration of working-age males who leave their families behind in the countryside is obviously a highly important factor in the case of Calcutta, as is the fact that many of the bustees are in reality rooming houses owned by a principal tenant or an absentee landlord. The form of tenure is also important in the case of many of the squatter "yards" of Kingston, Jamaica. Though family occupation is more normal in the Kingston case, there, too, the relationship is often that of tenants to principal tenant or landlord rather than a pattern of owner-occupation. Circular movement of purely temporary migrants is important in Africa. Again, prospects for eventual tenure also play a role of importance in many cases. Where control is firm (for example in Hong Kong, where extensions of squatter structures may be demolished by the authorities and the materials confiscated), it is usually not worth trying to improve a structure, whatever the family income.

Even allowing for the criticisms and qualifications made above, there is still considerable force in Professor Turner's argument: The criticism serves rather to reveal the complexity of the problem. The basic fact, which he rightly emphasized and which must be faced, is that urban housing problems in the Third World have now reached such formidable dimensions, and are likely to accelerate in serious-ness, that they are not capable of solution within the foreseeable future solely by Western-style methods, even given greatly improved capital inputs into housing and the possibility (which is doubtful in many cases even with the capital) of developing conventional construction capacities markedly larger than those at present in existence in most Third World countries. As the first section of this paper indicated, however, the economic and social forces at work in shaping the residential pattern of the contemporary Third World city must in these circum-stances be further evaluated. Physical planning must seek to turn such forces to advantage, for attempts to create wholly Western-style cities are likely to be doomed to failure, though this is not to say there is no future at all for the high-rise, minimal-standard housing scheme.

MARSHALL CLINARD approached the concept of self-help in the slum as a means of solving some of the pressing problems.

. . . The use of urban community development offers great hopes for the physical and social improvement of slum areas into which migrants move. Efforts are being made to organize local slum areas so that self-help may be stimulated among the residents to deal with sanitation, health, and illiteracy, as well as with delinquency, crime, and other antisocial activities, in this way changing the slum character of the area. Group practices have brought about the prob-lems of many of these areas, and group organization and effort can be effective in changing them. The objectives are to develop local community feeling and responsibility for improvements, discover indigenous leadership that will help to change the area, stimulate self-help and the cooperation of local people in the use of services provided for the people by the government, and make possible the decentralization of some of the services provided. The development of such an approach to slums and migrant problems can be made at the national and municipal levels through the creation of governmental agencies, as has been done in urban community development programs in such places as India, Pakistan, and Venezuela. Such programs can help with the absorption problems of urban migrants by helping them directly or by changing the type of areas into which they have moved.

People have made improvements in houses and courtyards. They have paved and repaired lanes and constructed drains. They have constructed common latrines, urinals, and bathing facilities. They have pooled their resources to pay for additional water supplies and for the first time have brought into the squatter area one single light-point by which their children, at least, can read at night. They have stimulated health improvements like immunization and health classes. They have conducted adult literacy classes. In some, particularly in Hong Kong, they have set up self-help libraries, newspapers, and reading rooms and acted also in the field of cooperative purchasing of food, organizing cultural programs, crafts, sewing classes, and food-preserving activities.

Such programs can help with the absorption problems of urban migrants by helping them directly or by changing the type of areas into which they have moved.

AREAS FOR GOVERNMENT ACTION

ROBERT J. CROOKS summarized the national institutional action to be taken, as well as that under the auspices of the United Nations.

. . . The experience gained to date indicates a number of critical areas in which governments can act to foster the progressive improvement of transitional settlements, in particular:

(1) Land. There is clear and rational evidence that the willingness of families in transitional areas to make capital improvements to their living environment relates directly to their expected ability to remain on the land they occupy.

(2) Employment. The relationship between the ability of transitional area inhabitants to improve their physical and social environment and the degree to which they can obtain adequate employment are direct and fundamental.

(3) Urban Planning. The physical capacity of an area to improve or continue an improvement process will depend on its location in relation to the urban area as a whole, its potential to acquire normal urban services such as water, electricity, and transportation, and the suitability of the site for residential purposes.

(4) Community Services. Health and education services, community development, and other social support affect both the willingness and ability of people to participate in a process of physical environmental improvement.

(5) Technical Assistance. Particularly in the use of building materials and construction techniques, technical assistance can directly improve the effectiveness with which popular resources are employed for environmental improvement.

(6) Finance and Credit. There is sufficient evidence of the powerful potential of community-oriented savings and credit programs tied to housing and home improvement to warrant serious and innovative effort to initiate schemes by which this potential can be realized.

(7) Legislative and Administrative Mechanisms. Present forms of departmental specialization commonly act to block comprehensive programs, for which, in any case, legislative authority may be inadequate.

United Nations concern in this problem area was identified by the General Assembly in 1960. During the past decade, reports by the Secretary-General and direction from the Committee on Housing, Building, and Planning, beginning with its first session in 1963, resulted in the meetings of expert groups, research, and interregional seminars, which developed the background for Resolution 1224 (XLII) of the United Nations Economic and Social Council (June 6, 1967). The Resolution calls for a search for alternative and comprehensive policies and public investment programs aimed at magnifying and speeding the progressive improvement process that can take place as a result of popular initiatives.

As directed by the Resolution, the Center for Housing, Building, and Planning, in conjunction with other U.N. departments and agencies, has developed proposals and engaged in preparatory activities toward establishing a series of pilot programs for slum and squatter settlement improvement. The objective of these activities is to aid governments in the formulation of effective long-range policies and programs that will radically increase the rate of progressive improvement in the living conditions of low-income urban dwellers. This work is complemented in the Center by efforts toward the compilation and analysis of information on magnitude and trends, development of methodology, and coordination of relevant research.

Based on experience gained in the past decade, the U.N. Center for Housing, Building, and Planning continues to stress the importance of achieving a major shift in attitude and emphasis from the current norms of national and international policies and programs that attempt to deal with transitional urban settlements. The most basic policy and program directions are the acceptance and support of the long-term existence of transitional areas and the anticipation of future transitional settlement growth.

Acceptance and Support of the Long-Term Existence of Transitional
Areas. In many cases, transitional urban settlements constitute
valuable actual or potential additions to the urban housing stock and
fixed capital investment at city and national scales. In conditions of
rapid urbanization and even more rapid growth of transitional areas,
through migration and natural population growth, vast clearance
schemes with or without high-cost public housing can only aggravate
the problems of people living in these areas. Such schemes may
generally be considered to be destroying the human environment
rather than improving it, as such measures commonly result in a
reduction of the limited stock of accommodation within the economic
grasp of transitional settlement dwellers, through physical elimination
and corresponding market pressure toward increased rents for the
remaining units. Public authorities at all levels should recognize
that, in general, measures aimed at eliminating transitional area
populations from the city will not succeed, nor can developing economies
afford to build conventional public housing for these people. Consistent
with a positive supportive attitude, governments should take action
wherever possible to extend linkages that could make normal urban
utilities and community services available to these areas on an appropriate scale, according to priorities established through the involvement of the residents themselves in the development process. Of
particular importance in encouraging the progressive improvement
of transitional urban areas is the degree to which the residents feel
a secure right to the land they occupy, and supportive programs
should treat this issue as a matter of high priority.

Anticipation of Future Transitional Settlement Growth. Governments
and international organizations concerned with the environment of
human settlement, should now be ready to accept the lessons offered
by experience, demographic projections, and economic realities, to
the effect that urbanization and the forces leading to the rapid growth
of transitional urban settlements will continue and grow in strength at
least until the end of this century. This attitude should lead naturally
toward preplanning for transitional settlement growth, in a manner
that will emphasize the positive aspects of the areas that have been
identified.

As mentioned earlier, clearance of slum and squatter areas, a
policy that is wholesale by its nature, constitutes a waste of popular
resource investment and often results in a net destruction of the living
environment. Governments and international organizations must
develop and use legal and administrative mechanisms that will make
planned land acquisition and development possible in urban areas in
advance of needs. Fundamental to the success of such preplanning
for transitional settlement growth is a comprehensive and coordinated

271

approach that will take into account not only the possibility of extending utilities and community facilities to the areas but also other key aspects, such as transportation and location in relation to jobs. This implies breaking down administrative rigidities and the traditional sectoral approach to planning and development at all levels.

The pressing need now is for countries to recognize the nature of urbanization in their development plans, to assess fully the current and potential extent of the problem of transitional urban settlements, to analyze their resources and the manner in which they are currently applied, and to establish the necessary major shift in attitude and emphasis. Some, but very few, member states have already made progress in this regard. What is now required is a commitment to the recognition.

CONCLUSIONS

Slums, ghettos, and transitional towns on the outskirts of the large cities have in some countries become one of the most pressing and serious problems. The great difficulty in dealing with them stems mainly from the fact that the problem comprises all the numerous aspects of what may be loosely termed the "social sciences." Another important difficulty in solving the problem is that it is still constantly growing, and, since in-migration into the towns has only just started in most developing countries, present slum conditions may only be a foreboding hint at what the future has in store.

Unfortunately, and in spite of great efforts being made, the problems are not likely to be solved in the near future, and, unless much more stress is placed on them, they are quite likely to continue to grow at alarming and disastrous rates in many of the developing countries.

12

**MEANS OF
IMPLEMENTATION**

In spite of a growing number of methods and textbooks on
national, regional, and urban planning, actual implementation
remains one of the most elusive and difficult tasks to accomplish.
This is mainly due to the fact that, while planning usually starts
with a definable aim and proceeds by methods that attempt to be
exact, execution of plans infringes on the unknown and often un-
definable complexities of political, public, and administrative
power struggles.

The realization that good plans do not of themselves guarantee
anything unless appropriate ways are found to implement them has
focused attention on the various executive and maintenance bodies.
It has become evident in recent years that new tools are needed—
administrative, political, and financial tools—to ensure that any
plans be optimally executed and that full control be retained both
over the processes of positive growth as well as over possible
processes of undesirable growth.

JOINING PLANNING TO EFFECTIVE POWER

JOHN FRIEDMANN explained these needs:

. . . In most countries, planning for specific sectors of the public
economy such as transport, housing, education, electric power, or
agriculture, is considerably more successful than either coordinated
intersectoral or spatial planning at the national level. The reason is
that sectoral planning is done by the very agencies that are in charge
of making the programed investments. For instance, a Department
of Transportation plans for the use of its own resources, including

its legal regulatory powers, in order to achieve intended, if usually quite limited, effects. A Rural Electrification Agency does likewise; the allocator of its investments is not the "unseen hand" of a competitive market but an explicit decision process in which technical factors are weighed alongside other considerations. Planning in these cases is used to guide the daily work of the agency. It provides the necessary information and analysis, produces future projects, furnishes evaluations of costs and benefits, and in a multiplicity of other ways is tied into the formulation of policies, program development, and project design.

Planning in this sense is effective because it is intimately joined to the exercise of power, that is, to control over the legal and monetary resources for carrying out intended actions. Where planning is so integrated with action, it must operate under a set of realistic constraints that make its contributions immediately relevant to the managers of power. Plans are usually formulated in terms of the available instruments for implementing programs; questions posed by the potential use of these instruments are the problems to which planning will generally respond. Sectoral planning is, therefore, closely linked with the available instruments of power.

At the national level, both intersectoral and spatial planning are further removed from the management of effective power than is sectoral planning. In most countries, the role of national planners is to advise on policy. Yet, as they are divorced from the instruments of action, national planners have no means of getting their advice accepted. Indeed, their advice is often judged irrelevant to the immediate needs of resource managers.

Various lecturers related experiences in their own countries as examples of the need for and possible solutions to administrative systems for undertaking implementation of development prospects.

ARIE SHACHAR explained the difficulties encountered in Israel during the first two decades of the population dispersal policy:

. . . In discussions of implementation measures of a national policy, careful attention should be given to a number of critical conditions.

Spatial planning authorities on a national scale are very seldom endowed with executive powers. The implementation measures of national programs such as housing, transportation, and industrial development are controlled and managed by the various sectoral agencies. The national plan, in its spatial context, is regarded as advice or as a guideline to be followed or disregarded by the various offices and agencies, which have effective powers and instruments for implementing the plans.

The Israeli situation is exactly the same in this respect, as the planning department has no executive powers and implementation is carried out by the various governmental offices such as the Ministries of Housing, Labor, Transport, Commerce, Industry, etc. There are several ways of overcoming the critical deficiency wherein national urbanization planning is divorced from executive power. Examples are (1) establishing a national ministry or agency for urban development, which will have the necessary financial resources and the regulatory powers to implement the urbanization policies, and (2) establishing a development corporation to deal specifically with critical elements of the urbanization policy.

The corporate authority must have ample financial and legal autonomy to carry out the plans. It is a remarkable result that, in spite of the fact that none of the above-mentioned institutional solutions were ever tried in Israel and the national planning bodies had no executive powers, still the implementation of urbanization policies followed the general schemes of the distribution of population quite carefully. The coordination between the planning department and the various implementing agencies was carried out by interministerial committees accompanied by a great deal of informal contact.

A national urbanization policy that would change the entire spatial organization of society must have a "sustained political commitment." In the Israeli case, the dispersion-of-population policy has been endorsed by all the governments from 1948 until the present time. This persistent political commitment at the highest levels of government has enabled the development towns to overcome periods of crisis and acute problems.

Implementation of the national urbanization policy was carried out by utilizing several policy instruments, most of them intended to support the development towns program, and very few measures were taken to limit the growth of the large urban agglomeration around Tel Aviv.

The development town program was implemented by the central authorities, which controlled and directed the basic instruments of the induced urbanization process—public housing and employment opportunities. The people who were to build and live in the development towns were the new immigrants who were directed from their port of arrival to one of the development towns. Few of the new towns benefited by the small out-migration movement of veterans moving in from the large cities and rural settlements. The assignment of migrants to a particular town was made according to the availability of housing or of employment opportunities within a short period of time after their settling in the new town. The spatial dimension of the housing policy was implemented by fixing annual quotas of houses to be built in each new town, according to the scheme of the planned distribution of population. The main incentive for migrants to stay in the development town was the provision of housing on the easiest terms available in the country. The houses were built by the government; during the period 1961-67, 43.1 percent of all units of public housing construction were built in the development towns. The rents there were heavily subsidized by the government, mainly during the first three years of residence. A comparison between availability and costs of housing in the large cities and the development towns resulted in a preference to stay in the latter at least for a period of adjustment to the new environment and culture.

The second major instrument for the implementation of the urbanization policy was the inducement of economic development, through financial incentives for investment in industry or through direct public investment in the physical infrastructure for industrial development, and by improving human resources, mainly through vocational training programs.

The above experiences led DAVID TANNE to propose the setting up of institutions to solve the problems; and, in spite of the relative success of Israel's urbanization policy so far, the need for far-reaching organizational change is strongly felt, as can be seen from the following statement.

. . . A comprehensive policy for planning may well be a working plan; however, unless it is supplemented by an institutional and conceptual infrastructure, it may well remain only a concept.

This institutional infrastructure is, in fact, part of a national governmental attitude toward planning—an understanding of the process of planning officially acknowledged.

This understanding is all too often acquired by a tortuous and painful course of repeated errors, and few countries have reached it. The case of Israel may serve as a good example of the pitfalls involved.

When the government was being organized in 1948, such unclear concepts as that of planning were haphazardly delegated to different authorities. Thus, while the Prime Minister's Office was preparing national plans, the Ministry of the Interior was preparing regional plans, and the Ministry of Labor was busy creating facts without any plans at all. In quite a few instances, towns were built and populated before the plans were even drawn. As the stress of new immigrants and housing needs lessened, a slow process of modification took place and various planning authorities were eliminated or brought under the same roof.

However, it is my contention that for an undertaking of national planning to succeed, more is needed than merely concentration of planning. For planning to succeed, there has to be harmonious streamlining from planning to execution and vice versa. This can exist only if both planning as well as execution are grouped under one heading.

This proposition, quite common and accepted on the single-project level, would necessitate major upheavals in most governmental structures. If, however, this is not done, instances are likely to occur in which towns are built without access roads, in which industry is developed in places without available manpower. The process of feedback is likely to continue its slow and unreliable course from one government office to another, instead of directly from the site back to the planning board.

This organizational obstacle is in many cases so huge and so effective that it can lead whole economies to total confusion. Conflicting interests—regional, ministerial, and personal—prevent the flow of information from one source to another, leak confusing details, and often divert execution off the right path. When planners have no part in execution and when those who carry out the plans do not share the planners' work, pandemonium is likely to ensue.

It is not suggested here that either of the two be subordinate to the other. It is suggested that in a modern state that maintains highly complex systems of organization, an authority has to be set up to include all the various and diverse aspects of national planning and all the varied means of execution and in which all elements would function together harmoniously.

Regional planning authorities were given the same attention by speakers in whose countries such projects figure prominently. JOHN FRIEDMANN introduced the subject.

. . . Regional development authorities are the leading exception to this condition of relative impotence. Established as semiautonomous agencies of the national government, they operate within the confines of a specific geographic area and control resources sufficient to carry out a variety of closely coordinated investment programs. The prototype of all these agencies is the Tennessee Valley Authority, established in 1933. The Guayana Corporation of Venezuela, the Cauca Valley Corporation in Colombia, and the Superintendency for the Development of the Northeast (SUDENE—Brazil) are more recent and equally well-known examples. On the urban scale, the foundation for the new capital of Brazil, the New York Port Authority, and a proposed Metropolitan Development Corporation for Valparaiso

(Chile) embody the same principle of fusing planning with effective power. In all these cases, planning focuses attention on the short-term future and is likely to be more concerned with strategies, programs, projects, and even operational details than with long-range plans that endeavor to portray an image of the finished work.

There is but little question that the corporate approach to the regional development has yielded impressive results whenever the powers of the development agency were commensurate with its mission. But these results have had to be bought at a cost. The authority of a regional agency extends over a defined geographic area that is only a small part of the national territory. Since none but the very largest countries have adequate financial and technical resources to undertake more than one or two concerted efforts of this kind simultaneously, use of the corporate approach has meant, in practice, that certain regions were favored at the expense of other areas. The justification for such a policy of imbalanced development has nearly always been based on arguments that stressed the overriding national importance of the regional scheme. Even so, the demonstration effect of a successful regional enterprise has often turned out to be difficult to control. Regions that considered themselves neglected frequently brought considerable pressure to bear on the government to mount similar efforts in their own areas. Although strenuously resisted by national planners who feared a geographic dispersion of resources and, more generally, a gradual attrition of their own powers to guide the over-all course of national development, these pressures often led to a multiplication of regional agencies and, consequently, to a dilution of resources for promoting development in any one area. Returning to the example of South America, both Venezuela and Colombia have six regional development agencies in operation, each with some resources of its own; Peru has blanketed the entire country with a series of Departmental Development Corporations; and Brazil has established, in addition to the powerful SUDENE, the Superintendency for the Development of Amazonia, the Foundation for the Development of Brazilia, and a number of other intensive regional programs.

The apprehensions of national planners appear to be well founded. Development authorities are potent institutions. Regionally based, they often succeed in obtaining the support of local populations and so become increasingly immune to central control and direction.

The experiences of Italy were presented by GABRIELE PESCATORE, of the Cassa per il Mezzogiorno.

. . . In 1950, the penetrating awareness of Southern Italy's development problems found concrete expression in legislation that set up the Cassa per il Mezzogiorno (Fund for the South—Law No. 646

of August 10, 1950), which was entrusted with the task of stimulating the economic and social revival of the southern regions through a plan of extraordinary activities, to be added to and coordinated with those of central and local public administrations.

The typical features of this task can be thus summarized:

(1) activity plans for several years, whereas normal administrations are bound to operate within the borders of annual budgets;

(2) intersectoral activities, namely, the possibility of operating at the same time and comprehensively in different sectors, also combining investments in infrastructure with incentives for stimulating productive investments;

(3) unity of activity management in the several phases of project planning, execution, and operation;

(4) time-saving concentration of public expenditure in both technical and financial phases, as the Cassa is not subject to the disbursement procedures encumbering ordinary administrations. In particular, the Cassa is free of the institutional controls placed on public administrations, because its constitution includes internal control similar to that of private corporations.

Cassa's activities to date have resulted in a massive program of public works for land reclamation, transformation, reforestation, and regulation of mountain watersheds; of integrated infrastructure (aqueducts, roads and transportation, tourist attractions, etc.); of a range of financial incentives for constructing, modernizing, or expanding productive projects in the sectors of industry, agriculture, hotels, handicrafts, and fishing; of combined operations in favor of the human element (professional and vocational schools, training centers, technical assistance, etc.). Funds allocated to the Cassa by institutional law and subsequent legislation between 1950 and 1969 have reached 4,995 billion lire ($8 billion) with annual allocations of around 1 percent of the national income.

Such sustained financial commitment has resulted in investments carried out in southern Italy for an over-all amount of about 9,000 billion lire ($14.4 billion) through 1970: 13.3 percent of them in general infrastructure; 22.5 percent in agriculture; 55.2 percent in industry; 3 percent in tourist promotion; 2.1 percent in improvement of the human element; and 3.9 percent in other activities. Another considerable number of direct and induced investments are under way at present.

The experiences of Japan were related by EIICHI ISOMURA, among others.

. . . It is only natural that local governments should demand decentralization of power. However, there is a conflict between the possibility of regional association and amalgamation.

In circumstances in which land and people have been under the rule of landlords and the inhabitants have been accustomed to this mode of life, the theory of amalgamation precedes the functional context. As the democratic way of thinking has become widespread in the postwar years, there has been much resistance to the attempt that cities, towns, and villages make to amalgamate with one another as though ordered from above.

The Local System Research Council, which is an advisory body to the Minister of Home Affairs, has recently recommended the adoption of an "association system" for the administration of Osaka and other big cities in broader area dimensions. A number of prefectures may be able to form an association for transportation, city water service, and sewerage system. However, there are some doubts about the degree to which this system as a whole could be made realistic.

Local Administration-Oriented Analysis (Province Versus Metropolis). Japan's local system is divided into the two phases of perfectures and cities, towns and villages. When this system is analyzed from the standpoint of development administration, the following four levels are evident:

(1) National Capital and Kinki Spheres. At this level, the plans that stretch over a number of prefectures are integrated and adjusted, and these functions could be described as an integral part of organization of the central government.

(2) Hokkaido has the Development Agency, which carries out the state's own measures for development. In other prefectures, however, each ministry has its own branch offices, which independently conduct administration. There is sufficient coordination between them and the prefectural level.

(3) Prefectural Level. Each prefecture has a planning department or office to formulate comprehensive programs. This organization serves as the machinery for adjustment with national policy and at the same time means intervention in planning on the level of cities, towns, and villages.

(4) Cities, Towns, and Villages. The question posed at this level concerns the big cities, whose planning functions are comparable with those of prefectures. In Japan, cities with a population of more than 100,000 are given the status of a designated city under the Local Autonomy Law, and some of the functions of prefectures are transferred to them.

What the author is concerned about here is the warning that perfectures, on the one hand, and cities, towns, and villages, on the other, are inclined toward dual administration in every facet of the local system as well as in planning. The perfectural system and the big-city system do exist according to the logic of compatibility in a country where land is limited, such as Japan. There is a strong current demanding concentration at least for regional development.

The most difficult and, perhaps, those that merit the greatest concern are the ways in which large metropolitan regions can be coordinated in a planning process. MORRIS HILL maintained that,

. . . In the face of the above conditions, metropolitan planning might be approached in any of the following ways:
(1) unitary metropolitan planning, whereby all public sectors in the metropolitan area are planned in detail, as an integral whole by a single planning agency;
(2) metropolitan framework plans, whereby the plans have loose general ties to detailed sector plans, prepared by individual jurisdiction, national or local;
(3) integrated metropolitan planning and policy-making, whereby planning by individual jurisdiction, national or local, general or sectoral, is performed in terms of a common set of objectives, planning guides, and criteria with a common approach to plan formulation and the scope of the metropolitan planning agency.
The particular approach chosen will depend on the particular governmental institutions in existence. In the case of the existence of a single metropolitan government, such as exists in metropolitan London, Tokyo, Toronto, or Winnipeg, the first approach is feasible and desirable. However, for most metropolitan areas in the world, the best that can be hoped for is the third approach. This is even the case in countries in which the national government performs the metropolitan planning function, because the often conflicting interests and activities of the several ministries involved still have to be coordinated. The second approach is more one of last resort than a preferred approach a priori.

JORGE HARDOY also took up the issue of metropolitan areas and examined their conditions in Latin America.

. . . Professor Hill has presented an outline of how we should develop the strategies for metropolitan experiences. From my experience of working in Latin America—it is the only place where I have ever worked—I think that in reality one can seldom use such an organized framework. In Latin America—and I assume also in most developing countries—the organization for planning is simply not there. My experience in Latin America shows that urbanization is a consequence of decisions largely made outside the framework of local or metropolitan agencies. This is essential in order to understand urbanization and to develop a strategy for urbanization at different levels. In any country of Latin America, local government is powerless financially and politically; and, unless we realize that, it is useless to go on discussing how to approach master planning studies or metropolitan planning studies, because the local governments, no matter how much they may want to do, are powerless.

In Latin America there is a tendency to centralize decisions on public investment. This is a trend that is not only traditional; it has also considerable political relevance to the present pace of development in Latin American countries. Stern gives about 12 out of the 20 Latin-American countries that have more than 85 percent of public investments centralized in the national government. Therefore, what the national government has to say and is doing is extremely relevant to what happens to the whole process of urbanization in the country. However, I am fully aware—and my own studies on the Cuban process have shown—that centralization calls for decentralization in evaluation and in the population's participation, which is very difficult to achieve where centralization is highly concentrated. However, I am willing to take the risk, because of increasing efficiency of the national governments. These are not very efficient in relation to provincial governments (which, too, are inefficient) and to local governments, which are most inefficient in our countries, with the exception of one or two of the major cities.

Yet, even if all the propositions were to be taken up, NATHANIEL LICHFIELD still visualized administrative difficulties.

. . . It would be wrong to believe that the problems of coordination, of rigidities and inflexibilities, do not exist even in the most highly organized countries. I put it even more strongly. Even in new towns in England, which are planned comprehensively, the rigidities and inflexibilities of the institutional structure are such, that instead of the houses, the schools, and the open spaces, etc., happening together, we always get imbalance, because of the institutional difficulties.

DECISION-MAKING ON URBAN DEVELOPMENT

Among the most difficult questions in urban planning is the dilemma of who is to decide and in what manner decisions are to be made. JORGE HARDOY examined the power structure of cities.

The Power Structure That Controls Decisions. The concept of urban reform will be a major topic of analysis and discussion during the next few years. It extends beyond simple changes in the urban and suburban land tenure system and consequently, in urban land uses. As a more radical and comprehensive concept, it should also include new systems of urban government and public investment, new ways of popular participation, and essentially a change in the power structure that controls decisions affecting the dynamics of urban growth and the internal structure of cities.

Urban reform is not a short-term policy. Its main objective should be the removal of the speculative tendencies that define the lines of physical growth in cities and of an urban ecology based on class discrimination. As land speculation and the inequalities of urban land distribution are a consequence of the sociopolitical system and of pressure groups controlling the urban scene, structural urban reform is impossible without changes in the power structure. Moreover, urban reform cannot be achieved over night. It requires the setting up of institutions, human and financial resources, and technology to plan and build cities, but, prior to this, appropriate legislation should be enacted that will imbue urban land ownership and housing with a different meaning.

LLOYD RODWIN raised a further aspect.

. . . One of the most difficult problems of plan-making generally and of urbanization strategy in particular is how to choose between multiple and conflicting goals. Some of the most obvious and difficult choices are between social and private costs, long- and short-term costs, capital and maintenance costs, and between social, economic, and political considerations. More specifically, in relation to the economics of urbanization, the big issues are choosing between concentration versus scatter, encouraging development in existing cities rather than development in new or lagging regions, and deciding on the proper balance between growth, employment, welfare, amenity, and other "values." Effective solutions must either serve these multiple goals or provide attractive compromises. The options, however, are often very limited, and, unfortunately, our mathematical models have less relevance when decision-makers compromise and seek satisfactory rather than optimum solutions, as they often do. These choices ought to be made clearer by pointing up rather than passing over the consequences, and by exploring more systematically their implications for policy and programing.

Certainly one of the first questions of interest is how decisions are made concerning urbanization investments. These decisions occur at the national, regional, and local levels, and they will vary, of course, in socialist and in mixed economies. Both kinds of economies, however, face some common problems in the way decisions are made for the urban subsystems of the national economic system. For example, provincial and regional authorities do not formally have a say, as a rule, in the way national capital allocations are made for infrastructure investments. In point of fact, however, they may, and often do, exert far more influence than one might suspect. In addition, some local and regional authorities play a significant role in shaping metropolitan and regional patterns and standards of development, in terms of what they do and what they do not do. We need to know more about the way investment decisions are made, formally and informally, and, in particular, whether certain kinds of cities and regions are systematically disadvantaged because of the way these processes operate and what this means for the national and regional economies.

In most countries, there are no urbanization policies as such. Decisions on urbanization investments are generally made implicitly and ad hoc by sector agencies (i.e., by ministries dealing with public works, housing, and industrial development, by households making decisions on housing, and by private firms). There has been no evaluation or cost-benefit studies of urban growth alternatives. They would also help to devise a technique for diagnosing such decision-making processes and to disclose important limitations of the current machinery and possible ways of getting around them.

The current dissatisfaction with existing growth patterns, however, will not help us to devise better alternatives unless we know the real weaknesses of the existing machinery and unless we explore carefully the pros and cons of new decision-making processes affecting urbanization. Many countries, among them Venezuela, Brazil, Salvador, Ghana, Indonesia, and Singapore, as well as Great Britain, France, United States, Rumania, Yugoslavia, Italy, Poland, Russia, and Japan have improvised or are now inprovising measures to encourage growth centers in lagging or resource development regions or even to establish national policies for urban or regional development. These countries, because they differ in size, location, and economic and social characteristics, can serve as possible laboratories and testing stations. We ought to learn what we can from their innovations and experiments. To do so, it would be important to establish the reasons for the creation of the new machinery and the urban development programs, the way they work, and their strengths and weaknesses. It would be particularly useful to compare the way such urban development decisions are made in various European countries such as Poland, Rumania, Yugoslavia, Italy, the USSR, France, and Britain, and in a number of different developing countries such as Venezuela, Brazil, Peru, Indonesia, Singapore, and India.

By way of example, one could examine the following: the adequacy of machinery to define development goals, not only aggregatively and by sectors but also spatially by cities and regions; the means that exist to coordinate development programs by sectors and by regions; the explicitness of the basic urban and regional development strategies; the quality of staff and training programs; the effectiveness of programs that enlist contributions from the private sector; the adequacy of local and regional accounting systems; the capacity of local and regional organizations to handle their responsibilities; and the provisions for evaluation and improvement of performance as a given program continues. Although such an examination would point up serious short-comings in each of the countries studied, it would also show that the concern in each country is with how to refine policies and to improve mechanisms for guiding urban development, not with how to get rid of them.

POPULATION PARTICIPATION IN
URBANIZATION PLANS

One of the most important observations made in recent years is that if people are to be affected by plans they should also be encouraged to participate in making them. LLOYD RODWIN maintained,

. . . Policy-makers often take inadequate account of what the local populace wants. Although such an attitude might have been acceptable in the past, today it is much less feasible or realistic. Many local leaders now argue that the inhabitants of different regions must have a greater voice in the administrative and political decisions that will affect their regions. And, whether one welcomes the trend or not, there is evidence that this view is spreading. For example, in the Guayana region of Venezuela, the Guayana Development Corporation was pressured to consult the local population, the merchants, political leaders, and even the humbler elements of society, whose values, in many respects, were different from those of the professional planners and the top leadership of the Corporation.

The local leaders wanted more emphasis placed on high em-ployment and labor-intensive activities than on a high rate of growth and the attraction of modern, capital-intensive enterprises. They favored low density, more self-help, and owner-occupied housing in places where migrants could find jobs and learn more easily about new opportunities. They objected to the criteria used by the Cor-poration for housing selection and welfare, which some of the local populace considered inappropriate for many of the families that the programs were intended to serve. Indeed, on some matters the Corporation, despite its great power and prestige, was even forced to reverse its position. Thus, it had been national custom to distribute public land held by the local community to those who had no land. In response to the pressures of the local leaders the Corporation literally had to agree to supply some of the public land owned by the Corporation to the new local community for distribution to the landless.

Other national programs have also been modified by local demands. In Turkey, local and regional pressures have forced more attention to be paid to development in the East, though "citizen participation" is still a long way off.

Because of this concern for decentralizing power, and because of the widespread interest of people in different parts of the world to play a more significant role in determining the conditions that shape their lives, we have to devise ways in which such options can occur. One of the lessons that we have learned and are trying to pass on is that the government should not be developing its programs from the capital, but rather from the region and that an effort should be made to give the people more local options, more local opportunities for decision-making. You have to give people a chance to do things themselves.

I think it is important to fight the feeling of government officials and people in central bureaucracies that they know best, that they have more information and know how to do the most effective job. To give a specific illustration: In many parts of the world, housing is being built by governments for people, particularly for migrants—the wrong kind of housing, inefficiently, at great cost, because those people think they know best what the migrants need. In point of fact, it is essential in most parts of the world—in Latin America, in Africa, in Asia—to reverse that policy and to help the migrants to build the housing that they can out of their own resources.

It does not matter if the conditions are not optimum, if the standards are not as high. If people sense that there is concern for their needs and that we are working together to try to cope with them, I think that we can get over the worst of it. But, when they feel that this is not so, then we are in for trouble, and rightly so.

Professor Rodwin then examined the "burden of democracy."

. . . I am a devotee of public participation. I know that many planners and politicians are not. I participated in a symposium a couple of weeks ago with Teddy Kollek, the Mayor of Jerusalem, who complained bitterly at attempts made by various groups in Jerusalem to state their positions on a number of issues—in particular, the beautification committee of the city, a citizens' body, and other bodies. I would say that in the final analysis this is what the politician and the planner has to learn to live with. Somehow or other we have to have a way of testing how our plans are affecting the public. Not every public is ready to participate in this, but, where the public is, it undoubtedly complicates the planning and implementation, as Mayor Kollek says it does.

In the United States, there has been an attempt made, though I am not sure it has been completely successful, where cities like Dallas are trying to involve the population in trying to define the metropolitan area. My general impression is that the group that tends to participate in an innovation of this kind is a very restricted, better-educated group in the metropolitan area.

Observations on this matter were also made by several politicians and administrators. ATO BEKELE HAILE, Deputy Vice-Mayor of Addis Ababa, Ethiopia, commented,

. . . I would say that citizen participation in local affairs would be desirable to a certain degree, but total handling by the communities of the cities themselves would be abandoning national responsibility to the total population of the nation; we feel that the destiny of the nation greatly depends on urbanization.

I understand the ideal of the letter of democracy—to involve the communities concerned as far as possible—but there should be some sort of material result from such participation. To my mind, communities lacking experience and know-how should not be involved too much in the decision-making of major policies; but they should be consulted on the minor ones and be informed of the major ones.

Our problem is one of overlapping—a great deal of mobility and a high rate of migration; we have stated this to be one of our problems. The national policy-makers cannot stand aside and look on, handing the problems over to the communities concerned, to do whatever they like. Later on, of course, there will be great problems that even the advanced countries face, just as the United States is facing now because it left its urban problems to local bodies, be they the state or the municipality. Now, when the crisis comes, it is not the crisis of the towns and it is not the crisis of the state—it is the crisis of the nation.

The Nepalese delegate, RAM C. MALHOTRA observed that,

. . . in Nepal fortunately we have all the good conditions—political stability, willing hard-working people, a bureaucracy devoted to the people, and, yet, progress has not been marked. I would reverse my position. My friend from Ethiopia said that the citizenry should not be given much power in decision-making. I would say that they should be given all the power in decision-making, in deciding what is good for them, their own priorities. But what the government should really do is to give them managerial power, managerial support, and I think management is the biggest problem in the developing countries, rather than lack of resources.

In ten years' experience, we found that we could not carry through our plans, not only because we did not have the resources or the machinery—the more important part was the organization—but most of the time it was because the people did not think that the most important priorities we laid down for them were the priorities they needed most in their own local areas.

Consequently, in 1961, we adopted a new constitution where the principles of participation as well as decentralization of power were included in the preamble. These are not only means but also goals— the higher goals of a higher standard of living, of a happier life, free of class exploitation, a classless society—that have been put in the constitution, as basic principles. Yet, with this accepted as a legal constitutional principle, the problem has been how to make it possible; how to make the people's participation a successful reality; how the decentralization of power can be realized to the utmost, to the optimum level.

FRANCISCO AGUIRRE, editor of the Diario de las Americas, made a proposal.

. . . I believe that everything you are doing is for the good of the people, and it is the people who really have to understand the work that you are planning. I am convinced that, if you take the publishers, the editors, and the writers of your respective countries into your confidence, you are going to be in a position to sell your ideas with great effectiveness to all the citizens of your countries. To close the gap will mean a lot to the future of our people, and it will not be difficult provided that you realize that in this era in which we are living, when the revolution in communications does not permit secrets to be kept very long without leaking out in some way or another, it is far better to win over that important public opinion that will certainly, in the majority of cases, back your ideals and your ideas.

I wish to remind you all of the importance of incorporating the news media in your plans. Professors, planners, executives, politicians—you will all be better off if you consider the need to obtain the backing of public opinion. As the publisher of Diario de las Americas, the only inter-American newspaper printed in Spanish in the United States, I know that one of the big problems that we have is to obtain the right information, at the right time.

INVESTMENT FINANCING OF URBAN DEVELOPMENT

The ways by which planning projects should be financed was also one of the most prominent features at the Conference. JOSÉ D. EPSTEIN, of the Inter-America Development Bank, introduced the subject.

. . . There is an important role to be played by external financing, and that, in fact, probably is one of the major differences between advanced and underdeveloped countries; whereas advanced countries do not have to depend on anything but their domestic financing, in underdeveloped countries, it is quite the reverse.

One of the tenets we all receive from classic, economic theories is that the newcomer has an advantage, but the classic theory is altogether wrong; in the main subject of the Conference, it has proven invalid.

There is not very much that advanced countries have been able to teach us. In fact, if anything, the underdeveloped countries are trying to avoid, not copy, experiences that we have heard and seen reflected from what has been happening elsewhere.

Much of what we have copied has brought hosts of new problems that we can probably only solve on our own. On that, just a small word of caution. . . . I think we must beware of the simple solutions. There are no simple solutions here.

One of the key factors in financing urban renewal and slum clearance in developing countries is that the initial aims were often set too high, whether for political reasons or through short-sightedness. These aims can, therefore, not be achieved unless standards are lowered. ROBERT SADOVE explained this in his paper.

. . . It is the view of this paper that the urban crisis requires a considerably wide range of possible choices in investment programs. Whenever an investment is proposed, the first step is to see whether a particular investment could not be altogether avoided by undertaking some other less costly course of development. For instance, many large-scale infrastructure works may have to be given up in favor of intensifying the use of existing land, transport, power, and other facilities. Locational factors will be critical. An attempt may have to be made to divert prospective growth of demand away from an already developed area to another area. Transport requirements may have to be reduced by shifting the location of employment opportunities. Such alternatives as these and many similar ones merit careful investigation in order to determine the real need for investment.

It is quite clear from the earlier discussions that, using existing standards, the urban growth problems cannot be overcome in any but the richest less developed countries if costs per capita of the order suggested by normal experience are accepted. Data from town planning organizations, consultants, and individual studies indicate costs per capita for social infrastructure and housing of "minimum" standards to be often above the $500 mark. Costs of providing employment probably represent at least equally as much. For the poorer countries, the alternative paths and/or lower standards of amenities suggested above will have to be sought. Strategies will have to be related to the income and resource capabilities of the country concerned as the earlier calculations exemplified—and these vary by a factor of over five times between the poorer and richer developing countries.

The argument of the paper, in summary, is that the magnitude of urban investments is such that much more than slight changes in project design will be required. The "substandard" and the "inadequate" may have to be accepted in the short run because otherwise half or nearly half of the population will continue to be excluded from the benefits of economic development.

For the poorer countries, alternative paths and/or lower standards of amenities must be specifically designed in light of the particular characteristics of the country involved. In East Pakistan, for example, roads were constructed, under the Rural Works Program, that in Western countries would clearly be considered substandard. The roads were mostly dirt and compacted by hand hammers or by sections of concrete pipe used as hand-pulled rollers. Nevertheless, the Program, which was in effect from 1962-67, helped to meet the province's need for a rural road network that could accommodate most conveyances, such as bicycles, rickshaws, and animal carts, and would begin to open up the province to agricultural marketing. By using labor-intensive methods of construction, capital costs were kept to a minimum. The high costs of maintaining the roads (which were subject to rapid deterioration) were acceptable to the province because of its existing labor surplus. Minimal-standard programs, such as this one, will tax to the limit the financial resources of most developing countries. Yet they are realistic programs; they represent a feasible means of dealing with basic rural or urban needs within limits set by a dearth of financial and physical resources.

The developing countries in their choice of urban investment alternatives may have to resolve the dilemma of excessive real demand for high and medium-income facilities against the equally real but unexpressed demand for minimal facilities of the low-income groups. But only in their choice of the latter will they effectively tackle the urban problem—the problem of providing adequate conditions of living for rapidly increasing urban populations. One is reminded in the difficulty of choice confronting the urban developing world of Paul Porter's comments regarding Greece's financially unrealistic recovery program after World War II. In the wisdom of Andrew Jackson, he said, "They will have to learn to elevate their sights a little lower."

LLOYD RODWIN pondered a different problem, the question of allocation and urbanization, in which cities to invest, when and how.

. . . in the main the facilities to accommodate future increases in population and economic activity will be located in existing cities, in new centers in the outer areas of big cities, or in the growth centers of resource development regions or of lagging regions. A major public policy issue is where, if at all, to encourage, or discourage, this development. It will not be easy, however, to make a wise choice, because of our ignorance about two basic matters, ignorance that will not be easy to dispel and that ought to be frankly recognized. First, there is a widespread belief that big cities beyond a certain size suffer from significant disadvantages, especially diseconomies of scale. Second, many policy-makers are convinced that it would be desirable to develop new "growth centers." The trouble with both views is that, although there is much evidence in favor of each, the underlying propositions are vague and nonoperational. The fact is that we do not really know when a city is too big or too congested, rather than merely poorly organized. Nor do we know, as yet, little more than the rudiments of how to convert an urban center into a "growth center." But this is not the first time (and probably not the last) that decision-makers have to manipulate forces they do not fully understand. This must be emphasized because the problems are too complicated to be decisively settled by any research—at least in the short run. There are simply too many problems of data inadequacies and analytical difficulties in trying to disentangle benefits and costs, social as well as private. What is more, past experience suggests that it is exceptionally difficult to cut the size or stop the growth of big cities: Indeed, we have almost no examples of successful efforts along these lines.
But, since there may be significant disadvantages in big cities as well as powerful reasons for wanting to encourage growth elsewhere, it might still be wise to steer development, where feasible, to targeted urban centers. Such a policy, without aiming to cut the growth of the big city to some arbitrary scale, could (1) promote urban centers in lagging or resource development regions; (2) avoid the squandering

of resources in scattered, dispersed developments (which would fail
to reach a critical size and might inhibit the "spread" effects of such
development throughout the region; and (3) reduce the rate of growth
of the big cities and, by easing the pressure on them, facilitate efforts
to reorganize and enhance the efficiency of the big metropolitan areas.

Pursuing these related policies, however, would require analysis
of the criteria for the choice of urban regions for development.
Someday we may invent powerful analytical techniques to evaluate
alternative choices of location, taking account of social as well as
economic considerations. But, meanwhile, we shall have to rely on
relatively simple pragmatic criteria. In doing so, we must consider
such factors as the development potential of different regions; constraints or special considerations affecting national growth (such as
shortages of exchange or common market problems); the feasibility
of locating leading economic growth sectors in growth centers; the
practicability of encouraging growth centers in declining or lagging
regions; and the probable development effects on the surrounding
hinterland of encouraging alternative growth centers.

JOHN FRIEDMANN, too, enlarged on this subject, outlining
the ways by which public investment can influence urban growth.

Direct Public Investment. This is the most widely used method for
implementing urban-regional development policies. The underlying
notion is that the provision of critical facilities in designated districts,
such as generating plants for electric power, transport facilities,
housing and other social services, and large manufacturing plants in
basic industries, will help establish conditions favorable to private
investors and so set in motion a self-sustaining process of regional
growth. Such investments are best carried out in coordinated
fashion according to a carefully worked-out program of development.
Isolated efforts, such as construction of an electric generating plant,
are not likely to produce significant changes in the attractiveness of
a region for private investors without supporting investments in other
facilities. This consideration argues strongly for the corporate
approach to urban-regional development planning. Even a tightly
coordinated approach, however, offers no guarantee that a cumulative
growth cycle will be initiated. For instance, the potential growth
center of Conception in Chile has proved incapable of attracting private
investments on a scale sufficient to allow this important provincial
city to compete with Santiago as the country's principal center of
manufacturing, this despite the general excellence of Conception's
facilities, including a leading private university. The city's remoteness
from national markets, its relatively high cost of living, the absence

of a diversified structure of private services to industry, and the extreme centralization of decision-making power in the nation's capital combine to militate against the self-supporting economic growth of the region. Further overhead investments or even the enlargement of the government's steel plant in the area would do little to encourage private investors unless some of the other conditions preventing spontaneous growth were to change. The situation may be radically transformed under the present socialist government of Chile as a result of both increased public ownership of industry and a general restructuring of the final output of manufacturing toward a greater emphasis on capital goods and working-class consumer products.

Examples of the failure of public investment programs to induce economic growth are probably more numerous, on balance, than the successful cases. Though public infrastructure may be necessary for urban-regional development, it is by no means a sufficient condition. Additional incentives, especially of a financial nature, may have to be offered to bring the private calculus of costs and benefits into harmony with policy designs. The social response of local communities to government incentives is especially relevant. Similar economic programs may not necessarily elicit similar community responses. A program may lead to the mobilization of the community in some cases while meeting with apathy or even passive resistance in others. This ability of the local community to organize itself for economic growth and development must be considered an important variable in the implementation of development strategies.

Financial Location Incentives. These are among the most popular devices for promoting the development of designated areas in private or mixed enterprise economies.

Principally, they include tax incentives, import tariff reductions, location subsidies, and investment credits. These measures are applied to individual firms in the hope of inducing them to invest their capital in the development areas. Experience has provided contradictory evidence concerning their effectiveness. Four major problems may be identified:

(1) It is politically difficult to restrict the geographic incidence of financial inducements to only a few areas. Yet the multiplication of areas eligible for favored treatment will encourage an excessive spread of industrial locations, dissipating the potential effectiveness of the incentives.

(2) Unless financial subsidies make up a substantial proportion of total variable costs in production dependent on location, they may not lead the industry to locate in areas that, in other respects, are lacking in decisive economic advantage. The subsidy must be at least sufficient to compensate the producer for higher costs of transport

of raw materials and/or finished products as well as for other costs
he may incur by locating outside existing core regions. Yet the provision of an adequate level of subsidy may place an excessive burden
on the public treasury and decelerate the over-all process of national
economic growth.

(3) Financial incentives may encourage the location of industry
in locations that are inefficient from the standpoint of private cost
accounting and thus reduce the over-all competitive position of national
industry in foreign markets. Additional export subsidies may, therefore, be required. This, however, would further raise the costs of
regional development to the nation.

(4) Withdrawal of financial incentives after the initial starting-
up period may lead to a shift of industries out of the region and back
to the core areas of the country. Should this happen, and the mere
threat to do so would be sufficient, a policy of permanent subsidization
might be required, resulting in a structural distortion of the resource
allocation pattern that would be difficult to reverse.

The most celebrated instance of the use of financial incentives
is the development program for the Brazilian Northeast. Some 600
industrial projects resulted from this program between 1960 and 1968.
Even so, the creation of new jobs has been unable to keep pace with
population growth in the region, and unemployment is reported to be
increasing. Moreover, the various financial incentives, such as the
50 percent relief in corporate income tax for an equivalent amount
of investment in the region, have had, on balance, a regressive effect
on the distribution of income.

The Northeast development effort is notable in that it combines
a number of the "success" elements, which have been discussed. It
is focused on a single region; it has acquired an institutional form in
the Superintendency for the Development of the Northeast (SUDENE);
it has survived several changes of government by acquiring a strong
political base in the region; and it has achieved a remarkable degree
of coordination in the use of development instruments.

An analytical critique of this program has been made by Professor Walter Stoehr in his comprehensive survey of regional development
policies in Latin America. His conclusions are worth citing at some
length, if only to demonstrate that even the very best of programs
may only partially succeed in what they set out to accomplish:

"The conviction that a direct strengthening of the economy and
the improvement of social welfare levels was essential for obtaining
a lasting effect led to the creation of SUDENE. Some 600 industrial
projects were the result between 1960 and 1968. A road and communications system was established, a modern educational system was
introduced, versatile professional opportunities were newly opened
in the region, and a change in the style of regional politics and

294

decision-making was initiated along with the opportunity for the states to participate in program formulation for the allocation of federal funds in the region. Of the original strategy components of SUDENE — intensification of industrial development, reorganization of agriculture, and relocation of population surpluses — only the first one was achieved to a major extent. Since the main incentives were for capital inputs, most of the new industries turned out to be highly capital-intensive, using modern technology; their contribution to the creation of regional income and the expansion of regional markets, however, was relatively small. In effect, these new industries remained modern enclaves within a large and backward area. They receive their capital and technology from the outside, mainly from the South-East, and shipped an increasing amount of their products to South-Eastern markets. The hoped for impact on the rural areas by absorbing manpower and creating additional income for rural population was not realized. Due to the lack of regional market expansion, these new industries created yet another problem for the nation: subsidized competition from the North-East emerged for some of the industries in the South-East, and in some sectors idle capacity arose due to the limited absorption possibilities of the national market.

"A great part of the income created by new industrialization flows back to the South-East. In addition, an instability has recently been created by pressure on the government to liberate the sale of newly established enterprises by their original tax-favored owners. This would indicate an inclination of investors in the South-East to withdraw their capital from the North-East as soon as they have secured their initial tax benefits.

"The rural sector has changed little relatively, first because practically all of the private capital under the tax savings legislation went into industrial rather than agricultural investment, and second, because the relocation of surplus agricultural labor as well as agricultural reform proceeded very slowly. Both have recently been de-emphasized even more because of fear that they would aggravate the unemployment problem still further.

"In summary, three key problems have arisen in connection with the program for the North-East. The first lies in a failure to create a self-sustained process of regional growth with decreasing dependency on extra-regional inputs. To a large extent, this may be ascribed to the lack of a sufficient regional multiplier effect under which growth would increasingly be based on regional savings, and regional markets would be enlarged. The second problem results from a failure of the development process to diffuse from the few industrial enclaves to the rest of the region. The third problem is the insufficient compatibility between the development of the North-East and national development criteria."

CONCLUSIONS

The need to join planning to effective power is one of the most real and pressing requirements of modern regional and urban planning. Traditional political systems, legislative, administrative, and executive alike, are more often than not wholly inadequate for the new roles of urbanization, where the needs are so great and the processes so rapid that they have to be divorced from any of the systems that are based upon periodicity and political influence.

The same holds true for the financing operative system, which, if correctly used, holds the destiny of effective planning in its power.

ORGANIZATION OF THE SIXTH REHOVOT CONFERENCE

The Sixth Rehovot Conference was organized by the Continuation Committee of the International Conference on Science in the Advancement of New States. It was sponsored jointly by the Hebrew University of Jerusalem and the Weizmann Institute of Science.

HONORARY PRESIDENTS

Abba EBAN
Minister for Foreign Affairs,
Israel
Abraham HARMAN
President of the Hebrew
University of Jerusalem

Ze'ev SHAREF
Minister of Housing,
Israel
Prof. Albert B. SABIN
President of the Weizmann
Institute of Science

CHAIRMAN OF THE REHOVOT CONFERENCES
Abba EBAN
Minister for Foreign Affairs, Israel

SECRETARY-GENERAL
Dr. Amos MANOR

SCIENTIFIC PREPARATORY COMMITTEE
Joint Chairmen:

Dr. Raanan WEITZ
Head, Settlement Department,
Jewish Agency and Settlement
Study Center

David TANNE
Chairman of the Board of
Directors, Tefachot Bank

Members:

Y. ABT
Ministry of Agriculture
Prof. D. AMIRAN
Hebrew University of Jerusalem
Prof. Ch. BEN-SHACHAR
University of Tel Aviv
Dr. E. COHEN
Hebrew University of Jerusalem

Y. DASH
Ministry of the Interior
Prof. A. ECKSTEIN
Bar-Ilan University
Prof. Y. ELON
Technion, Haifa
Y. HESS
Ministry for Foreign Affairs

D. KOCHAV
  Tahal: Water Planning for
  Israel
M. KUHN
  Architect
Y. H. LANDAU
  Jewish Agency for Israel
Prof. N. LICHFIELD
  University College of London
Dr. D. PINES
  University of Tel Aviv

A. ROKACH
  Settlement Study Center
S. SHAKED
  Architect
A. SHARON
  Architect
J. SLIPJER
  Formerly at Ministry of Housing
Y. TAMIR
  Azorim Mortgage Bank

SCIENTIFIC SECRETARIES

A. ROKACH, Coordinator
  Settlement Study Center
G. BAR-LEV
  Settlement Study Center
N. BEN-ELIAH
  Settlement Study Center
E. COMFORTI
  Architect, Ministry of
  Housing

Dr. H. LAU-YONE
  Technion, Haifa
J. MARGOLIS
  Settlement Study Center
N. MENUCHEN
  University of Tel Aviv
R. WEILER
  Architect

CONFERENCE SECRETARIES
Mrs. Rahel HAIK
Mrs. Faye RIMON

PRESS OFFICERS
Mr. Nechemie MEYERS
Mr. Ilan EFRATI

ACKNOWLEDGMENTS

The assistance rendered by government and public institutions abroad as well as in Israel is gratefully acknowledged.

ABROAD: Agency for International Development, Washington, D.C.
           Inter-American Development Bank, Washington, D.C.
           Organization of American States, Washington, D.C.
           The Asia Foundation, San Francisco
           The Axel Springer Foundation, Berlin

IN ISRAEL: The Ministry for Foreign Affairs
           The Ministry of Housing
           The Rothschild Trust

LIST OF PARTICIPANTS*

AFRICA

CAMEROON
Mr. Marc-Emile N'DIFO
  Director, Town Planning and
  Housing Division, Ministry of
  Urban Development

CENTRAL AFRICAN REPUBLIC
Mr. Antoine KANGA
  Director of Urbanization

**DEMOCRATIC REPUBLIC
OF CONGO**
H. E. Colonel L. J. BOTETI
  Ambassador of the Democratic
  Republic of Congo in Israel

DAHOMEY
H. E. Mama AROUNA
  Minister of the Interior
  and Security

ETHIOPIA
H. E. Ato Bekele HAILE
  Vice-Mayor, City of
  Addis Ababa

THE GAMBIA
H. E. Sherif M. DIBBA, M.P.
  Vice President and Minister
  of Finance
Alhaji The Hon. Yaya CEESAY,
M.P.
  Minister for Local Government,
  Lands and Mines

Mr. S. M. B. FYE
  Assistant Secretary, Development Unit, President's Office
Mr. E. C. SOWE, Jr.
  Permanent Secretary, Ministry
  for Local Government, Lands
  and Mines

GHANA
The Hon. Dr. Jones OFORI-
ATTA, M.P.
  Ministerial Secretary, The
  Prime Minister's Office,
  Economic Planning Division
Mr. Sampson K. AMPAH
  Regional Planning Officer,
  Ministry of Finance and
  Economic Planning
Mr. Joseph E. BANNERMAN
  Regional Planning Officer,
  Public Service Commission
Mr. Elubatel S. BOADI
  Rural Planning Officer,
  Ministry of Youth and Rural
  Development

IVORY COAST
H. E. Alexis THIERRY-LEBBE
  Minister of Construction and
  Urbanization
Mr. Henri CAMES
  Head, Abidjan Regional
  Urbanization Institute (AURA),
  Ministry of Planning

---

*Positions held at time of Conference.

Mr. Roger NICADIE
Planning Service for Regional
Activities, Ministry of planning
Père Claude A. L. J. PAIRAULT
Director, Ethno-Sociological
Institute, Professor at the Uni-
versity of Abidjan

KENYA
The Hon. Matthews Joseph
OGUTU, M.P. Assistant,
Minister for Local Government
Mr. Henry OGOLA
Agricultural Planner, Ministry
of Agriculture
Mr. James Mwangi WANYEKI
Principal Finance Officer,
Ministry of Local Government

LESOTHO
Mr. Manasse Ephraim SELLO
Assistant Secretary, Ministry
of the Interior

LIBERIA
The Hon. Cyril BRIGHT
Secretary for Development
and Planning

MALAGASY REPUBLIC
H. E. Eugene LECHAT
Vice President of the
Malagasy Republic
Mr. Willy R. ANDRIAMBELO
Head, Department for Urbani-
zation and Housing, Ministry
of Supply
Dr. Roger ANDRIANTAVY
Mr. José RAVELOMANANTSOA
Director General of SIEMAD,
State Housing Company

MALAWI
Mr. James A. K. MUNTHALI
Planning Officer, Physical
Planning Division, Zomba

MAURITIUS
H. E. Hurrypersad RAMNARAIN
Minister of Cooperation
Mr. Guy E. M. DANJOUX
Chief Officer, Ministry of
Housing, Lands and Town and
Country Planning

NIGERIA
Mr. Mustapha K. GBAJA-
BIAMILA
Member, Lagos City Council
Caretaker Committee
Prof. Akin MABOGUNJE
Professor of Geography,
University of Ibadan

SENEGAL
Mr. Mousse Daby DIAGNE
Director of Town Planning
and Housing, Ministry of
Public Works, Urbanization
and Transportation

SIERRA LEONE
The Hon. Manfred Onike COLE
Minister of Housing and
Country Planning
Mr. L. D. DEIGH
Acting Permanent Secretary,
Ministry of Housing and
Country Planning

TCHAD
Mr. Valentin NGAKOUTOU
Director of Planning

TOGO
H. E. Jean TEVI
  Minister of Finance, Economy
  and Planning
Mr. Koudjolou Henri DOGO
  Director of Planning Com-
  mission

UGANDA
Mr. John ODONGO
  Senior Planner, Department of
  Town and Regional Planning,
  Ministry of Public Service and
  Local Administration

UPPER VOLTA
H. E. François LOMPO
  Minister of Public Works,
  Transportation and Urbani-
  zation
Mr. Abel Isaac TRAORE
  Director of Urbanization and
  Architecture

ZAMBIA
Mr. P. M. MUYNANGWA
  Commissioner of Town and
  Country Planning

ASIA AND THE MEDITERRANEAN

CYPRUS
Mr. Andreas DAVERONAS
  Town Planning Officer, Depart-
  ment of Town Planning and
  Housing, Ministry of Interior
Mr. Constantinos P. IOANNIDES
  Director, Department of Town
  Planning and Housing, Ministry
  of Interior
Mr. Andreas M. JACOVIDES
  Agricultural Officer, Ministry
  of Agriculture and Natural
  Resources

HONG KONG
Prof. Denis John DWYER
  Professor of Geography and
  Head of Department of
  Geography and Geology, Uni-
  versity of Hong Kong

ISRAEL
Miss Tora ARAZI
  Geographer, Settlement Study
  Center, Rehovot
Prof. Morris HILL
  Faculty of Architecture and
  Town Planning and Department

of Industrial Engineering and
Management, Technion-Israel
Institute of Technology, Haifa
Dr. David PINES
  Head, Center for Urban and
  Regional Studies, Faculty of
  Social Sciences, University
  of Tel Aviv
Prof. Arie SHACHAR
  Professor of Geography,
  Department of Geography,
  Hebrew University of
  Jerusalem
Mr. David TANNE
  Chairman, Board of Directors,
  Tefachot Bank
Dr. Raanan WEITZ
  Head, Settlement Department
  of Jewish Agency and Head
  of Settlement Study Center,
  Rehovot

JAPAN
Prof. Masahiko HONJO
  Department of Urban
  Engineering, University of
  Tokyo

Prof. Eiichi ISOMURA
President, Tokyo University

KHMERE (CAMBODIA)
Mr. Vann MOLYVANN
Architect and Head,
Department of Urban
Planning, Ministry of
Public Works

KOREA
Mr. Jong Wan CHOI
Vice Mayor of Seoul Metro-
politan Government
Prof. Yung-Hee RHO
Chairman, Department of
Urban and Regional Planning,
Graduate School of Public
Administration, Seoul National
University

LAOS
Mr. Manorak LUANGKHOT
Director of Housing and
Urbanization, Ministry of
Public Works and Trans-
portation
Mr. Phak SAVANN
Director-General, Ministry of
Public Works and Transportation
Mr. Thongkhanh VONG-
SYPRASOMTV
Head of Engineering Services
in the Vientiane District

NEPAL
The Hon. Ram C. MALHOTRA
Member-Secretary, National
Planning Commission
Mr. Puspa Man JOSHI
Planner, Secretariat of
National Planning Commission
Mr. Govind REGMI
Geographer

PHILIPPINES
Senator Helena Z. BENITEZ
Chairman, Commission on
Housing and Urban Develop-
ment and Resettlement, The
Senate
H. E. Dr. Rafaelita H. SORIANO
Ambassador of The Philippines
in Israel
Miss Yolanda EXCONDE
Senior Research Assistant,
Institute of Planning, Univer-
sity of The Philippines
Mrs. Rosario JIMENEZ
Senior Research Assistant,
Institute of Planning, Univer-
sity of The Philippines
Mr. Jaime SENGA
Regional Planner, Laguna Lake
Development Authority

SINGAPORE
Mr. A. G. S. DANARAJ
Senior Planner, Development
Control Division, Ministry
of National Development
Mr. TAN Chok Kian
Permanent Secretary,
Ministry of Finance

THAILAND
Mr. Thavil GITSOMCHAI
Economist, National Economic
Development Board
Dr. Malai HUVANANDANA
Adviser to the Ministry of
Interior; Rector of National
Institute of Development
Administration
Mr. Om HUVANANDANA
Lecturer in Economics,
Thannasat University
Mr. Prasart JUNHAMAN
Acting Chief, Regional Planning

Division; Senior Planner,
Department of Town and
Country Planning, Ministry
of Interior
Mr. Somsakdi KEAWKINGKEO
Regional Planner and
Lecturer, Faculty of Social
Sciences, Chiangmai Univer-
sity
Mr. Somwung SOOKYING
Economist, National
Economic Development
Board

Miss Chiraphon SUPHANASARN
Economist, National Economic
Development Board

TURKEY
Dr. Yilmaz GURER
Deputy Under-Secretary,
Ministry of Reconstruction
Mr. Irfan GIRGIN
Assistant Manager, Division
of Agricultural Settlement
Planning, Ministry of Rural
Affairs

CENTRAL AND SOUTH AMERICA

ARGENTINA
Prof. Julio GAMBA
Dean, Faculty of Economics,
University of Buenos Aires
Dr. Jorge E. HARDOY
Senior Researcher, Instituto
Torcuato di Tella, Center of
Urban and Regional Studies,
University of Buenos Aires
Mr. Ricardo F. MAGNANI
Perfecture of Gran Rosario
Ing. Walter H. PIAGGIO
Representative of CONADE,
Perfecture of Gran Rosario
Ing. Horacio F. PREMOLI
Director of Technical Depart-
ment, Town Planning Commis-
sion Municipality of Rosario

BOLIVIA
Arq. Mario RIVERO
Executive Director, National
Housing Council

BRAZIL
Mr. Leo Serejo Pinto de ABREU
National Housing Bank

CHILE
Dr. Fernando PEDRAO
Regional Institute of Social
Planning

COLOMBIA
Mr. Roberto ARENAS B.
Director, Department of
Planning

COSTA RICA
H. E. Gonzalo J. FACIOS
Minister for Foreign Affairs
H. E. Rev. Benjamin NUÑEZ
Ambassador of Costa Rica
in Israel

DOMINICAN REPUBLIC
H. E. Francisco Gilberto VIL-
LANUEVA
Minister Without Portfolio,
Director-General of the
Dominican Agronomy Institute
Mr. Miguel GONZALES
Personal Assistant to Minister
F. G. Villaneuva

Dr. José Mañuel PITTALUGA
Director Manager, National
Housing Bank

ECUADOR
Dr. Cordero Bejar FEBRES
Economist, National Institution
for Planning and Economic
Coordination

EL SALVADOR
Arq. Mario Miguel BARRIERE
Head, Department of Urban
and Regional Planning, National
Council for Planning and
Economic Coordination

GUATEMALA
Lic. Mañuel COLOM ARGUETA
Mayor of Guatemala City
Arq. Federico FAHSEN
Executive Assistant to Secretary
General, National Council for
Economic Planning

HAITI
Mr. Antoine F. MATHELIER
Co-Director, Bas Boen
Project, Department of
Agriculture

JAMAICA
Mr. Edgar S. STEER
Agricultural Economist,
Ministry of Agriculture
and Fisheries

MEXICO
Lic. Roberto Rios ELIZONDO
Secretary-General, Institute
of Social Insurance
Dr. Edmundo FLORES
Professor of Economics,
National University of Mexico

Mr. Garcia Francisco TAPIA
Civil Engineer, Institute of
Resources
Ing. Luis UNIKEL
El Colegio de Mexico

NICARAGUA
Dr. Francisco AGUIRRE
Editor, Diario de las Americas
(Washington, D.C.)

PANAMA
Lic. José Benjamin SOKOL
Deputy Director-General for
Planning and Administration
at the Presidency

PERU
Arg. Santiago AGURTO
Executive Secretary, Commis-
sion for the Reconstruction
of the Affected Zone
Mr. Ayala Alfredo BARCENA
Director of Projects and
Technical Assistance, Northern
Regional Development Office
Mr. Alarcon Magno L. HERRERA
Planning Officer, Ministry of
Agriculture
Mr. Luis Lopez JIMENEZ
Senior Director, Ministry of
Housing

URUGUAY
Arq. Ildefonso AROZTEGUI
Director of National Housing

VENEZUELA
Dr. Carlos ACEDO MENDOZA
President, FUNDACOMUN—
Foundation for Community
Development
Dr. Nelson Geigel LOPE-BELLO
Attorney—Urban Development

NORTH AMERICA

UNITED STATES OF AMERICA
Prof. William ALONSO
  Professor of Regional Planning,
  Institute of Urban and Regional
  Development, University of
  California, Berkeley
Prof. Joel BERGSMAN
  Director, Urban Economic
  Development and Growth,
  The Urban Institute,
  Washington, D.C.
Prof. Brian J. L. BERRY
  Professor of Geography,
  Center for Urban Studies,
  University of Chicago
Dr. Marion CLAWSON
  Director, Land Use and
  Management Program,
  Resources for the Future,
  Washington, D.C.
Dr. Marshall B. CLINARD
  Professor in the Department
  of Sociology, University of
  Wisconsin
Prof. John FRIEDMANN
  Professor of Planning,
  Economics, and Geography,
  Head, Urban Planning Program,
  School of Architecture and
  Urban Planning, University of
  California, Los Angeles
Prof. Walter ISARD
  Professor in Regional Science
  Department, Wharton School of
  Finance and Commerce,
  University of Pennsylvania

Prof. Edwin S. MILLS
  Professor of Economics,
  Public Affairs and Urban
  Studies, Department of
  Economics, Princeton
  University, New Jersey
Prof. Chester RAPKIN
  Professor of Urban Planning;
  Director, Institute of Urban
  Environment, School of
  Architecture, Columbia
  University of New York
Prof. Lloyd RODWIN
  Professor of Land Economics,
  Head, Department of Urban
  Studies and Planning and
  Director of Special Program
  for Urban Studies of Develop-
  ing Areas, Massachusetts
  Institute of Technology
Dr. John W. SOMMER
  Assistant Professor of
  Geography, Dartmouth
  College, New Hampshire
Prof. John F. C. TURNER
  Lecturer at the Department
  of Urban Studies and Plan-
  ning, Special Program for
  Urban and Regional Studies
  in Developing Areas, Mas-
  sachusetts Institute of
  Technology
Prof. Robert C. WEAVER
  Professor of Economics, and
  President of Baruch College,
  City University of New York

EUROPE

BELGIUM
Prof. P. LACONTE
  Institute of Urbanization and
  Territorial Administration,

Catholic University of
Louvain
Prof. Lucien LEBACQ
  Faculty of Applied Economic

Sciences, Centre Univer-
sitaire de l-État, Mons
Prof. Jozef MORTELMANS
Faculty of Engineering,
Catholic University of Louvain

FRANCE
Prof. Jacques Raoul BOUDEVILLE
Professor of Economic Sciences
at Faculty of Law and Political
Science, University of Paris
Mr. Jean CANAUX
Inspector General of Con-
struction; Director of the Re-
search Center on Urbanization

FEDERAL REPUBLIC OF
GERMANY
Prof. Dr. Edwin von BOVENTER
Professor of Economics,
University of Munich, Head,
Institute for Empirical
Economic Research

GREAT BRITAIN
Mr. Robert E. BOOTE
Deputy Director of the
United Kingdom Conservancy,
Natural Environment Research
Council
Dr. Leslie GINSBURG
Planning Adviser at the Civic
Trust
Prof. Nathaniel LICHFIELD
Professor of the Economics of
Environmental Planning, School
of Environmental Studies,
Department of Town Planning,
University College, London
Prof. Gerald WIBBERLEY
Professor of Countryside
Planning, School of Rural

Economics and Related
Studies, Wye College,
University of London

ITALY
Prof. Gabriel SCIMENI
Professor of Economics,
Director of the Institute of
Urbanistics, Faculty of
Architecture, University of
Rome

THE NETHERLANDS
Mr. Willem DAM
Head, Information Department,
Ministry of Housing and
Physical Planning
Dr. P. J. van DOOREN
Director, Department of
Social Research, Royal
Tropical Institute

RUMANIA
Mr. Gheorghe NEGOITA
Researcher, Research Institute
for Agricultural Economics
Arq. Gheorghe PAVLU
Director, Institute of Sys-
tematization and Architecture
Mr. Nicolae STANESCU
Economist, Ministry of
Agriculture and Forestry
Arq. Constantin Aurelian TRISCU
Secretary, Union of Architects

SPAIN
Mr. ANGELET
Information and Documentation
Center, Urbanization Branch,
Ministry of Housing
Mr. Fernando FERNANDEZ
RODRIGUEZ
Head, Department of Regional

306

Studies, Economic and Social
Development Plan
Mr. Francisco F. LONGORIA
Head, Department of Technical
Studies, Urbanization Branch,
Ministry of Housing

SWITZERLAND
Prof. Walter W. CUSTER
Department of Architecture,
ORTS, Regional and Country
Planning, Swiss Federal
Institute of Technology

INTERNATIONAL ORGANIZATIONS

AGENCY FOR INTERNATIONAL
DEVELOPMENT (AID), Washington,
D.C.
Mr. William MINER
Director, Urban Development
Staff, Technical Assistance
Bureau
Mr. Harold ROBINSON
Chief, Housing and Urban
Development, Latin America
Bureau

INTER-AMERICAN DEVELOP-
MENT BANK (IDB), Washington,
D.C.
Dr. Thomas CAROL
Dr. José D. EPSTEIN
Treasurer

INTER-AMERICAN INSTITUTE
OF AGRICULTURE,
Costa Rica
Mr. José ARAUGO
Director-General

INTERNATIONAL BANK FOR
RECONSTRUCTION AND DEVEL-
OPMENT (WORLD BANK), Wash-
ington, D.C.
Mr. Bernard CHADENET
Deputy Director of Projects
Mr. Robert A. SADOVE
Director, Special Projects
Department
Dr. Albert WATERSTON
Lecturer, Economic

Development Institute of the
World Bank; Professor of
Economics at The American
University, Washington, D.C.

INTERNATIONAL LABOUR
OFFICE (ILO), Geneva
Mr. Jorge MENDEZ
Chief, Employment Planning
and Promotion Department

ORGANIZATION OF AMERICAN
STATES (OAS) Division of
Urban Development
Mr. Juan ASTICA
Regional Coordinator,
Buenos Aires, Argentina
Mr. Osvaldo BEDINI
Deputy Chief, Inter-American
Project in Urban and Regional
Planning (PIAPUR), Lima,
Peru
Dr. Ernesto COHEN
Academic Coordinator,
Inter-American Project in
Urban and Regional Planning
(PIAPUR)
Mr. Marcos Antonio CUEVAS
Regional Coordinator, Rio
de Janeiro, Brazil
Mr. Philip HUBER
Chief, Division of Urban
Development Department of
Social Affairs, Washington,
D.C.

ORGANIZATION FOR ECONOMIC
COOPERATION AND DEVELOP-
MENT (OECD), Paris
Mr. J. G. ROBERTS
  Administrator, Technical
  Cooperation Service

UNITED NATIONS CENTER
FOR HOUSING, BUILDING, AND
PLANNING
United Nations, New York
Mr. Robert J. CROOKS
  Director

UNITED NATIONS DEVELOP-
MENT PROGRAM (UNDP)
Mr. David MORSE
  Senior Consultant; Chairman,

Policy and Planning Commit-
tee, United Nations, New
York
Dr. Anatole A. SOLOW
  Director, U.N. Special Fund
  Project on Municipal De-
  velopment and Administration
  (Ven-18), Caracas, Venezuela

UNITED NATIONS EDUCA-
TIONAL SCIENTIFIC AND
CULTURAL ORGANIZATION
(UNESCO), Paris
Prof. Walter MANSHARD
  Director, Department of
  Environmental Sciences and
  Natural Resources

RAANAN WEITZ is Head of the Land Settlement Department of the Jewish Agency, and also of the Settlement Study Centre at Rehovot. He is on the Board of Governors of several universities in Israel, and author of numerous books and articles on agricultural development, rural settlement, regional planning, and urbanization. Dr. Weitz was Joint Chairman, with Mr. David Tanne, of the Scientific Preparatory Committee of the Sixth Rehovot Conference, on which this volume is based.

THE CASE FOR DEVELOPMENT

Prepared by United Nations Centre for Economic
and Social Information
Foreword by Philippe de Seynes

THE ENIGMA OF ECONOMIC GROWTH

David Horowitz

PLANNING FOR URBAN GROWTH
British Perspectives on the Planning Process

Edited by John L. Taylor

URBAN GOVERNMENT FOR RIO DE JANEIRO

Ivan L. Richardson

URBAN GOVERNMENT FOR VALENCIA, VENEZUELA

Mark W. Cannon
R. Scott Fosler
Robert E. Witherspoon